EMPIRE OR DEMOCRACY?

N.B.

It is suggested that members should always look through the *Left News*, which comes with each monthly book, immediately. Every month it contains full particulars and descriptions of the various categories of forthcoming extra books at special Club prices, together with a card on which members who wish to obtain any of these books can order them: important articles by Laski, Strachey, and others: an editorial by Victor Gollancz commenting on the progress of the Club and announcing future developments: and an article by Dr. Lewis (entitled *The Groups Month by Month*) which gives a picture, that cannot be obtained in any other way, of the activities of the Left Book Club considered as a movement.

EMPIRE OR DEMOCRACY?

A Study of The Colonial Question

By LEONARD BARNES

Author of

Caliban in Africa, The Duty of Empire, etc.

LONDON

VICTOR GOLLANCZ LTD

1939

PRINTED IN GREAT BRITAIN BY RICHARD CLAY AND COMPANY, LTD. (r.u.),
BUNGAY, SUFFOLK.

FOREWORD

I HAD better make it clear that where I speak of Empire or imperialism I am not thinking of Canada, Australia, New Zealand, South Africa, or their relations to this country. Though British interests still exercise various veiled forms of control over those countries or practise intervention in them in spite of constitutional pretences, the Dominions stand to Britain in much the same relation as other small countries, such as Denmark, Holland, or Portugal, with whom we happen to be on friendly diplomatic terms. Their powers of self-government are, within limits, real. What I mean by imperialism is the forcible subjecting to British rule of India, Ceylon, tropical Africa, the West Indies, and the rest of the so-called dependencies and mandated territories; and by the Empire I mean the territories under the British flag which are so subjected.

J. F. Horrabin has been good enough to allow me to use his inimitable maps and diagrams. For permission to reproduce the diagrams on pages 57 and 143 I have to thank the Editor of the *Economist* and the Editor of *Africa* respectively. In several chapters I have incorporated material previously contributed by me to *Reynolds News*, the *Political Quarterly*, and *Empire : A Monthly Record*. Chapter VIII is drawn largely from an essay which I contributed to a volume entitled " The British Civil Servant ", and published by Messrs. Allen & Unwin.

L. B.

CONTENTS

A 2

MAPS AND DIAGRAMS

PART I

THE CLAIMS AND THE CLAIMANTS

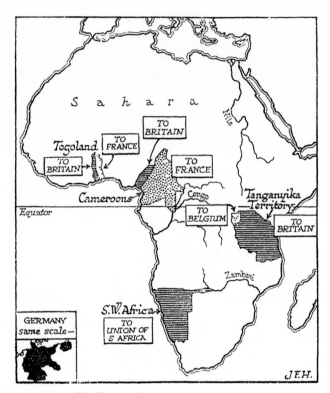

The Former German Colonies in Africa

CHAPTER I

THE NEW COLONIAL CLAIMS

§ 1. WHAT THE CLAIMS ARE

HITLER demands the return of Germany's former colonies. That is the form which his general claim for what he calls colonial equality has come to assume. High official quarters in Berlin have stated that no further formulation of this demand is to be expected, for Hitler looks to Britain to put forward in due course proposals for the settlement of the question.*

The ideas entertained by the German Government and the National-Socialist Party on the colonial issue have been given fairly clear definition. The suggestion that there should be a re-distribution of mandates and that Germany should become a mandatory power is rejected by both. So, also, are all suggestions that small colony-owning countries like Portugal or Belgium should make colonial sacrifices in order to spare Britain the pain of returning mandated territory. This, it is declared, would spoil Germany's moral case and confuse an issue which is otherwise clear.†

On the other hand, the Paris correspondent of the *Manchester Guardian* in a message published on November 10th stated that " Germany has admitted the principle of substituting territories of equivalent value for those that once belonged to her ". There have been many rumours of semi-official suggestions in Berlin that Germany would accept instead of her old colonies a continuous strip on

---

* *Daily Telegraph*, October 13th, 1938.
† *Observer*, October 30th, 1938.

the West Coast of Africa, including all or part of Nigeria, the Cameroons, and contributions farther south from France, Belgium, and Portugal.* Madagascar has also been mentioned as a possible French concession.†

The main lines along which German colonial propaganda developed during 1938 were as follows:

    1. Germany demands colonial territory because she is over-populated.

    2. She has an indisputable right to own overseas colonies.

    3. She has a right to the recovery of all her former colonies.

Special prominence was given to colonial possessions as hall-marking the status of a great power. Germany's former Asiatic possessions did not receive specific mention. The heaviest emphasis was placed on South-West Africa.

In practice, Germany's claim seems to be limited at present to her old non-Asiatic possessions. Hitler is credibly reported to have assured Japan that whatever he demands in Africa, he will not seek the return of the former German islands in the Pacific now held (technically under mandate from the League of Nations) by the Japanese.‡ It is recognised, however, that in Hitler's diplomatic technique any demand he makes is a minimum, a starting-point for further demands. Germany is understood to want her former colonies not merely that a wrong may be righted, but in order to have a nucleus for a new overseas colonial empire. The former colonies are to be that nucleus.

On the other hand, German assurances have been given that there will be no war over the colonial issue, and that the maintenance of the British Empire is regarded as a positive factor in German foreign policy. Hitler himself is reported to have said that it would be a terrible blow

    * See *Manchester Guardian*, November 2nd.
    † Ibid., November 10th.
    ‡ *Daily Mirror*, October 28th, 1938.

to him if the Indians seceded from the British Empire.*
He is known to have observed to Mr. Neville Chamberlain
at Godesberg, " There is one awkward question—the
colonies. But that is not a matter for war; there will be
no mobilisation about that." †

German intentions are seen in a different light in non-
German quarters. Authorities in Moscow, for example,
take the view that the German Air Line Berlin–Baghdad–
Teheran–Kabul, German economic penetration in Turkey
and Iran, and the visits (in the weeks that followed the
Munich agreement) of German ministers to the countries
of the Near East are all evidence of the increasing rivalry
between Britain and Germany for the control of the Near
East and the route to India. The Kaiser's actions as
Protector of Islam are, we are told, child's play compared
to the subversive activities now being developed by Hitler's
Germany in the Arab countries. " Hitherto a question
of propaganda and diplomacy, the colonial question has
now assumed a military and political aspect." ‡

Support for this kind of view is afforded by an article
in the *Sunday Sun* of March 14th, 1937. The article was
by Adolf Hitler, and entitled " Why I Want Germany's
Colonies Back ". In it the author observed, " Germany's
lost lands will only return to the bosom of our common
Reich by the stroke of a mighty sword ".

However that may be, Hitler's expectation is that the
colonial question will soon be settled in his favour. Dr.
Schacht, when President of the Reichsbank, is reported
accordingly to have set up a special department in the
Bank to study problems concerning the preparation of new
colonial currencies. For technical reasons, the reichsmark
will not be introduced as the regular currency in any
colonial territories which Germany may recover.§

* *Observer*, October 2nd, 1938.
† This assurance was repeated as late as January 7th, 1939, in
Goering's paper, the *National Zeitung*.
‡ *Izvestia*, October 23rd, 1938.
§ *Daily Telegraph*, October 13th, 1938.

Germany is not the only country which has colonial demands to put forward. As long ago as February 1933 the Government of Poland made a declaration in which it recorded its right to claim a colonial mandate sooner or later.

In August 1935 an article appeared in the *Polish Economist* dealing with Poland's right to colonial possessions. The article was reproduced on August 13th, 1935, in the official journal of the Polish Government. The article asked quite simply and directly that the allocation of mandates in respect of the former German colonies should be revised, and that the revision should take the desires of Poland into account. It also gave expression to an argument which runs through most public discussion of the subject in Poland. " The German possessions comprised territory more than 7½ times greater than the territory of Poland. Most of these possessions are in Africa. Since about 9% of the territory of pre-war Germany was returned to Poland, it would only be just that Poland should receive a corresponding part of the former German colonies. Poland has never renounced the right to claim such a part, and she possesses legal title to make the claim." *

The argument that the Polish claim to colonies should be proportionate to the amount of pre-war German territory now incorporated in Poland does not figure so prominently in Polish propaganda to-day as it did three years ago. The claim itself, however, does.

It was first put forward officially by the Foreign Office in Warsaw on July 31st, 1936. In the *communiqué* then issued it was said to be the duty of the League of Nations to deal with the matter without delay. Territories in South America and South Africa were claimed as best suited for Polish immigration and colonisation.

The acute Jewish problem in Poland and the fact that Poland as a whole had the greatest natural increase of

* See " Le Problème Colonial ", by O. Louwers (Brussels, 1936).

population in Europe were mentioned as justifying the claim. It was added that countries with a great amount of capital at low interest (meaning British and France) should provide under the League's guarantee the capital needed for Polish colonial enterprise.

Nor should it be assumed that those countries which are elaborately equipped in a military sense are the only ones that do not find the existing colonial situation altogether to their taste. As evidence of such wider dissatisfaction, one might quote the Norwegian paper *Nationen*, which in its issue of May 11th, 1929, went so far as to propose that Norway should be granted a mandate from the League of Nations in respect of the old German possessions in East Africa. Similarly, the Foreign Minister of Denmark, M. Munch, in a broadcast on October 14th, 1935, alluded to the question of the " open door ", and claimed access for all to the natural resources of colonial territories. These are merely characteristic examples of an attitude which finds continuous expression in the smaller countries of Europe, an attitude of polite protest at the increasing economic exclusiveness of the imperialist powers.

More striking and less civil was a scene which took place in the Italian Chamber of Deputies on November 30th, 1938. Count Ciano, the Foreign Minister, had just wound up a speech with a vague and platitudinous peroration, when the Deputies burst into a storm of cheering and shouted " Tunisia ". The Rome correspondent of *The Times* reported the episode as a " demonstration deliberately planned to express a demand ".

In the succeeding days the Italian press buckled to the task of outlining Italy's various aspirations. Italy must see to the " complete protection of all the persons of Italian race and language ". She must " achieve the reparation of injustices, the compensation of wrongs ancient and new ". She must obtain " those frontier rectifications which are necessary to give a better arrange-

ment of Europe and the colonies ". The revisions of
frontier more particularly indicated were those of the
department of Nice, which was ceded by Italy to France
in 1860, and of Tunisia, which was occupied by France
in 1881, to the extreme annoyance of Italy, who even
then aspired to possess it. These suggestions were under-
lined by the semi-official Signor Gayda, who observed that
" the Italian nation is ready to march, if necessary, even
against France ".* A few days later Italy's claim was
extended to cover Corsica and a share in the Suez Canal.
By December 11th an Italian newspaper, *L'Assalto*, was
adding, " France will have to admit that Jibuti (in French
Somaliland) must now become a part of Italy, a country
which is the lord and master of all Ethiopia ".

All this is an ironical commentary on the " accord "
on which Mussolini and Laval entered early in 1935 and
which was intended to be a full settlement of all the
colonial differences then existing between France and
Italy. At that time, four short years ago, the long-
standing colonial quarrel between the two countries was
thought to have been liquidated. Moreover, liquidation
was not regarded as an end in itself; it was to provide
the conditions necessary for a common programme of
action in Europe at a time when the German challenge
to French continental hegemony was reaching a critical
stage.† But the Rome–Paris axis came to nothing, and
to-day Italy is bent on squeezing France for coveted
territories and strategic positions, while Germany con-
currently extorts similar Danegeld from the British
Empire.

The Mussolini–Laval agreement of 1935 was formally
denounced by the Italian Government in December 1938
as an official step in support of the new Italian claims
against France.

* See *The Times*, December 3rd, 1938.
† See " Les Clauses Coloniales dans Les Accords Franco-Italiens du
7 Janvier, 1935 ", by Paul Goiffon.

§ 2. THE NATURE OF THE PROBLEM

What, then, is the problem raised by these various claims and these various forms of disapproval of the colonial *status quo*? It is essential to answer the question clearly. What we popularly term the colonial problem is not one problem, but two. There is the immediate problem, which is largely one of political expediency, of what to do about the colonial demands of Germany and the rest; and there is the long-term problem, which involves fundamental sociological considerations, of what to do with colonial empires. One solution may fit both; indeed, it is the task of statesmanship to find a solution that does fit both. But it is of the first importance that the two should not be confused as they were in 1919. The colonial problem properly understood is not just a wrangle and a rivalry between great powers: it is a question of right and wrong. Ultimately, its solution depends on ordinary people understanding that colonial empires are wrong.

By distributing Germany's colonies (and for that matter Turkey's too) at the end of the last war, the powers took a short step forward and a long step back. The mandate system in itself can, if you like, be regarded as an advance in colonial theory. It sketched the outlines of a new liberal-idealist conception of empire. But it was also used to conceal the fact that a few powers, all of them hardened imperialists, were seizing the colonies of another power as the prize of victory.

The pushing of the German and Italian colonial claims to the forefront of the diplomatic stage requires that the ambiguity inherent in the shuffling procedure by which the mandate system was first set up should be resolved.

Was what happened in 1919 simply that the British and French Empires added to their already vast areas at Germany's expense? If so, Germany has at least as good a case for demanding her colonies back as Britain and France have for retaining them. All three are highly industrialised countries, all have big guns, all have a feeling of superiority to the dark races. On the level of power politics the only difference is that Germany lost one empire by losing a war, while Britain and France gained a second empire each by winning it; and that Germany to-day has rather bigger guns than either France or Britain. There is little scope for moral arguments here. At the same time, nothing can be plainer than that the colonial problem will never be solved by adding one nation to the list of " haves " and subtracting one from the list of " have nots ".

On the other hand, did Britain and France really mean what they said when they established the mandate system and forwent the outright annexation of the ex-German colonies? Did they genuinely believe that the " well-being and development of primitive peoples form a sacred trust of civilisation "? Were they frankly discarding the old imperialist assumptions and the tradition of national possession? If so, they provided themselves with grounds that were valid then, and which remain valid now, for refusing the restoration of her colonies to Germany, and indeed the satisfaction of any country's colonial claims. They did indeed offer themselves and the world what they and the world need even more urgently to-day than in 1919—an escape from the endless vicious circle of the division of the spoils. But, in that case, it is high time they proved their sincerity by advancing farther along the new road and completing the break with imperialism.

CHAPTER II

INTERESTED ATTITUDES

§ 1. IMPERIALIST RIVALRIES 1914–18

AT the end of the last European War the German colonies were disposed of in the following way:

German East Africa (375,000 sq. m.), mandated to Great Britain (Tanganyika) and Belgium (Ruanda-Urundi, 20,550 sq. m.).

South-West Africa (322,394 sq. m.), mandated to the Union of South Africa.

Cameroons (307,995 sq. m.), mandated to Britain (34,236 sq. m.) and France.

Togoland (33,700 sq. m.), mandated to Britain (12,600 sq. m.) and France.

German New Guinea : Kaiser Wilhelm's Land (93,000 sq. m.), Bismarck Archipelago (1,115 sq. m.), German Solomon Is. (4,000 sq. m.), mandated to Australia.

Samoan Islands (1,200 sq. m.), mandated to New Zealand.

Nauru (5,396 acres), mandated to the British Empire.

Pacific Islands : Caroline, Marshall, Belew, and Marianne (or Ladrone) Islands, mandated to Japan.

How did these arrangements come to be made?

As the European War was professedly fought for idealist purposes, the annexation of colonies was not emphasised as a war aim. Part of Lloyd George's evidence * suggests that even as late as the end of 1916 nothing had been said on the Allied side about colonies. " No country ", says

---

* " The Truth about the Peace Treaties ", Vol. 1.

Lloyd George, " was prepared to perpetuate the horrors of such a war merely for the sake of wresting the German colonies from German control. Had Germany and her Allies accepted in substance our terms, peace could have been established in the month of January 1917 instead of November 1918 without the surrender by Germany of one of her overseas possessions."

Elsewhere,* however, he prints a memorandum by General Smuts on war aims, which gives the impression that a few months later not only Smuts himself but two Committees of the Cabinet had very different ideas in mind. The Smuts memorandum (dated April 29th, 1917) stressed the need of defining and limiting Britain's war aims " at this very late stage of this long and exhausting struggle ", and proceeded to limit them to four. At the head of this severely shortened list came the destruction of the German colonial system, with a view to the future security of all communications vital to the British Empire. " This has already been done—an achievement of enormous value which ought not to be endangered at the peace negotiations."

As for the Germans, a memorandum prepared for the Imperial German Cabinet in 1918 expressed a demand for a colonial empire that would give Germany " not only a great part of what we won in order to be economically independent of England, but a means of stifling England's home at any moment with the help of our navy and the man-power latent in this future dominion ". The dominion was to be in Africa, and to extend from the Atlantic to the Indian Ocean. France, Belgium, and Portugal, as well as Britain, were all to have contributed their share. These designs were no doubt taken into account by the Allies in considering how the colonial question was to be treated.

Later in 1918 negotiations which led up to the armistice were opened on the basis of President Wilson's fourteen points (first published to the world on January 8th, 1918).

* " Memoirs ", Vol. 3, p. 1531.

Of these points the fifth read as follows: " A free, open-minded, and absolutely impartial adjustment of all colonial claims, based upon a strict observance of the principle that in determining all such questions of sovereignty the interests of the populations concerned must have equal weight with the equitable claims of the government whose title is to be determined ".

This, in the words of J. M. Keynes,* was a wise and magnanimous programme. In the words of Lloyd George, it was a vague statement capable of a variety of interpretations. Anyway, on November 5th, 1918, it became part of a solemn contract to which all the great powers of the world put their signatures. On the faith of these signatures, the armistice itself was signed six days later.

By the time the Peace Conference met in Paris other aspects of the case had come to seem more important. It was then only remembered that the ex-German colonies had been won in fair fight in a war in which Germany was held to have been the aggressor. Not a voice, therefore, was raised in favour of returning them. Nor, one may add, was any voice raised in favour of consulting the African populations concerned, or of giving their interests equal weight with the governmental claims which were under discussion. " All were agreed ", said President Wilson, " to oppose the restoration of German colonies." Lloyd George adds the comment that " the revelations as to the military, naval, and aerial use which the Germans intended to make of their colonies in the future were responsible for that unanimity ". The fact that the territories involved had inhabitants of their own seems to have been quite forgotten.

It is evident that the views of the Dominions were given great weight in influential circles in the Conference. The Union of South Africa was vehemently opposed to the continuance of German proximity and intrigue in South-West Africa. The encouragement given by the Germans of

* " Economic Consequences of the Peace ", p. 58.

that territory to Beyers and his fellow-rebels against the authority of an Afrikaner Government in 1914 determined, so Lloyd George tells us, the attitude of Botha and Smuts.

The same witness adds, " As to East Africa, the South African Union considered the presence of a vast territory under German control to be a constant menace to Rhodesia and South Africa and a block to the realisation of the great Rhodes dream of a Cape-to-Cairo route. Australia disliked the prospect of Germany with a jumping-off ground so near to the Australian shores in New Guinea and the Solomon Islands. New Zealand took the same view about Samoa."

The above outline of the story serves to show the currents and cross-currents of imperial ambition by which the various players in the drama were swayed. What emerges most plainly is that the decisive consideration against returning Germany's colonies was strategic.*

§ 2. COLONIES AT VERSAILLES

In the end, by Article 119 of the Treaty of Versailles, Germany ceded to her victors " all her rights and titles over her overseas possessions ".

It was a comprehensive gesture, covering not only German sovereignty, but German property, private and public alike.

All Government property in the German colonies, including railways, was required to be surrendered without payment. The German Government, however, remained liable for any debt which might have been incurred for the purchase or construction of such property or for

---

* This fact raises a question which is very relevant to our current situation to-day. If it was right to exclude Germany from Africa because it was strategically inconvenient to us or to South Africa to have her there. it was also right to draw the frontiers of Czechoslovakia with an eye to the same principle. The defenders of the Munich agreement have now repudiated that principle in relation to Central Europe. Will they insist on repudiating it in relation to Africa too?

the development of the colonies generally (Articles 120 and 257).

As for private property, the Allied and Associated powers reserved, and later exercised, the right " to retain and liquidate all property, rights, and interests belonging to German nationals or companies controlled by them " within the former German colonies (Articles 121 and 297*b*).

This wholesale expropriation of private property was carried out without the Allies affording any compensation to the individuals expropriated. The proceeds were employed first to meet private debts due to Allied nationals from any German nationals, and, second, to meet claims due from Austrian, Hungarian, Bulgarian, or Turkish nationals. Any balance remaining after these claims had been met was either returned direct to Germany or retained by the liquidating power. If retained, it was carried to Germany's credit in the Reparation account.

In short, as Keynes commented at the time, " not only were German sovereignty and influence extirpated from the whole of her former oversea possessions, but the persons and property of her nationals resident or owning property in those parts were deprived of legal status and legal security ".*

The principal Allied and Associated powers were, besides Britain and the Dominions, the U.S.A., France, Belgium, Italy, and Japan. The treaty placed these countries in the position of partners in the colonies so renounced and made over by Germany.

The question remained how the colonies were to be apportioned among the partners. The allocation was made, in the manner described at the beginning of this chapter, by the Allied Supreme Council at the Peace Conference in May 1919. To the various territories thus allotted was applied the so-called mandate system. An outline of the mandate system was embodied in Article 22

* Op. cit., p. 63.

of the Covenant of the League of Nations, which was signed at the same time as the Treaty.*

In other words, while the above-mentioned countries were, and presumably are, the legal owners or sovereigns of the ex-German colonies, they have made a double delegation of their sovereignty: to the League as supervisor, and to the several mandatory Governments as administrators.† Acceptance of a mandate by various of the Allied and Associated powers conveyed no new ownership to them individually, but merely laid them under certain duties of administration in conformity with the terms of the mandate in each case, and in trust for the inhabitants of the mandated territories.

One of these duties is the rendering of an annual report to the Council of the League. The Permanent Mandates Commission was set up to receive and discuss such reports and to act in regard to them as agent of the League Council.

§ 3. TOWARDS COLONIAL REVISION

This scheme for the government of the ex-German colonies still remains in force. Whenever proposals have been mooted for modifying it, official assurances have been given that there would be no change in the control of the mandated territories. Nevertheless, it has been widely realised that the mandate arrangements were not altogether satisfactory in themselves and that, in so far as they represented an advance on the old imperialist systems, there was no reason why the mandate principle should in its application stop short at the colonies which changed hands at Versailles.

Many organisations, therefore, notably the Labour Party and various sections of the peace movement, addressed

* See appendix to this chapter, page 40.

† This is the view of the matter taken by many authorities (see e.g., "Mandates", by Freda White). But the point is not free from controversy, and others hold that sovereignty is vested in the League of Nations, for which the various mandatories hold the territories on trust. (See *Manchester Guardian*, November 4th, 1938.)

themselves to the task of working out schemes for the extension and improvement of the mandate system. The question was, for example, considered in detail by the Annual Conference of the Labour Party at Hastings in 1933, and the policy of the party was laid down in a statement on the colonies. In that statement it was declared that the more advanced colonies should be assisted to self-government, and that the mandate system should be accepted for all colonies inhabited mainly by peoples of primitive culture. The latter phrase was further explained by drawing a distinction between colonies inhabited by peoples of European culture, such as the West Indies, those inhabited by peoples of oriental culture, such as Ceylon, Malaya, and the Straits Settlements, and those inhabited by peoples of primitive culture, such as certain African and Pacific territories.*

Similarly, the National Peace Council published in June 1936 a statement on peace and colonial policy, which declared that " all countries (including protectorates) having peoples of primitive culture not at present capable of self-government should be brought within a strengthened mandate system ", firstly in order to accelerate the training of native populations in self-government, and secondly to ensure that that training should not be such as to obstruct a general advance towards world prosperity and world peace.

Again, in July 1938 the British League of Nations Union sponsored the following resoluton at the 22nd Plenary Congress of the International Federation of League of Nations Societies:

" That this Congress,

" Being convinced that the mandate system for colonial territories is superior to national administration without international control,

" Advocates the transfer where practicable of non-self-governing colonial territories held by the various

* " The Colonial Empire ", October 1933. (Labour Party.)

colonial powers to the mandate system subject to two
fundamental principles

" 1. Any change must be on such terms as will safeguard the existing interests of the populations concerned,
and must be subject to the free consent of these populations.

" 2. It must secure equal opportunities for the trade
and commerce of all Members of the League."

No British Government, however, made any move in
regard to any international aspect of the colonial question
until Sir Samuel Hoare, speaking as Foreign Secretary at
the Assembly of the League of Nations in September 1935,
during the early stages of Mussolini's Abyssinian campaign,
declared his readiness to discuss the question of access to
colonial raw materials.

The course taken by French thinking on the colonial
problem throughout all this period was marked by a certain forgetfulness that there was a French colonial empire
at all, and by a tendency to view the matter as primarily
one between Britain and Germany. The French saw
justification for this attitude in the fact that the only
territorial gains which France made at Germany's expense
in the 1919 Peace settlement were parts of the Cameroons
and of Togoland.

All the same, the French Government did publish on
April 8th, 1936, a memorandum and peace proposals
which included a paragraph dealing with the colonial
question. The document was prepared and issued immediately after Hitler's re-occupation of the Rhineland.*

More recently this accommodating spirit seems to have

---

* The paragraph read as follows : " The double necessity for a
common reservoir of raw materials and for territory for expansion for
surplus European production should lead to a revision of certain colonial
statutes, not in the domain of political sovereignty but from the point of
view of equality of economic rights and the co-operation of credit
between European States, which, having assured themselves of collective
security and mutual assistance, will accordingly have to be considered as
associates, and not as rivals ".

flagged. There was a phase shortly after Munich when Daladier appeared for a while to be ready to consider a Franco-German settlement which would include the transfer of certain colonies lying outside the African " zone of security ". But parliamentary pressure became so strong and many sections of public opinion so vociferous that he later denied in categorical terms any intention of giving away anything. The powerful agitation in France against the surrender of any colonies sprang up during November 1938, and was a curious phenomenon, especially when one remembers the extremely weak strategical position of France *vis-à-vis* the two claimants for slices of her Empire. " The average Frenchman is not acutely Empire-minded; yet the outcry against any surrender of colonies to Germany was perfectly genuine; it was a remarkable reaction against the humiliation of Munich, against Hitler's threats that he would ' take ' the colonies if he did not get them, and against the pogroms. The anxiety shown by M. Monnerville, the Negro deputy, at the prospect of being ' handed over to the Nazis ' had a profound effect. I am told that in Senegal extracts from ' Mein Kampf ' were circulated among the natives—extracts in which Hitler refers to the Negroes as ' ape-headed creatures '—and the effect was devastating." *

So far the British Government has declined to consider any extension of the mandate system, or even of the Open Door, to British dependencies. Both questions were debated in the House of Lords on February 17th, 1937, and in regard to both, the Government spokesman's response was negative. All the Government has publicly offered to do is to negotiate with Germany with a view to modifying the working of imperial preference in certain colonies in respect of certain commodities. This gesture was made in consequence of the Report of the Geneva Committee on Raw Materials. Since then there have been signs of a shift of opinion in Government circles,

* *New Statesman*, November 26th, 1938.

but the shift is in the direction of passing the hat round the imperial powers in order to collect some gifts of colonial territory for Germany, the hope evidently being that if Germany's importunities should become really tiresome, some judicious largesse of this kind might keep her quiet for a while longer. There has been no indication of willingness on the Government's part to make any move which might be read as an admission that the customary assumptions of imperialism are open to question.

With the Halifax mission to Germany in November 1937, the colonial question entered a new phase. German policy had by then succeeded in bringing it into close relation with the European question. It became clear that Britain and France from their side were thenceforward contemplating concessions to the Central Powers over a wide field. An indication of some of the possible concessions was given in the *communiqué* that the Prime Minister read to the House of Commons on November 30th, 1937, when reporting on the London discussions with MM. Chautemps and Delbos, which followed the Hitler–Halifax conversations. "A preliminary examination was made of the colonial question in all its aspects."

Three provisos were added: (1) that the colonial question could not be considered in isolation, (2) that it would involve a number of other countries, and (3) that it would require extended study.

After this announcement by Mr. Chamberlain, no further overt step was taken until the publication of the van Zeeland Report in January 1938.* Perhaps the passages in the Report which dealt with the colonial question were not strikingly happy or courageous. They seem to have left little impression in any quarter.

---

* The relevant passages were these:
" With a view to assisting the solution of the colonial problem, it has been suggested that the régime of mandates should be revised, that the national element should be removed, and that the system should be made completely international, both from the economic and the political point of view.

§ 4. REACTIONS IN THE EMPIRE

The last section affords evidence of a growing popular realisation that you cannot found a peace system on armed commercial empires which seek exclusive controls and narrow national advantages in large sections of the earth; in a word, that empire and peace will not and cannot mix. Contrariwise, it is also true that the strategic considerations which decided the Allies against returning Germany her colonies at the end of the war have perhaps even greater weight to-day, and are certainly quite as strongly felt in the outlying parts of the Empire.*

Chamberlain's Government is, therefore, in an awkward position, with Hitler waiting to be appeased on one side, on another his own party and the British Empire, Dominions and colonies alike, shouting " Hands Off ", and on a third the progressives urging him to abandon the

---

" In the case of colonies properly so called, it would perhaps be opportune to seek for the means of generalising the system of the Open Door which obtains in the basin of the Congo Convention, a system the general result of which it is impossible to criticise.

" In those colonies where such a régime cannot be organised, certain circles have recommended that the possibility be examined of creating privileged companies whose activities will be strictly limited to the economic sphere, and whose capital would be divided internationally in such a way as to offer real guarantees of impartiality.

" With regard to raw materials, a most interesting proposal has been formulated tending to the supply of colonial goods in exchange for industrial products. An agreement would be concluded between a colony and an industrial state, and colonial goods supplied would be carried to an account and paid for by the execution in return of important public works, bridges, railways, ports, etc. The intermediate finance would be provided by the metropolitan State."

* Serious constitutional difficulties in Empire relations might arise from this position. Cf. A. Berriedale Keith, " The Dominions as Sovereign States ", p. 56 : " It cannot be denied that a difficult position would be created if in certain circumstances Britain should find it advisable to meet German claims for restoration of territory in Africa, and Germany should desire to put pressure on the Union of South Africa to make a like concession. For Britain to risk a conflict with Germany over an issue on which concession to Germany seemed desirable, or even morally incumbent, and on which the Union held a different view, would obviously raise a very serious situation for the Empire, and it is easy to understand that consideration for the position of the Union has counted largely in the refusal of Britain to seek to meet the not unnatural desires of Germany on this head."

imperialist principle altogether. To complete the picture, we have to visualise Italy strongly supporting the German claims, Germany strongly supporting the Italian claims, and the smaller imperial countries like Belgium, Portugal,* and Holland, all vowing that their colonial possessions shall not be sacrificed to ease Chamberlain's difficulties. With these sentiments official Germany, for her own reasons, heartily concurs.

The movement of protest against any contemplated surrender of British colonial or mandated territory began to assume considerable proportions, particularly in Africa, immediately after the Munich agreement. In October the Association of East African Chambers of Commerce called on the British Government to make an irrevocable declaration that Tanganyika should remain an integral part of British East Africa, and urging that the three territories of Kenya, Uganda, and Tanganyika should be formed into a fiscal and administrative Union under British Government control.†

On October 18th, the Tanganyika League met at its Nairobi headquarters, and decided to urge that the most vigorous action should be taken to prevent the return of ex-German colonies. The League has the support not only of the British element, but also of the South African Dutch element in East Africa.‡

On October 15th, a body calling itself the South-West Africa League was formed in Windhoek, South-West Africa. Its objects were described as being to oppose the return of South-West Africa to Germany and to co-operate with Tanganyika in her efforts to oppose the return of that territory.§

On October 19th, the Southern Rhodesian Parliament

---

* In Portugal, the pro-Government newspaper *O Seculo* held the German demand to be quite reasonable. " Let her colonies be given back as soon as possible", this paper said. (*Manchester Guardian*, November 5th, 1938.)

† *Manchester Guardian*, October 29th, 1938.
‡ Ibid., October 19th.   § Ibid., October 17th.

adopted unanimously a motion urging that the British Government should summon a meeting of the heads of the Dominions and colonies to decide upon a policy regarding " the continued holding or relinquishment of mandated territories ".*

At the same time local societies and movements were coming into being in every town of any note in the whole of British South and East Africa, with a view to giving effect to a militant " Hands-off-Africa " policy. It is hardly too much to say that the only sections of opinion in all that region which favoured the return of colonies were the extreme nationalists who follow Dr. D. F. Malan in South Africa, and a handful of clergy of pacifist leanings.

Similar protests were made by the Indian residents in Tanganyika, who are much more numerous than the Europeans, and appeals addressed by them to the Indian National Congress. The appeals state that many millions of Indian money are invested in Tanganyika property, industry, and plantations, and that this capital would probably be lost in the event of the cession of the territory to Germany.† The Indians have reason for such misgiving, as they were specially prominent in buying up ex-German property which was compulsorily liquidated under the terms of the Treaty of Versailles.

The response from India was to insist on the need for self-determination in the matter of transfer for the people of Tanganyika, and Subhas Chandra Bose, the Congress President, issued a statement on October 21st, in which he declared that " the people of Tanganyika are not cattle, that they can be bought and sold at the sweet will of the Big Powers ".‡

The attitude of the Union of South Africa is not less unyielding. The Union is moved by imperialist impulses of its own, and since the virtual annexation of South-West Africa after a military conquest by Union troops,

* *Manchester Guardian*, October 19th.
† *Daily Worker*, October 21st.   ‡ Ibid., October 22nd.

B

this imperialism has extended until it has blossomed forth, not only in a determination to retain that territory, but in the declaration, in the face of German and other imperialist interests, of what amounts to a Monroe Doctrine for the whole of Africa south of the equator. On November 16th, 1938, General Smuts declared that the Union would fight for South-West Africa.

In this spirit, Oswald Pirow, the Union Minister of Defence, began in the latter half of October a journey . which took him through East Africa to Lisbon, Salamanca, London, Rome, and Berlin.* At Kisumu in East Africa, he had important private discussions with the leaders of the Tanganyika League and the European members of the Kenya and Tanganyika Legislative Councils.† In Lisbon, he was reported to have taken the attitude that the return of German colonies must be opposed; and at the same time to have offered the closest co-operation with the Portuguese Government in measures for the protection of the Portuguese colonies, Angola and Mozambique.‡

Much South African merchandise is exported by way of Lourenço Marques, and goods are imported by the same route. Pirow is understood to have asked for assurances that means of defending the port would be available and would be used. The Portuguese, on their side, were thought to be strongly inclined to reach agreement with the South African Government.§

Pirow's general outlook, which is probably shared by most South Africans, may be summed by saying that it combines a firm refusal to surrender the Union's mandate with a great anxiety to persuade other people to make sacrifices for Germany's appeasement.

Meanwhile, German activities were going ahead both in South-West Africa and in Tanganyika.‖ The German

* See also p. 251.   † *Manchester Guardian*, October 24th.
‡ *Observer*, October 30th. § *Liverpool Daily Post*, October 29th, 1938.
‖ On November 1st posters of the Tanganyika League in Arusha were reported to have been torn down from their boardings, allegedly by Nazis. (*Manchester Guardian*, November 2nd.)

PIROWETTE

element is numerically more important in South-West Africa. The population of the territory consists of 330,000 Africans and about 30,000 Europeans. Among the latter are 9,000 Germans, of whom 6,000 are naturalised British subjects and 3,000 German nationals.

Already by 1935 a subsidised Nazi organisation had become so active that the South African 'Government felt obliged to ban organisations using political uniforms and claiming the return of South-West Africa to Germany. Since then, the Nazi movement has continued to flourish, but in semi-secret or camouflaged forms. Trained propagandists are sent out from Germany at frequent intervals; in the schools, Nazi propaganda is spread by German teachers. The best students are granted a further course of study in Germany itself.

The *Johannesburg Star* of June 22nd, 1938, reports that " should it come to the notice of the Nazi agents that any German is anti-Nazi, he is summoned by a local Committee of agents and führers to appear at a certain address and explain his conduct. He may escape with a fine, which is paid to the Winterhilfe. If disciplinary measures do not have the desired effect, the culprit is placed on the black list, and instructions are given to Germans not to support him in business and to ostracise him socially. If he has any relatives in Germany, the Gestapo is informed, and pressure is exerted on them to bring the recalcitrant to heel in South-West Africa, or in the Union for that matter ".

In this manner opposition is broken down among the Germans themselves, and the appearance of a united front in favour of the German colonial claims is presented. In the words of Albert Voights, a leading local Nazi, old-fashioned Germans have to stand back " to make room for men who have fully grasped the National-Socialist conception ".

The official attitude in Australia took much the same shape as that of official South Africa. Several members

of the Australian Cabinet, including W. M. Hughes and
Earle Page, thought it necessary during October 1938 to
state clearly that the return of New Guinea to Germany
could never be considered. Their strongly worded
reminders that official Australian opinion was unshakeable
on this question were obviously directed against German
propaganda in the western Pacific. There are still some
German settlers in New Guinea who have not escaped
the eagle eye of the Nazis. The party would not allow
them to be any more forgetful than Germans in Africa
of where their allegiance rightly lies.*

The whole story of the handling of the colonial issue by
the Allies since the war bears a melancholy resemblance
to their handling of the disarmament issue. They forcibly
disarmed Germany, on the informal but still explicit
understanding that that was a prelude to voluntary disarmament by themselves, and indeed by all members of
the League of Nations. By failing to honour this understanding they wrecked the whole scheme for a world of
disarmed democracies and prepared the way for a world
of fascist States carrying a range of national armaments
never before dreamed of. In the same way they forcibly
deprived Germany of her colonies, and then applied the
mandate principle to them. If they had gone on to
apply the same principle to their own colonies (which the
logic of the situation clearly demanded), the colonial
question as we now know it and have to face it would
not have arisen.

Given a little good will and a little open-mindedness on
the part of Allied Governments, Africa as an international
problem could have been quietly disposed of any time
during the fifteen years which followed the war. But
neither good will nor open-mindedness was available, and
the blunder that was being perpetrated in the field of
disarmament at so huge a cost to the world was blindly
repeated in the colonial field at an additional cost which

* See *Daily Telegraph*, November 4th, 1938.

our rulers are only now beginning to reckon up. The Allies might have strengthened the foundations of universal peace by making small concessions freely, at a time when concessions would have been a virtue and a grace. Having refused to do this, the prospect is that they will be obliged, in deference to threats of violence, to salvage an unsubstantial vestige of a strictly localised peace by making large concessions at a time when concessions have become a betrayal and a crime.

No one seems enamoured of the prospect, neither Dominions nor colonies nor white men nor black men nor brown men. In the same fashion the Munich terms were unwelcome to all the people of Czechoslovakia. But Chamberlain knew how to deal with them. Perhaps he will be able to impress on the Empire how desirable it is that a sacrifice should sometimes be made for the general good. He made the Czechs save peace once; maybe he has arguments to persuade Oswald Pirow and the Tanganyika League to save it a second time. It would mean a bit of a scene—a first-class family row in the Empire. That can but be painful to a sensitive man. But not so painful as incurring the displeasure of Adolf Hitler.

At one moment the displeasure of Hitler seemed to preoccupy the British Government; at another the displeasure of British subjects in Africa. In this second mood Malcolm MacDonald, the Secretary of State for the Colonies, authorised the Governor of Nigeria to state in the Legislative Council that the British Government had no intention of considering the transfer of Nigeria from British administration. This statement was made on November 28th, 1938. A similar one had been made in Tanganyika a week or so earlier. On December 7th MacDonald himself made a more general declaration in the House of Commons as follows:—

" I do not believe that there is to-day any section of opinion in this country which is disposed to hand over to any other country the care of any of the territories or peoples for whose government we are responsible either as a colonial or as a mandatory power. (Cheers from all sides.)

" That is a view that is shared by the Government. (Cheers from all sides.)

" We are not discussing this matter, we are not considering it. It is not now an issue in practical politics."

This sounds almost categorical, if not quite. But members were not satisfied. MacDonald was pressed to say whether the " now " of his last sentence was used in the sense of " no longer " or as indicating a reserved opinion. There were long cries of " Answer, answer ". But answer came there none. MacDonald kept his seat and held his tongue.

In Berlin the statement was received with mixed irritation and scepticism. Germany, it was remarked, did not intend to allow the door to be closed on her colonial claims by a British Minister.

Members of Parliament and Germans alike perhaps remembered a similar episode of exactly three months before. On September 7th, *The Times* had published a leader suggesting the cession of the Sudeten areas of Czechoslovakia to Germany. The suggestion was at once officially repudiated by the Foreign Office as " in no way representing the views of the British Government ". Yet by the end of September the British Government had not only embraced the repudiated policy, but had forced it on a horrified Czechoslovakia while defending it as essential both to peace and justice.

Two other pledges given by Chamberlain's Government are worth noting. On November 14th, 1938, Chamberlain promised that he would not arrange the transfer of colonies or mandates without consulting Parliament. Later in the same week Britain's obligation to defend Portugal's colonies was officially admitted.

APPENDIX TO CHAPTER II

Article 22 of the League of Nations Covenant
(Mandatories. Control of Colonies and Territories)

To those colonies and territories which as a consequence of the late war have ceased to be under the sovereignty of the States which formerly governed them and which are inhabited by people not yet able to stand by themselves under the strenuous conditions of the modern world, there should be applied the principle that the well-being and development of such peoples form a sacred trust of civilisation and that securities for the performance of this trust should be embodied in this Covenant.

The best method of giving practical effect to this principle is that the tutelage of such peoples should be entrusted to advanced nations who by reason of their resources, their experience or their geographical position can best undertake this responsibility, and who are willing to accept it, and that this tutelage should be exercised by them as Mandatories on behalf of the League.

The character of the mandate must differ according to the stage of the development of the people, the geographical situation of the territory, its economic conditions and other similar circumstances.

Certain communities formerly belonging to the Turkish Empire have reached a stage of development where their existence as independent nations can be provisionally recognised subject to the rendering of administrative advice and assistance by a Mandatory until such time as they are able to stand alone. The wishes of these communities must be a principal consideration in the selection of the Mandatory.

Other peoples, especially those of Central Africa, are at such a stage that the Mandatory must be responsible for the administration of the territory under conditions which will guarantee freedom of conscience and religion, subject only to the maintenance of public order and morals, the prohibition of abuses such as the slave trade, the arms traffic and the liquor traffic, and the prevention of the establishment of fortifications or military and naval bases and of military training of the natives for other than police purposes and the defence of territory, and will also secure equal opportunities for the trade and commerce of other Members of the League.

There are territories, such as South-West Africa and certain of the South Pacific Islands, which, owing to the sparseness of their population, or their small size, or their remoteness from the centres of civilisation, or their geographical contiguity to the territory of the Mandatory, and other circumstances, can be best administered under the laws of the Mandatory as integral portions of its territory, subject to the safeguards above-mentioned in the interests of the indigenous population.

In every case of mandate, the Mandatory shall render to the Council an annual report in reference to the territory committed to its charge.

The degree of authority, control, or administration to be exercised by the Mandatory shall, if not previously agreed upon by the Members of the League, be explicitly defined in each case by the Council.

A permanent Commission shall be constituted to receive and examine the annual reports of the Mandatories and to advise the Council on all matters relating to the observance of the mandates.

CHAPTER III

GERMAN COLONIAL POLICY

"Take every care that the strength of our people is anchored securely not on colonies, but on the soil of the home country in Europe."—Adolf Hitler, "Mein Kampf", p. 754.

§ 1. BACK TO BISMARCK

IT seems a far cry from the above observation of the Führer to the German government's present agitation for colonies as vital to the national existence of Germany. Indeed, the attitudes of official Germany towards the colonial question have always been remarkably inconsistent. Even to-day, while that Germany clamours for colonies with a single and united voice, it justifies the clamour with a bundle of arguments so self-discrepant that clearly no kind of regard has been paid to logic in assembling them.

It is worth remembering that Bismarck's colonial policy was marked by similar vacillations to those of the National-Socialist Party. Bismarck undoubtedly approached the issue with some sympathy for the view of the Manchester School that colonies were an endless source of trouble and expense. Moreover, he regarded with disrelish the prospect that colonial expansion might drive him to build a fleet, and thereby to enrol England among his enemies. But between 1883 and 1885 he came to display a considerable interest in colonies, and joined with apparent zest in the scramble for Africa. In this period of less than two years he acquired South-West Africa, the Cameroons, Togoland, and New Guinea.

The usual account of this *volte face* has been that the pressure of public opinion, worked up to a pitch of jingo

42

enthusiasm by the propaganda of the Gesellschaft für Deutsche Kolonisation, overbore his better judgement and forced him into some colonial adventures. This account is called in question by A. J. P. Taylor, who in a recent book has sought to show that Bismarck's truculent behaviour towards Britain was not due to direct rivalry in the game of colonial grab. Bismarck continued to attach little value to the acquisition of a colonial empire for its own sake. His main object was the creation of a conflict, or the appearance of conflict, between Germany and Britain. He happened to be flirting with a scheme for a Franco–German entente, and his quarrels with Britain over colonies were to form a guarantee of the seriousness and sincerity of his overtures to the French.*

We should not ignore the possibility that a dominant motive of Hitler's may equally be the creation of nuisance values and the reassurance of his collaborators in Tokio and Rome somewhat after Bismarck's style. During the first years of his rule Hitler accepted, apparently without reserve, Bismarck's view that colonies would have little economic value for Germany, and that they might prove a positive danger, since their defence would commit Germany to entry on a naval construction race with Britain. This would be likely to drive Britain into alliance with Germany's enemies, as in 1914. In any case, to read the documents connected with the phase of Bismarck's ostensible interest in colonies is to gain an insight into the sordid complexities of diplomatic strife and intrigue such as perennially end in war. Any reader who has not fallen a prey to complete cynicism will be sickened by them. But they continue. Indeed, they are doubtless being repeated at this moment in the chancelleries of the great powers.

§ 2. POST-WAR FEELING IN GERMANY

The annihilation of the German empire in the circumstances of Versailles was widely felt by German patriots as

* See A. J. P. Taylor, " Germany's First Bid for Colonies, 1884/5".

a great national loss. But the sense of loss attached to colonies was only one item in the wider sense of loss attached to military defeat. So that the question of colonies as a specific issue received little attention once the general humiliation of the peace treaty had been forced upon the country. In the confusion of the early 1920's, again, few Germans had time or energy to devote to the colonial question. But in 1924 signs of a revival of interest began to be perceptible. In the German memorandum dealing with Germany's possible entry into the League of Nations, the following reference appears: " Germany expect that in due time she will be given an active share in the working of the mandate system of the League of Nations ". It was in 1924 also that Dr. H. Schacht drew the outlines of a scheme for the formation of a chartered company in which German finance and German personnel would undertake the development of certain areas of Central Africa. An echo of this scheme reappears in the van Zeeland Report of 1938.

By 1926 the vanguard of a movement for the return of Germany's colonies began to come into prominence. In this year Dr. A. H. Schnee, a former governor of German East Africa who had served for a short while on the mandates commission of the League, published a book entitled, " German Colonisation, Past and Future ". Here he submitted the mandate system to sharp criticism and demanded the return of Germany's former colonies to her unrestricted rule. When the National-Socialist Party came to power in 1933, they appointed Schnee head of the Hochschule für Politik in Berlin.

At the time when Briand and Stresemann were drawing Germany and France closer together, Stresemann himself ventured to touch on the question of colonies. Speaking to an audience of Germans in Geneva on September 21st, 1926, he declared that Germany had the same right to possess colonies as any other nation. The speech was regarded as a grave indiscretion in British and French circles. In general it may be said that apart from Schacht and a small group of former colonial officials, there was little interest in the colonial question under the Weimar Republic, and certainly no popular enthusiasm about it. After the Allies had rapped Stresemann over the knuckles for his audacity in 1926, the subject was completely dropped for seven years. Then in February 1933, within a few weeks of his seizure of power, Hitler declared, " As for our colonies overseas, we have certainly not renounced our colonial aspirations ". Yet it was still not open to everyone to re-echo these exalted sentiments. When, in the summer of the same year, Hugenberg made a reference at the World Economic Conference to Germany's desire to recover her former colonies, the lapse was made a pretext for dropping him from the Cabinet.

Thenceforward little was heard of the colonial issue, and such mention as was made of it by leading members of the National-Socialist Party suggested that it was considered of small importance and no urgency. As late as the spring of 1935 Hitler was reported to have told Sir John Simon and Anthony Eden during their conversations in Berlin that he was still not convinced that colonies would be economically advantageous to Germany.*

The year 1935, however, marks the end of official indifference in Germany. Goering, himself the son of a colonial official, was the first of the Nazi leaders to make a strong point of the need to recover the colonies. Official opinion steadily fell into line with him. In March 1935 the Chamber of Industry and Commerce demanded that the colonies should be restored. The activities of the colonial societies and propaganda organisations began to increase. By the summer there were at least ten such societies, of which the most prominent were the Reichs-kolonialbund and the Deutsche Kolonialgesellschaft. Colonial training-schools were opened in Göttingen and other German towns. Instruction provided in them covered

* *Daily Telegraph,* March 29th, 1935

all aspects of colonial administration. Picked students were drafted at the conclusion of the course to Tanganyika and South-West Africa.

Throughout 1936 the campaign gathered momentum and received wide support in the press. In the middle of the year the Deutsche Kolonialgesellschaft was dissolved and replaced by the colonial department of the National-Socialist Party under the direction of General Ritter von Epp. The official leadership of the campaign was in this way assumed by the party.

By 1937 the utterances of the party leaders began to take on a certain tone of menace. Hitler observed in a speech on January 30th, " To-day Germany lives in a time of fierce struggle for foodstuffs and raw materials. . . . Therefore the demand for colonies will be ever and again raised for our so densely populated country as a matter of course." In the spring a great German colonial exhibition was opened at Frankfurt, and in the summer similar ones were opened at Munich and Dusseldorf. At Munich loud-speakers were alleged to have announced from time to time, " We are going to build a gigantic fleet in order to keep our connections with our possessions abroad and to develop them. We are going to get our colonies back, for no great nation can go for any length of time without colonies." *

The second half of 1937 was full of colonial alarms and excursions. Mussolini during his visit to Germany demanded a place for that country in the African sun, and in frequent newspaper articles afterwards called on Britain and France to cede colonies to Germany. In Germany itself colonial demands were given louder and louder voice.†

* *Manchester Guardian*, August 10th, 1937.
† The above account of the development of the colonial campaign in Germany is drawn in the main from an unpublished memorandum prepared by the League of Nations Union.

§ 3. GERMANS AS COLONISERS

Alongside this question of what Germans have thought or think about the desirability of colonies, we have to raise the question of their actual performance as colonial administrators. In the thirty years between 1884 and 1914 how did the record of their rule in Africa compare with that of other imperial powers ?

When the German protest against confiscation of the colonies was considered at the peace conference, the allied statesmen brushed it aside with the remark that " Germany's failure in the domain of colonial civilisation is so evident that the allied and associated powers cannot give her a second chance nor abandon thirteen or fourteen million natives once more to a fate from which the war delivered them ".

The Allies took this view partly no doubt because they desired to assume control of the German colonies themselves, and partly on the basis of certain official publications giving information as to the treatment of Africans by Germany.* These blue books were a bunch of atrocity stories about Germany's behaviour towards subject races. Few people nowadays take them as evidence of any special immorality on Germany's part. Their accuracy, so far as they go, is not denied. But it would be possible with equal accuracy to make similar collections of atrocity stories for all imperial powers in Africa. In fact, this has been done by the Germans themselves as a kind of reprisal, giving particular attention to French and British treatment of subject peoples. The German documents, however, receive little publicity in Britain or France.

It is difficult, perhaps impossible, to weigh impartially the record of Germany against that of other countries. Probably the best attempt we can make is to consider

* " Report on the Natives of S.W. Africa and their Treatment by Germany ", 1918. (Cd. 9146.)
" Papers relating to Certain Trials in German S.W. Africa ", 1916. (Cd. 8371.)

representative and authoritative opinions which have been expressed on the matter.

Lugard, who saw the Germans at work in Africa, thinks that " they have set us an example in the thorough and practical way in which they have set about to develop their territories, but that as regards tact with the natives the advantage perhaps rests with us ".*

Sir Harry Johnston, writing in 1899, says of East Africa, " The Arabs are becoming reconciled to German rule, while on the other hand German officials are learning the art of dealing tactfully with subject races ". Johnston sums up his general judgement as follows : " I fancy when history takes a review of the foundation of these African states that the unmixed Teuton (Dutchman or German) is on first contact with subject races apt to be harsh and even brutal, but that he is no fool and wins the respect of the negro and the Asiatic, who admire brute force ; while his own good nature in time induces a softening of manners when the native has ceased to rebel and begun to cringe ". †

Leonard Woolf, after carefully balancing the evidence and the relevant circumstances, comes to the conclusion that the only possible verdict upon the facts is that the German state proved itself absolutely unfit to own African colonies. He goes on to add, what the Allies at Versailles omitted to mention, that the facts also prove all European states to be absolutely unfit to own African colonies. " It would ", he says, " be absurd to deny that European civilisation, through the machinery of state and trade, has carried some considerable benefits into Africa ; but the autocratic dominion of European over African has been accompanied by such horrible cruelty, exploitation, and injustice that it is difficult not to believe that the balance of good in the

* F. D. Lugard, " The Rise of our East African Empire ", 1893. Pt. i, p. 402, cited by Leonard Woolf in " Empire and Commerce in Africa ", p. 257.
† Sir H. H. Johnston, " The History of Colonization of Africa by Alien Races ", 1899, p. 258 (also cited by Woolf, ibid.).

world would have been and would be infinitely greater, if the European and his state had never entered Africa." *

Further interesting evidence has lately been made available about German rule in the Cameroons. Mr. Harry R. Rudin in a monograph based on the German colonial archives up to 1914 considers that " Germany's colonial accomplishments . . . constitute a real and unusual achievement and entitle her to very high rank as a successful colonial power, a view quite different from that reached in 1919 ".† Mr. Rudin does not make it perfectly clear whether he reaches this judgement out of gratitude to the German authorities who let him see their papers, or on a summing up of the facts which he himself gives. Among these facts we find that Germany never fully " pacified " her natives. " After 1884 there was scarcely a year without open hostilities in some part of the country." In 1914 the most important and advanced tribe was on the verge of rebellion. When war broke out, the Germans, " believing ", as Mr. Rudin puts it, " in prevention as well as in punishing what was regarded as high treason ", hanged their enlightened paramount chief, Manga Bell.

One other study ought also to be taken into account.‡ Miss Townsend's book surveys the whole field of German colonial enterprise, and Professor Carlton Hayes of Colombia University has summed up her work by saying that she " presents ample evidence for her belief that Germany's colonial administration was neither better nor worse than that of any other colonial power similarly circumstanced ".

If we attempt to weigh the whole evidence thus made available for us, it seems safest to conclude with Rudin and Townsend that all imperial powers are much of a muchness in their dealings with subject races; and with Woolf that European nations in general, instead of swopping atrocity

* See Woolf, op. cit., p. 259.
† " Germans in the Cameroons ", 1884–1914.
‡ " The Rise and Fall of Germany's Colonial Empire, 1884–1919 ", by Mary Evelyn Townsend.

stories about one another, might preferably join in making open confession of a sin common to them all, common indeed to all white races, and possibly common to all mankind—" We cannot trust ourselves to be impartial and just in our dealings with a weaker people living on the same soil ". * At any rate it is important to be clear that the refusal to return colonies to Germany, if it is to be made, cannot be grounded on any pre-war maladministration which distinguished Germany from other countries.

§ 4. NATIVE POLICY OF THE NAZIS

But after all what we really want to know is not so much what the Germans did before 1914 as what they are likely to do in 1940. As if to satisfy our curiosity on this point, a pamphlet was published in Germany in December 1938 entitled " The Colonial Question and Racial Thought ". The author, Dr. Günther Hecht, expert on colonial racial problems in the racial-political office of the National-Socialist Party, laid down the racial principles which were to govern the future treatment of natives by their German rulers.

The National-Socialist Party, Hecht informs us, will not uproot the native by forcing baptism upon him, nor will his equality with Europeans be preached to him. Natives will not be allowed to leave German colonies for Europe on any pretext. " Coloured people will, however, be allowed their full rights of existence in their home land." No native will be able to become a German citizen. The German racial law will be extended to the colonies.

Native schools will not teach any " European matter ", since, if that were done, Europe would have to be presented to the natives as the peak of cultural development, and they would therefore lose faith in their own powers. But local culture will be fostered side by side with " an introduction to the understanding of European civilisation ". In principle higher schools and universities will be closed to

* See also " Australia ", by W. K. Hancock, p. 80.

natives. Special theatres, cinemas, and other places of amusement and recreation will be erected for them.

This programme, Hecht concludes, will stand in opposition to the " levelling and anti-racial teaching of equality of the democratic colonial policy ". * We shall see in Part III how levelling and equalitarian the colonial policy of the so-called democratic powers actually is. Meanwhile we may agree with Hecht that from his own scheme the democratic tendency seems to have been successfully excluded.

* See *The Times*, December 12th, 1938.

CHAPTER IV

DOES GERMANY NEED COLONIES?

§ 1. PRESTIGE

WE turn now to a group of questions which may be framed as follows. Why are colonies valued? Is the kind of value colonies possess relevant to Germany's present situation? If so, in what special ways are colonies likely to help Germany? If not, why does she cry for them so insistently? Is it simply because of some vague feeling that they would be nice things to have?

You may think it odd of them, but the Germans at the moment seem to find in just such a vague feeling the decisive reasons for wanting colonies. It riles them that a bunch of little one-eyed countries with few guns and no great superfluity of butter—countries like Holland, Belgium, and Portugal—should own extensive colonial empires, while Germany herself has none. Here we are once more in the presence of the charmingly immature notion, so dearly cherished by our own imperialists also, that colonies are essential to the status of a great power. You may have colonies and not be a great power, but you cannot be a great power and not have colonies.

Sometimes, indeed, the claim is put higher, and colonies are represented as being a necessary attribute even of nationhood. This notion has been carried to its logical extreme by von Ribbentrop, who holds that " every nation in the world, even the smallest, has the right of possessing colonies ". He evidently feels that by conceding the right to the small nations he is strengthening the claim of a great

52

nation like Germany. The bigger the nation, the better the claim. He does not seem to have reflected that in a world arranged on this basis there would be no one left to be a colony. As in the old Spanish army, we should be all generals and no privates—unless of course we all undertook to perform as one another's colonies. It is, however, unlikely that the Nazis interpret colonial equality in this sense.

Beyond the general view of colonies as a kind of court dress which every accredited great power is entitled to wear, the Germans have special " moral " grounds for wanting colonies. To the sensitive nationalism of Hitler's régime it seems that only by the recovery of Germany's colonies can the " colonial guilt lie " be finally scotched. The " lie " is sometimes said to have been informally withdrawn by the Allies when Germany was told, as far back as 1926, before she entered the League of Nations, that it was perfectly open to her to hold a mandate, if at any time she happened to possess a territory with regard to which she wished to undertake mandatory obligations. But we can readily understand that to the German eye there seemed to be an element of mockery both in this somewhat barren gesture and in the soapy hypotheticality of the diplomatic phrase. Anyway, in a speech to the Reichstag in 1936 Hitler made the colonial question a point of honour. It is the one item in the hated *Diktat* of Versailles that remains unrevised. Hitler's claim to colonies is thus first and foremost an integral part of his claim to full all-round equality with other powers.

By assigning priority to " moral " considerations such as these, the Germans by no means intend to suggest that colony-ownership lacks any more material interest or advantage for them. There are four traditional reasons why colonies are thought to be valuable, and the Germans adduce all of them in support of their claim. First, as a source of raw materials; second, as markets for exportable goods; third, as fields of investment; and fourth, as outlets for surplus population.* Orthodox British spokesmen, from their side, try to show that on one ground or another none of the four applies very significantly to Germany's present problems. The argument proceeds somehow after this fashion.

§ 2. RAW MATERIALS

The chief raw materials are not in the main drawn from colonies in the strict sense of the term—i.e., territories subject to the control of other states. They are drawn from the territories of sovereign nations. The most important exceptions are rubber, tin, copper, palm oil, and certain foodstuffs. Moreover, there are in fact very few instances at present of discrimination in relation to access to raw materials against countries which do not possess colonies. It may, of course, be argued that this situation is liable to change at any time.

Various restriction schemes have been set up by producers in the interests of producers; and the number of such schemes is increasing. They often cause some international friction, as in the case of the Stevenson rubber restriction scheme, which was keenly resented in the United States. True, they do not differentiate in terms between one type of consumer and another, and hence cannot be accused of directly discriminating against " have-not " powers. In practice, however, they raise the price of raw materials or prevent it falling, with the result that countries short of foreign exchange tend to have their trading difficulties increased. Germany and Italy are among the number of such countries.

Again, control of some types of raw materials is desired for strategic reasons. An example is afforded by Britain's interest in the near-Eastern oil supply, and consequently in the Haifa pipe-line, which is unquestionably one of the

* For a detailed account of the questions which fall under these various heads, see the Chatham House publications : " Raw Materials and Colonies ", " The Colonial Problem ", and " Germany's Claim to Colonies ".

main reasons why the British are in Palestine. In other cases, such as those of copper and tin, which involve restriction as well as control, the scheme may nominally bear equally on countries A and B, but be resented more in B because it has been instituted by A. Various suggestions have been made that any unfairness might be met by an international agreement promising equal supplies to all consumers, and giving consumer countries representation on the control boards.*

Countries with exchange restrictions would no doubt find the purchase of raw materials easier if they possessed colonies within their own currency areas, though probably in that case they would have to face other difficulties. But British, and to a lesser extent French and Belgian, writers are wont to stress the fact that when Germany did possess colonies she did not make much use of them from the economic point of view. The whole of Africa produces only 3.7% of the world's raw material supplies, as compared with Europe's (including U.S.S.R.) 36.9%, North America's 31.9%, and Asia's 20.1%. The former German colonies produced the following proportion of the world's supply of the materials specified.†

	%
Useful metals	0
Gold	0.1
Rubber	0.2
Cotton	0.1
Copra	0.2
Ground nuts	0.9
Palm oil	5.2
Coffee	0.5
Cocoa	6

The ensemble is not very striking.

Before the war Germany drew from her colonies 0.6%

* See e.g., Sir Arthur Salter in " Peace and the Colonial Problem ".
† See " Raw Materials and Colonies ", published by the Royal Institute of International Affairs.

of her raw material requirements. Dr. Schacht has specified the essential raw materials as coal, iron, mineral oil, cotton, rubber, and copper. Of these only cotton is produced on an economic basis in any former German colony (in Tanganyika). And quantitatively this production is very small.

To this line of argument the German reply is that there is no fair comparison between the pre-war and the post-war positions. Pre-war Germany was not short of raw materials, she had ample foreign exchange and trading opportunities, and therefore had no pressing need to exploit her colonies to the full. Did she possess those colonies to-day, " their development through German labour and German capital and credit in German currency would be pursued with the greatest vigour, and infinitely more raw materials and food-stuffs would be produced than is the case to-day under the rule of the mandatory powers ". * Dr. Eicke, a director of the Reichsbank, has estimated that about 15% of Germany's essential imports could be provided to-day by her former colonies. More recently, the *Economist* (November 26th, 1938) mentioned a German calculation according to which Germany would obtain 10% of her yearly imports on the basis of present output in these colonies, and would soon raise that percentage to 20 if they were under her control. (The diagram on page 57 shows the total exports from the former colonies in 1934 as a percentage of German imports from all sources.)

§ 3. MARKETS

When we pass on to consider colonies as markets for exports, we soon find that there is a marked tendency for trade to follow the flag, even without compulsion or open discrimination. This has been the British experience, for example, in Tanganyika. In that territory there were trade and business connections with German firms dating from the pre-war period, and the open door was doubly

* Dr. Schacht, speaking at Frankfurt on December 9th, 1936.

The Former German Colonies

POPULATION AND TRADE

	Europeans.	Natives.	Total Exports, 1936.
	Most recent years.		
East Africa . . .	9,400 *	8,500,000	£5,000,000
S.W. Africa . . .	30,700 †	300,000	3,000,000
Cameroons . . .	2,700	3,200,000	2,500,000
Togo	400	1,100,000	750,000
New Guinea . . .	3,800 ‡	500,000 §	2,000,000
Nauru . . .	200	2,000	500,000
W. Samoa . . .	600	55,000	250,000
Marianne Is., etc. . .	100 ‖	50,000	1,000,000 ¶

* 30 per cent. German; also 33,000 Asiatics. † 30 per cent. speak German at home. ‡ Of which 500 are Germans. § Areas under Government control only. ‖ Also 52,000 Japanese. ¶ 1934.

Principal source for figures and diagrams: "Germany's Claim to Colonies", Royal Institute of International Affairs. 2s.

[By Courtesy of *The Economist.*

guaranteed by the terms of the mandate and by the Congo Basin treaties. Yet the dominant trade position passed from Germany to Britain. Favourable trade positions can evidently be secured by other means than preferential tariffs.

But generally speaking the policy in the British and French, and to a lesser extent the Dutch, empires has been to draw the economic bonds of empire closer by protectionist devices. In 1922 the United States Tariff Commission estimated that even though there were then important preferential arrangements between various countries in the British Empire, only 5% of British trade was affected by them. Since 1931–2, however, the Ottawa Agreements and other structural changes in the system of world trade have altered this situation to such an extent that now more than half the total volume of British trade is within the circle of British preference. There can be no doubt that the Ottawa Agreements and others similar to them have been one of the most important factors in creating the difficulties felt by Germany and Italy in their external trade. A number of British writers, recognising this, have put forward the suggestion that there should be an international convention guaranteeing the open door in all colonial territories.

As we shall discover in Part III, it is important to remember that so long as the present methods of development are followed in colonial areas, it is impossible that colonies should form important markets for any country, owing to the low standard of living among native populations. The position in the British Empire to-day is that the colonies absorb about 10% of British export trade, or about 1% of the output that makes up the national income. For other countries with less extensive colonial areas the proportion is likely to be even smaller.

Apart from tariff discrimination, Germany's position in colonial markets is adversely affected in two further ways. First, on a basis of multilateral trade raw materials can be acquired by the sale of exports to any country. But the recent growth of exclusively bilateral trade makes such purchases more dependent on the sale of goods directly to the producers of raw materials. Direct sales are plainly easier for countries which have close political relations with these producers. Countries such as Germany and Italy are justified in claiming that the lack of these relations is a special handicap to them in so far as bilaterial trade has replaced multilateral in the world at large.

In the second place, a colony-owning country has a certain advantage in being able to pay for imports either in its own currency or in a colonial currency which can be freely bought at a fixed price in terms of its own. Since in this case imports do not have to be paid for in foreign exchange, such a country may obtain them either by what amounts to a forced credit or in exchange for goods which could not be otherwise sold abroad at remunerative prices.*

§ 4. FIELDS OF INVESTMENT

When it comes to the question of investment in colonial areas, the British Empire, in common with most others, shows a certain amount of anti-foreign discrimination, both direct and indirect. We may note, however, that the countries that are demanding colonial territories at the moment are those which have the least surplus capital to dispose of. Abyssinia, for instance, is a burden on Italy's home resources, and is likely to remain so for many years to come. The same thing would be true of any undeveloped areas handed over to Germany at present. On the other hand, it may be argued that shortage of capital is not a very relevant difficulty in the way of the development of colonies, if one assumes that Germany would be working within her own economic and currency systems. The essential factor would be that she would have control over the labour supply. Furthermore, she would presumably hope for a

* For a fuller discussion see Leonard Barnes," The Future of Colonies ', pp. 13 ff.

loan in any negotiations for the return of colonies. We saw that Poland, for example, has expressed this hope with the utmost bluntness.

§ 5. EMIGRATION

As a result of the war, Germany lost 10% of her population, but 15.4% of her arable land. This must be made good by colonies. Germany must have room for expansion. The Germans are a virile race, and as such have a right to expect that less virile races will make room for them.

" Germany has too little living room for her population. She has made every effort, and certainly much greater effort than any other nation, to extract from her present limited space all that is necessary to secure the life of the nation. In spite of all these efforts the space is not sufficient." *

So runs the German argument. From the British side this rejoinder is made. The important fact to bear in mind in considering colonies as fields for emigration is that the dependent territories are for the most part tropical, and hence unsuitable for European settlement on a large scale. It has become almost a familiar gibe to recall that there were only some 20,000 Germans in the German colonies before the war—less than the number of Germans domiciled in Paris at the time. In the British African dependencies, in spite of great efforts to establish white settlers, there are at present less than 30,000. On this basis the relief afforded to the annual increase in German population by the return of colonies would be only some 3 or 4%. Colonies, it seems, will not provide a solution for over-population in any country, except at an enormous public cost. (As we pointed out above, the " have-not " countries are lacking in capital.)

There is another general consideration of some significance —namely, that extensive voluntary emigration is possible only to countries with higher standards of wages and

* Dr. Schacht, December 9th, 1936.

income than obtain in the countries in which the potential emigrants live. This in practice limits the fields of large-scale emigration to sovereign states such as the U.S.A., Australia, Canada, New Zealand, and so on.

Moreover, Germany cannot have it both ways. It is unreasonable to maintain that at present there is little or no unemployment in her country, and yet to complain that she has a large surplus population for the relief of which she must acquire colonies. We may perhaps assume that considerable real unemployment exists in Germany; in other words, that her work-creating policy absorbs many men in work which would not normally be undertaken by private enterprise, but which is made available by the state largely as a method of keeping men physically fit and capable of working in the future. But even on this assumption, Germany is not alone in suffering from unemployment. Nor are colonies the cure for this complaint, since Holland, France, and Britain, possessors of the largest colonial empires, all suffer chronically from it.

Again, it is noteworthy that thousands of Italians and other workers are being brought into Germany to work on the land. This addition to Germany's labour force is not easy to square with the demand for colonies on the ground that they are needed for living room. Germans themselves seem to be aware of the inconsistency here, and in their discussions about colonies the problem of Germany's surplus population no longer plays an important part.

§ 6. THE CURRENCY QUESTION

We can see, then, that there has in effect been considerable economic discrimination against the countries which are now demanding colonies. It has come about partly as the result of the peace settlement and partly as a reflection of the economic difficulties of the post-war period in general. It may even be said that the worst international effects of agreements such as Ottawa have arisen not from any direct discrimination, but from the fact that they tend to break up the whole system of multilateral trade. This dislocation has borne most hardly on particular countries, notably Germany and Italy. It is not in the main due to action taken in colonial markets. It is due firstly to the tariff policy of the United States, secondly to French quotas and commercial policy, and thirdly to British protectionist policy and Empire preference in the years since 1931.

For these reasons, among others, Germany has been reduced to strange straits in order to acquire the foreign currency needed to pay for her imports. One device is to barter German machinery for Smyrna figs, and to reckon the price of the figs at 40% above world prices. Germans themselves are too frugal to eat Smyrna figs. The figs are therefore exported from Germany to London, and sold in London at a price by which Germany loses the extra 40% she originally paid. In this way she secures currency from Britain which she uses to buy the materials she wants from the countries willing to supply them.*

In the opinion of the committee of the Council of the League of Nations which investigated the problem of access to raw materials and published a report in September 1937, the question of ability to pay for raw materials presents more serious difficulties than that of their supply. But the difficulties of payment are, so the committee believes, largely due to the financial and economic policies of certain countries or of their rearmament.

This, of course, is a familiar argument from the German side. Dr. Schacht has even insisted that Germany cannot obtain raw materials without colonies because only in her own territories will her own currency find acceptance. If we go on to ask how it comes about that German currency is unacceptable elsewhere, we find the following answer is commonly given. Germany, it is said, is afraid openly to devalue the mark, as almost every other country in the world has devalued its currency. Her pride forbids

* R. S. Hudson, Secretary to the Department of Overseas Trade, in the House of Commons, November 30th, 1938.

her to enter into a general currency agreement, and she prefers to manipulate her blocked marks and barter agreements in order that her foreign trade may serve the aims of her foreign policy.*

The fact is that while Germany, in common with other countries accustomed to rely on international trade for the proper balance of their national economy, no doubt suffered from the post-war heightening of the barriers to international trade, she herself has been one of the worst offenders in this matter. Most economists agree that German foreign exchange difficulties have been brought about very largely by German financial and political policy. Her currency is over-valued by something like 40%, which means that she can export, and thus obtain foreign exchange, only with great difficulty.

Her policy of economic self-sufficiency accentuates her export difficulties, and her vast rearmament plan also has the same effect, since it draws all available resources into home production, so that little attention is given to the export traders. Rearmament also forces German internal price-levels still further above world price-levels, with the consequence that her currency becomes increasingly over-valued. Any country must expect to find its foreign trade gravely hampered if it insists on maintaining a system of currency and exchange control, registered and blocked marks, clearing agreements, and the rest.

§ 7. POWER CONSIDERATIONS

There is, however, a certain unreality in discussing either Germany's claim to colonies or the colonial question in general in terms of everyday bread-and-butter economics. In so far as Germany is sincerely and seriously interested in acquiring tropical colonies at all, her interest is deeply tinged with a militaristic and coercive colour. What concerns her is not equal access to raw materials, for

* See *Manchester Guardian*, January 28th, 1937.

example, but the possibility of controlling sources of raw
materials from which she would be able to exclude other
countries. She is not concerned with other people's
open doors, but with getting hold of a door of her own
that she can shut.

Again, as we saw in Chapter II, the real reason why
France and Britain are not prepared to give up African
territory lies in its strategic and military importance. It
is for precisely corresponding reasons that Germany covets
African territory—because if she possessed it she would
by that very fact have outflanked the defence arrangements of the British and French empires, and would have
provided herself with the man-power for a black army into
the bargain.

Last, and perhaps most important, is the desire to
exploit cheap labour. As a broad generalisation we may
say that wages in the older industrial countries are on the
average some four times as great as those paid for similar
work in colonial areas. This huge inequality of labour
costs in a world which is otherwise becoming more uniform
holds out very attractive possibilities to the financier and
the industrialist.

As Richard Palmer reminds us in a valuable essay,
" Other things being equal, the rate of profit will depend
on the cost of labour. The patchy development of industrial capitalism should therefore lead to a flow of capital
down the standard of living gradient from the older
industrial countries to the new ones where labour is still
unorganised."

Hitherto other things—that is to say, natural resources
and the efficiency of labour—have not been equal, but
they are now tending to become equal, and the tendency
can be speeded up whenever it pays powerful interests to
do so. Meanwhile, the gap between the cost of home
labour and the cost of colonial labour narrows, if at all,
very slowly. Hence Palmer foresees " a prospect of radical
changes in the centre of gravity of world industry during

the next half century and the development of a new phase of imperialist exploitation." *

Colonies overseas, in fact, may come to be used to restore to the economy of the older industrial countries that element of profit to which so much violence is done by totalitarian regimentation at home.

§ 8. GERMAN COLONIES IN EUROPE

In view of Munich, and the consequent heightening of German influence all over the south-east of Europe, the question may be asked whether the range of natural resources now available for the German economy is not so extensive as to render tropical possessions superfluous. There is no doubt that in post-Munich Europe Germany can command new supplies, such as Hungarian wheat and Roumanian oil, which have altered the general economic outlook greatly to Germany's advantage. But the inference drawn by official Germany is not that African colonies are unnecessary, but that still more land in Europe is a still more urgent need.† Austria and the Sudeten areas, it is argued, are on balance importers of foodstuffs and raw materials. Their incorporation in the Reich increases Germany's previous shortage of these things, and it is doubtful whether the increased shortage can be fully made good by the four-year plan, even with the aid of " intensive trading " in the Balkans. Such doubts could, however, be set at rest if Russia, " the country which complements the Reich ", were to be brought within the German sphere of influence. According to *The Times*, the Nazis are contemplating a military attack on the Soviet Union with this end in view.

The passage is a striking one, and deserves quotation in full :—

* " Science and World Resources ", by Richard Palmer (*Fact*, December 1938).
† See *The Times* (Berlin correspondent), November 10th, 1938.

C

" In National-Socialist circles it is suggested that M. Stalin's present progress means that the break-up of Russia from within may not be so far distant. In that case the Russian Ukraine, with its rich resources, might be linked by way of what is now the Polish Ukraine and the Carpatho-Ukraine (Ruthenia) to the industries of the Reich. It is not a fantastic thought that the façade of friendly relations between Poland and the Reich is maintained against the day when common action may be required to turn to mutual advantage a collapse of Communist Russia. The Reich, in any case, can afford to be friendly, in view of the influence which could be exerted from its satellite, the Carpatho-Ukraine, on the Ukrainian population in Poland.

" How far the Reich Government cherish these aims is not clear. The most that can be said is that they are openly discussed in National-Socialist circles here (*i.e.*, in Berlin). Their realisation seems to depend, however, on events not under the control of the Reich unless, *as seems highly probable*, resort were had to military action before a Russian collapse."

§ 9. NUISANCE VALUES

The probability, then, seems to be that Germany will keep the colonial agitation going at full blast, not so much because in her more realistic moments she attaches first-class importance to the possession of colonies, as because the agitation itself carries with it solid diplomatic advantages.

This is the view taken by Harold Nicolson, who has confessed, " I do not believe that Hitler's major objective is the return of the colonies. I believe that what he desires is to extend the might of Germany to the south-east of Europe and to strike in the direction of Odessa or the Aegean. To execute that policy he must obtain protection in the rear . . . and that in its turn entails some agreement with England. . . . All he can offer is not to rob her of her possessions. And in order to enhance the value of that offer he has organised this colonial agitation." *

The *Economist* substantially agrees. " The Nazis ", it observes, " are astute enough to realise that so long as Britain can be scared into worrying about colonial concessions, they have much to gain by waiting, and in the eyes of the world everything to gain by refusing to consider rumoured ' arrangements ' which would include the colonies of countries like Portugal and Belgium. Meanwhile their propaganda works day and night to create an atmosphere outside Germany in which the real question will not be ' Ought Germany to have colonies? ' but ' Which colonies ought Germany to have? ' In that way they will drive the hardest bargain, and conceding Powers receive the smallest return for their concessions." †

§ 10. SCIENCE AND WEALTH

There is one last consideration on which this chapter should close. The problem raised by the German claim to colonise is both a problem of politics and a problem of human geography. When we view it in the latter aspect, we have to admit that the political entity covered by the term " post-war Germany " was rather poor in natural resources. This is plainly true if we direct our attention to the physical supplies of essential materials available on her own soil. She was poor in all such materials except coal, nitrates, and potash. She produced only 80% of her food supply, and was in particular short of fats, coffee, tobacco, tropical oils and fruits, and many other things, of some of which the loss of her colonies had deprived her.‡

* *Northern Daily Telegraph*, January 10th, 1938.
† November 5th, 1938.
‡ See Leonard Barnes, " The Future of Colonies ".

Even if we extend the meaning of the term "natural resources", as we legitimately may, to include accumulations of capital and many kinds of technical knowledge and skill, the impression of post-war Germany's poverty remains valid. The Versailles Treaty aimed at, and to a considerable extent achieved, the systematic destruction of : (1) Germany's overseas commerce as represented by her mercantile marine, her colonies, her foreign investments, her exports, and the overseas connections of her merchants; (2) her coal and iron resources and the industries built on them; and, to a less extent, (3) her transport and tariff system.* These were the main factors on which her economic structure depended. The Treaty could not destroy the skill of German workmen and technicians, and in this form of resource Germany remained rich. But little enough else was left.

Thus, if God had had occasion to remake the nations in 1920, and had happened to have a glass of blessings standing by, Germany would presumably have been offered an extra helping to put her level with the enemies who had dispersed or annexed her previous store. But what God failed to do in 1920, science is in its own gradual fashion achieving all the while. It used to be said that concentrations of natural resources do not always coincide with concentrations of population, and that it is the work of international statesmanship to put people and resources in the most fruitful possible touch with one another. In view of the melancholy way in which international statesmanship has botched the job, it is some comfort to learn, what Richard Palmer tells us, that as science brings into human use substitute materials and alternative forms and sources of power, " a general tendency manifests itself towards relative uniformity in the distribution of the world's resources ". This tendency, Palmer suggests, has to be taken as one of the premises in any discussion of the prospects of civilisation.

* See J. M. Keynes, " Economic Consequences of the Peace ", p. 60.

Palmer shows that the twentieth century has thrown the basic materials of our civilisation into the melting-pot. " Coal and steel and copper, silk and wool and cotton, wood and rubber and oil have served us well. Some of them will continue to serve us either in their present form or in new and unexpected shapes. But beside them are growing up a host of new materials created by the chemist or made possible by new sources of power. Some of these new materials are already better and cheaper than the natural products that they are replacing. Others are better, but not yet so cheap, and so are used only for special purposes. Others again are cheaper but not so good. And these things are not standing still. . . . The general trend of development is towards the production of material substitutes which are not only as good or better than the natural product, but cheaper also.

" The organic chemist is giving us the freedom of a world of materials. Increasingly, he is able to choose his starting-point according to local convenience. . . . We can make sugar from cane, beet, or wood; in the tropics, in temperate climates, in the sub-arctic. We can make rubber or textile fibres from coal or oil or wood, whichever is locally abundant, or from any source of cellulose grown with cheap nitrogenous fertilisers. . . . The ancient framework of climate and soil and mineral wealth is becoming less rigid as science enables us to make the most of what we happen to have." *

This factor of the influence of scientific progress on the aspect of the population problem which we have been considering is generally neglected or even ignored. But the moment it is mentioned its importance is obvious. Everyone is aware, either dimly or acutely, that the pattern of industry and the pattern of trade are continually undergoing change. Few people have yet understood clearly enough to want to explore the political and economic consequences, that the pattern, and therefore in effect

* Richard Palmer, *op. cit.*

the distribution, of world resources are changing too. What is more, the change is in the direction of increasing equality.

In a rational world this would open up a new approach to difficulties of the sort Germany is said to be labouring under. The real problem of raw materials would be seen not as a matter of territorial expansion, but as one of science and technology. Perhaps after all colonies are becoming superfluous, and the four-year plan in its technological aspect is one of the influences tending to make them so.

But if colonies are to be considered superfluous for Germany, the question arises whether they are not super-fluous for everyone else. This question must now be faced, and in Part II we shall inquire what kind of people, if any people at all, are the real beneficiaries of imperial systems as we know them and see them at work.

PART II

WHAT ARE EMPIRES WORTH—
AND TO WHOM?

CHAPTER V

INVESTMENT

§ 1. THE AMOUNT AND THE YIELD

AVERAGE standards of living in Britain are higher than in most European countries. Many people believe that this superiority is directly connected with Britain's control of great colonial possessions.

What are the facts? How big is the investment income that comes to this country from abroad? Who gets and spends it? How far is it dependent on our imperial domination of subject peoples?

The average total of overseas investment income recorded by the Inland Revenue for the whole pre-slump decade was something over £200 millions a year. After declining to about £150 millions in the depth of the slump, it is now back again to near the £200 million mark.

This figure represents roughly one twentieth of our total national income; so that, if we suddenly lost it all, our position would be like that of a man who, having enjoyed an income of £400 in one year, found himself obliged to rub along on £380 the next. It would be a great nuisance, but it would not break us. And it would be only a fraction of the loss which the slump itself imposed on us.

But perhaps a truer picture is given by the statement that something like one quarter of our total imports is delivered to us, gratis, by foreign and Empire countries as a tribute upon the capital they have borrowed from British investors in the past. Getting something for nothing always sounds pleasant. We must remember, however,

C 2

that free imports, just because they are free, are not available to purchase current British exports. So it seems reasonable at any rate to inquire whether British export trade might not receive a healthy stimulus from the abolition of the tribute system.

The £200 millions of tribute represent the yield on a total capital estimated by Sir Robert Kindersley, of the Bank of England, at £3,764 millions in 1936.* Of this capital far the larger proportion is invested in foreign countries and in the self-governing Dominions. If (still following the Kindersley survey) we try to analyse how much of it is sunk in the dependent Empire, with which we are here primarily concerned, we get these approximate results: †

	£ million.
India and Ceylon	438
Malaya	84
East Africa	31
West Africa	37
Other British territories	49
	£639

The *Economist* (November 20th, 1937) estimates that the average rate of yield on British capital overseas has varied between 5 and 7% of the nominal amount of the capital. Take the intermediate figure of 6% as the probable yield on the £639 millions of the above table, and you find that the whole dependent Empire brings Britain in an investment income of about £38 millions a year.

* *Economic Journal*, December 1937.

† Kindersley, of course, is concerned to find the amount of active capital overseas bringing in a return to investors in Britain. His figures do not take into account capital losses sustained by such investors. Still less do they attempt to measure the total amount of capital that has as a matter of history been invested in British dependencies.

His figures for East and West Africa together come to £68 millions. It is instructive to compare this with a figure of £284 millions given by S. H. Frankel for the same territories in his "Capital Investment in Africa". Frankel is measuring the total cash subscribed for investment, and his figure therefore includes cash subscribed by foreign investors as well as British. It also includes the losses made by both. Even so, the discrepancy is very great. It looks as though someone must have lost a lot of money somewhere.

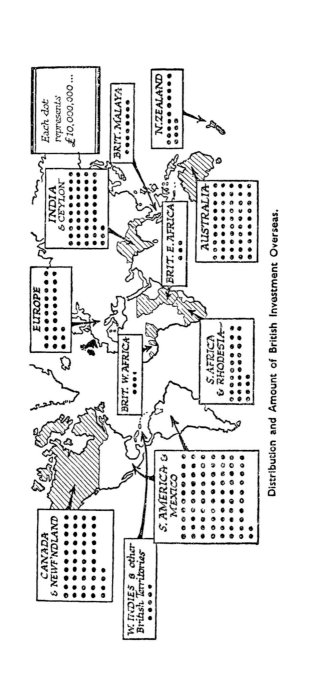

Each dot represents £10,000,000 ...

BRIT. MALAYA

N.ZEALAND

INDIA & CEYLON

EUROPE

BRIT. E.AFRICA

AUSTRALIA

BRIT. W.AFRICA

S.AFRICA & RHODESIA

CANADA & NEWF'NDLAND

W.INDIES & other British territories

S.AMERICA & MEXICO

Distribution and Amount of British Investment Overseas.

This is less than one-fifth of our total overseas investment income, and less than one-hundredth of our total
national income. If the investment yield from all the
dependent Empire were suddenly cut off, our position
would be like that of a man whose income was reduced
from £400 to £396 a year.

Clearly, if the liberation of the dependencies could be
bought by foregoing £38 millions, the bargain would be
astonishingly cheap at the price. But there is no reason
to think that such liberation would involve the loss of all
the £38 millions, or indeed of any part of it. The achievement of self-government by the dependencies would not
necessarily, or even probably, be accompanied by the
repudiation of their overseas indebtedness. It was not
so accompanied when the Dominions reached their
sovereign status. Why should anyone suppose it would
be in the case of India or Africa? The constitutional
history of the British Empire tells heavily against any such
supposition.

§ 2. WHERE THE MONEY GOES

Among what kinds of enterprise are the £639 millions
of investment in the dependent Empire distributed?
Here is Kindersley's answer summarised.

£ millions.

	Govt. and Municipal.	Railways.	Public Utilities	Mines.	Miscell- aneous.	Total.
India and Cey- lon	256	84	7	12	79	438
Malaya	6	—	4	7	67	84
Other British territories (including E. andW. Africa)	59	4	6	25	23	117.
	321	88	17	44	169	639

Finally, we may note that in recent years the Empire
as a whole (and therefore, *a fortiori*, the dependent Empire)
has ceased to have much significance as a field for new

British investment. The table below shows the change from pre-war days.

New Capital Issues in London 1911–13 and 1934–36 *
(Home Government borrowings excluded)

Class of borrower. Percentage of Total Issues.

	1911–13.	1934–36.
United Kingdom	18	84.5
British Empire	35	15
Foreign	47	0.5

This is very striking evidence of the present preoccupation of the British market with domestic issues. Nor is it the whole story. For capital formerly invested overseas is being repaid and redeemed, and over the period since 1932 this repatriation of capital has outbalanced our new overseas lending by some £76 millions.†

To sum up, then, we may say that the dependent Empire (including the great territories of India and tropical Africa) no longer plays a part of any special importance in our national economy from the investment point of view. Britain still receives from it, by way of tribute on past lendings, some £38 millions a year, most of which goes into the pockets of a few big industrial and financial concerns, and which cannot, by any stretch of imagination, be thought to compensate the common people of this country for the overhead costs of maintaining imperial rule.

* See *Economist*, September 11th, 1937.
† *Ibid.*, October 30th, 1937.

CHAPTER VI

TRADE

It is common belief that Britain's trade with the Empire is vital to her national survival. In order to preserve the life-lines of commerce that link us to Empire countries, we spend year after year hundreds of millions of pounds on the Royal Navy and other warlike establishments. Is this good business? What is the real social value of Empire trade for the common people of Britain?

The judgement that Empire trade is a vital necessity implies two things:

1. that overseas trade is in some sense preferable to home trade;

2. that, within the field of overseas trade, trade with Empire countries is in some sense preferable to trade with foreign countries.

There is perhaps a third implication also: namely that, within any limits likely to be realised, the more Empire trade we do, the better off we shall become.

How do these ideas square with the facts?

First let us get the broad proportions of the picture right. A generation ago it was calculated that some 18% of the total product of British industry was sold abroad; to-day the percentage has fallen to 12. In fact, nearly nine tenths of the output of our labour and capital is now sold at home. The home market is of overwhelming importance when compared with the overseas market.

Of the 12% which is sold abroad, more than half goes

to foreign, as distinct from Empire, countries. Allowing for this, we shall not be far out if we say that some 5% is absorbed by the Empire as a whole, and a mere 2% by the dependent parts of the Empire (India and the colonies, etc.).

This does not mean that Britain might, without serious loss or discomfort, suddenly dispense with overseas markets, or even with the markets of the dependent Empire. Are not the distressed areas living, or rather dying, evidence of what the loss of export markets can do to us, so long as our economic system lacks the flexibility to adjust itself to external change?

The question of supplies is perhaps more important still. Everyone knows that Britain must buy from overseas certain food and materials that she cannot produce, or can produce only at great disadvantage. True, as we saw in dealing with investment, one quarter of all our imports of this kind comes to us free in the form of interest on the capital we have lent to other countries in the past. But the other three quarters have to be paid for by our current exports of British goods and services.

Here is the economic necessity which orthodox imperialists are fond of emphasising. Unless we are ready to sink into the final madness of self-sufficiency, some considerable external trade is, and will remain, essential for our economic health. That is nowhere disputed. What is denied by the anti-imperialist forces is that such trade can be had only by withholding political freedom from 400 millions of Indians and Africans.

We have to realise, then, that, as J. A. Hobson puts it,* the value of overseas markets is to be measured not by the aggregate value of the goods we sell in them, but by the superior gain from selling those goods overseas as compared with selling them (or corresponding quantities of other goods) at home. And superior gain is not always, or perhaps ever, the same as higher profit.

* " Imperialism ", p. 30.

§ 2. HOME DEMAND

Imperialists speak of colonies as outlets for surplus goods, assuming that home demand is a fixed amount (x) and that goods produced in excess of x must therefore be sold abroad or not sold at all. The assumption is a false one. It is doubtful whether such things as surplus goods have ever yet existed, except as a function of the maldistribution of the national income. In any case, to quote Hobson again, " there is no necessary limit to the quantity of capital and labour that can be employed in supplying the home market ".

No doubt, in order to secure the maximum production that is technically possible for the world as a whole, a highly developed system of international (or rather interregional) exchange would be necessary. But such a system would be based on the principle of comparative real costs, and would cover only a relatively small fringe of the commodities produced in any given region.

There is certainly no warrant for the traditional British assumption of " the more external trade, the better ". It is probable that Britain in the past has done more external trade than was beneficial from the economic point of view.

In general, nations, as their real wealth expands, tend to transfer their energies more and more to distribution, services, and elaborate forms of industry which are less suited to external trade than are simpler goods. In this sense, it may be a sign of economic progress if the relative size and growth of a country's external trade decline.

Has the vast outlay of energy and money on imperial expansion involved an increase in trade with the Empire as compared with foreign trade ?

The diagrams give the answer to this question and to several others as well.

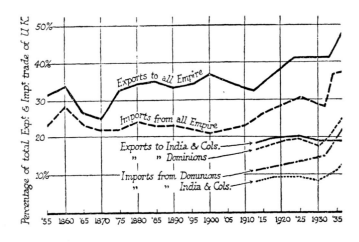

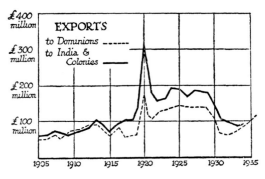

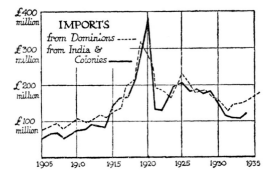

§ 3. EFFECTS OF IMPERIAL PREFERENCE

Exports to the Empire were one third of our total exports in 1860; they were also one third in 1915. Imports from the Empire were 29% of our total imports in 1860, and 26% in 1915. This in spite of the fact that between the two dates " foreign countries " were reduced by millions of square miles of territory and tens of millions of population which were conquered for the Empire and went to swell its resources.

Since the great war, exports to the Empire have risen to 49% of our total exports, and Empire imports have risen to 38% of our total imports.

Three points are worth noticing about this.

(1) Imperialism had no appreciable influence on the direction taken by our overseas trade until preferential tariff and monetary arrangements (which culminated in the Ottawa Agreements of 1932) began to be applied during and after the war.

(2) The increase in the ratio of trade with the Empire took place step by step with the deepening of international tension which has brought us to the brink of the second world war. It was, in fact, achieved at the cost of intensified poverty and distress in many parts of the world, notably Italy, Japan, and Germany.

(3) In the last fifteen years, while the ratio of our Empire trade has been rising, the money value of that trade has been falling.

What, then, are we to conclude? In the first place, there is nothing sacred about overseas trade, whether with Empire or foreign countries.

Broadly speaking, the most beneficial and serviceable kind of trade is the trade we do among ourselves—the operations of the home market. It is towards bringing these to an orderly and coherent system that economic policy should be first directed.

True enough, there is along the margin of our economic

life a strip, now wider and now narrower, which is the proper field of overseas trade. Rational planning would not seek to enlarge this strip relatively to the field of home trade; nor, within the strip itself, to enlarge the Empire portion relatively to the foreign portion.

It would seek so to arrange our exchanges with the outside world that goods and services not essential to a given standard of living for the people of Britain were exported to pay for external goods and services that were essential to such a standard.

In other words, it would use as its criterion the common economic benefit of all sections of our population. Our present system of preferential Empire trade is valued not as such a common benefit, but as a private privilege from which certain industrial and merchant interests actually profit in their particular businesses, and from which others hope to profit in theirs.

In the last analysis that privilege is sought after for two reasons: because it enables those who enjoy it to exclude their foreign competitors from valuable markets, and because it carries with it the right to exploit cheap colonial labour up to a total man-power of over 400 million.

CHAPTER VII

JOBS

§ 1. PUBLIC ASSISTANCE FOR THE WELL-TO-DO

" THE British Empire is a gigantic system of outdoor
relief for the British governing classes." Some such statement has been variously attributed to James Mill and to
John Bright speaking in the middle of the nineteenth
century, and is still widely held to correspond with the
facts. Bertrand Russell sees this outlet as operating to
Britain's advantage. " Social life in Britain ", he says in
one of his unkinder moments, " has remained compara-
tively free from the impulses that seem repulsive in German
nationalism because the Empire has been a cesspool for
British moral refuse." * And what in this way is Britain's
gain has, when viewed from the colonial end, been an
injury to the colonies—the mere transfusion of bad blood
from the centre to the circumference.

German and Italian spokesmen have laid emphasis on
the value that German and Italian colonies might have as
fields of employment for their middle classes.† It has even
been suggested, apparently quite seriously, that, if in the
early 1930's Germany, for example, had had an empire
like the British in which to place a proportion of her ex-
student population, middle-class unemployment would not
have filled the ranks of the Brown Shirts, and the Nazi
Revolution would not have taken place. If so, the British
Empire may conceivably have prevented a similar revolution in Britain, and may thus have qualified to take its
place as a force preservative of democracy and liberalism.

* " Freedom and Organisation ", p. 415.
† For an illuminating discussion of this point see H. N. Brailsford,
"Why Capitalism means War ", pp. 76 ff.

The conclusion is too paradoxical. Moreover, whatever lowering of the potentialities of fascism might be achieved by draining off " surplus " middle-class youth to the colonies would almost certainly be offset by the return home of retired colonial officials and business employees with enlarged spleens and hobnail livers. It is a two-way traffic. Mr. G. T. Garratt has suggested that these pensioners with colonial and Indian service, who have spent their active careers exercising petty dictatorships of their own over Asiatic or African servants, form the handiest of all raw material for a fascist movement at home.*

§ 2. OFFICIAL POSTS AND PENSIONS

The number of European British subjects serving in official positions in the non-self-governing parts of the Empire to-day seems to be, on a conservative estimate, approximately 20,000, made up as follows. The figures are based on information supplied by the India Office, the Colonial Office, and the Crown Agents for the Colonies.

TABLE I

India	(Civil)	.	.	.	.	6,055
	(Military)		.	.	.	3,635
Colonies, etc.	(Civil)	.	.	.	.	9,000
	(Military)		.	.	.	500
						19,190

The emoluments of these posts are paid from colonial or Indian revenues. They may all be taken as between £250 and £1,000 a year, except some hundreds which are above the latter figure.

To these figures must be added retired officials drawing pensions from colonial or Indian funds. It is difficult to arrive at any precise figure here, but there is good reason

* See " The Shadow of the Swastika ".

to suppose that there must be at least as many pensioners as serving officials. Again, we have not included the British army in India, nor the personnel of the Royal Navy serving overseas. Both these elements exist, and occupy the positions which they do occupy because of the existence of the Empire.

§ 3. UNOFFICIAL EMPLOYMENT

There have also to be taken into account the presumably larger numbers of European British subjects who are in unofficial employment in the Empire. The existence of their jobs, though less directly than that of official jobs, is to no small extent associated with the political control which is so advantageous to British trade. Can we get any idea of what these unofficial jobs amount to?

If we study the tables given by R. R. Kuczynski in his book on Colonial Population, we find that the total white population of British tropical Africa, including the Sudan but excluding Southern Rhodesia, comes out in round figures at 60,000. The corresponding figure for all the West Indian colonies, including Bermuda and British Guiana, is approximately 90,000; and for Ceylon, Malaya, and Hong Kong approximately 50,000.

We thus get the following table:—

TABLE II

Total White Population

Tropical African colonies, etc.		.	.	.	60,000
West Indian	,,	.	.	.	90,000
Eastern	,,	.	.	.	50,000
					200,000

Now let us divide this total by 3 in order to arrive at the number of earners—i.e., of people in jobs. The divisor is almost certainly too high, but since we cannot tell what the true divisor is, let us for the moment use 3 and keep on the conservative side. This would give us 66,000 as the number of jobs. But we have already counted 9,500 (say 10,000) of these in Table I, and must therefore deduct them now from our 66,000. We are thus left with 56,000. Again, allowance has to be made for heads of households who are permanently settled in the colonies (mostly in the West Indies, but also in Kenya and Northern Rhodesia), and so do not fall into our category of temporary migrants from England. We will assume—it is no more than a guess —that 20,000 is the right allowance here. It brings the figure down to 36,000.

If now we make the same calculation using 2 as divisor instead of 3, we get a final figure of 70,000 in place of our previous 36,000. We will assume that the true figure lies somewhere in between these extremes.

On this showing, then, there are between 36,000 and 70,000 unofficial jobs in the colonies, etc., which are filled by people from England who work in them for a term of years and then come home again to settle down. The holders of these jobs are not of course paid, as are the people in Table I, from the public funds of the colonies in which they work. But they are paid out of the general social income of those colonies, and not out of Britain's social income.

Next we have to ask, What is the corresponding position as regards India? The 1931 census shows the total of British subjects of pure European descent in India and Burma as 300,000 in round figures. If we follow the same procedure as in the case of the colonies and divide by 3, we get a gross total of 100,000 jobs in these countries. Take away 10,000 for those already counted in Table I, and (say) another 10,000 as an allowance for Europeans who may not have come from Britain or may not return there. That leaves a net total of 80,000. The alternative calculation, using 2 as divisor, gives 130,000.

We can now make up a final table.

TABLE III

	Lower Limit	Upper Limit
Serving officials (India and colonies, etc.)	20,000	20,000
Officials retired on pension (do.) . .	20,000	20,000
Unofficial employees (Colonies, etc.) .	36,000	70,000
do. (India and Burma) .	80,000	130,000
	156,000	240,000

§ 4. UPPER-CLASS LIVES

Obviously no sort of exactness can be claimed for any of these figures, except possibly the first. But they do give an approximate idea of the order of magnitude of the field of employment which the dependent Empire offers to the middle-class youth of this country. We can be pretty sure that in fact our lower total is too small, partly for the reasons given above, and partly because no account has been taken of such semi-colonial countries as Egypt, Iraq, and Palestine. In the United Kingdom there are calculated to be rather under 2 million persons who draw incomes of not less than £250 and not more than £1,000. Speaking in the roughest way, therefore, we may estimate that India and the colonies furnish an aggregate reinforcement of some 10% to this group in our society.

As the dependencies move towards autonomy, their operative staffs, both official and unofficial, will be drawn more and more from the indigenous peoples concerned, and the number of imported Europeans will gradually dwindle away. Meanwhile it is clear that historically the influence of British colonial expansion on the development of the class-structure in Britain has been significant, and that the influence persists unimpaired in our own time.

Many of the people who now find employment in the Empire would no doubt, if such posts were not open to them, be employed in some capacity at home. But it is improbable that they would be anything like so well provided for. One might perhaps say that one of the

main advantages of the Empire from this standpoint is
that it enables middle-class persons to live upper-class lives,
on condition of their removing to the tropics to do so.
Furthermore, the pressure on the labour market for the
middle classes at home is very appreciably reduced by
this outlet.

CHAPTER VIII

THE COLONIAL SERVICE

§ 1. PAY

Now that we have a rough idea of the number of jobs in the Empire, it is worth looking a little more closely into the character and the conditions of them. No study has been made of unofficial employment in the Empire. But plenty of information is available about the public services, the terms on which appointments are made, and the kind of people who fill them.

The following table gives an approximate record of the number of official posts filled annually from this country. The precipitous drop after 1930 reflects the severity of the shock dealt to the dependencies by the great slump.

1922	1923	1924	1925	1926	1927	1928
523	679	940	1094	1167	1089	1299
1929	1930	1931	1932	1933	1934	1935
1118	1189	392	243	299	421	529

The large majority of all these appointments carry *initial* emoluments whose value ranges from £400 to £700 a year. Their average value appears to be somewhat over £500. The investigations of Colin Clark into the national income of this country and its distribution lead to the conclusion that only some 4% of the occupied population enjoy incomes of £500 and over. A job in the colonial service therefore admits a man at the outset of his career straight to membership of this exclusive aristocracy (though his salary, we may repeat, is part of the social income not of this country, but of the dependency which pays it).

As to the amounts which colonial officials may expect

to be earning at the close of their careers in the service, it is difficult to generalise. But of the administrative services proper it may be said that the customary salary scales rise to £1,000 a year in tropical Africa, and to £1,800 a year in the Asiatic dependencies. There are also higher posts above these scales. Anything above £1,000 puts its recipient into the same income-group as the top 1½% of earners in Britain.

Rewards of this order of magnitude for helping to fulfil a sacred trust can hardly be called niggardly. Seen from the standpoint of the native populations from whose tax-payments they are met, they represent almost unimaginable wealth. And we should remember that attached to the substantial rates of salary are valuable pension rights, and that regulations further provide for long full-pay leave after each prescribed tour of service, together with free return passages to England, and free or assisted passages for wives and children. Tours of service may vary from twelve months in some parts of Africa to four years in the Far East and elsewhere.

On retirement, the holder of a pensionable appointment —and the majority of colonial service appointments are pensionable—may expect to draw a pension of as much as two-thirds of his final salary after thirty odd years of tropical service; or a proportionately smaller pension for shorter service, subject to a minimum period of years.

But enrolments in the colonial service have also to be considered in comparison with those offered by alternative careers open to possible recruits. The Warren Fisher Report * argued strongly for a standard of remuneration generally higher even than the present, on the ground that " the remuneration and opportunities offered in other public appointments and in business are an increasingly important competitive factor ".

Some may question whether this argument has much weight, except perhaps during periods of universal boom

* Cmd. 3554.

such as the world is unlikely to see for many years to come. A stronger argument is that it is essential that the representatives and agents of Britain among the so-called backward races should be of the highest types we are capable of producing. If it is a fact—and the Colonial Office believes it is—that such types cannot be secured without offering remuneration on the existing scale, then that scale must be regarded as having *de facto* justification.

Certainly, the standard of personnel entering the colonial service has immensely improved since the war, and the improvement has gone hand in hand with improvements in the general conditions of service. Certainly, too, there is evidence of the disastrous results of trying to economise on the salaries of officials (e.g., in the South African Protectorates). It is important that terms of service should not be of a kind to include any positive encouragement to supplement official remuneration " on the side ".

§ 2. OFFICERS AND GENTLEMEN

As to the qualifications demanded of candidates, the competitive examination for Ceylon cadetships is the same as that for the Home Civil Service and the Indian Civil Service; it is well known that the standard of intellectual ability needed for any prospect of success in the examination is high. For appointments filled by the Crown Agents for the Colonies the necessary qualifications are technical rather than general. In the wide range of administrative, scientific, and professional appointments dealt with by the Colonial Office, selection depends on educational attainments, on professional or other training and experience, and on character and personal fitness. Broadly speaking, it may be said that a university degree, normally with honours, is practically essential in the conditions of to-day.

Furthermore, selected candidates are required to undergo courses of special training before they assume duty overseas, and their final appointment is conditional on their satisfactory progress at the course. A system of agricultural scholarships has been set up, which involves one year's training at home, and a second year at the Imperial College of Tropical Agriculture in Trinidad. A similar scholarship scheme exists in connection with veterinary appointments. There are one-year courses for education, forestry, survey, and police candidates. And administrative cadets take a course at Oxford or Cambridge, also lasting for a year, which includes instruction in the principles of law, evidence and legal procedure; elementary surveying and field engineering; colonial history, geography, anthropology; tropical economic products, agriculture, forestry; tropical hygiene and sanitation; phonetics and various native languages.

What is meant by character and personal fitness in candidates depends on the traditions of the service and on the beliefs, desires, and experiences of colonial Governors and of the Director of Recruitment and his staff at the Colonial Office. It is not easy to devise an accurate objective measurement of these sentiments. But we can to some extent study their effects by looking at the actual sources from which university candidates are drawn. The Warren Fisher Report goes into this question, and gives the following interesting table. The figures show the total

Cambridge . . . 211	Wales 11
Oxford . . . 198	Durham . . . 10
London . . . 108	Manchester . . . 10
Edinburgh . . . 91	National University of
Glasgow . . . 48	Ireland . . . 8
Trinity College, Dublin 41	Reading . . . 7
Dominions and Over-	Sheffield . . . 5
seas 35	Exeter University College 1
Aberdeen . . . 34	Nottingham do. . . 1
Agricultural Colleges . 30	—
Birmingham . . 16	Total, Oxford and Cam-
Leeds . . . 14	bridge . . . 409
Liverpool . . . 13	—
Belfast 12	Total, other Universities 518
Bristol . . . 12	—
St. Andrews . . 11	Grand total . . 927

number of candidates selected from each university during the three years 1927–29 by the Secretary of State for posts for which a degree is needed.

From further analysis, as we learn on the same authority, it appears that London is by far the largest source of supply for medical appointments. Oxford and Cambridge lead in educational appointments, with London third at a long interval. In the administrative services, which in the view of the Report are in many ways the most attractive and important, Oxford and Cambridge are again far ahead of the rest. Taking the non-scientific services as a whole, the results for 1927–29 were: Oxford 173, Cambridge 168, other universities 91. The newer universities, on the other hand, supply most of the specialist and scientific recruits. In other words, we may say that the administrators come mainly from families belonging to the employer class, and that the specialists come mainly from families belonging to the employed class.

In a curious and somewhat uneasy passage, the Report goes on to recommend the extension of the field of recruitment so as to embrace all the home universities and if possible the universities in the Dominions. Especially should a greater effort be made to attract administrative recruits from home universities other than Oxford and Cambridge. (Here the word " attract ", with its implication that the preponderance of recruits from the old universities is due to some lethargy on the part of possible candidates in the new, is ingeniously chosen.) But, the Report adds, " We do not mean to suggest that applicants are likely to be recruited from other centres in such numbers as may be expected from Oxford and Cambridge ".

Nothing is said in explanation of the supposed advantages of associating the Dominions with the work of " imperial trusteeship ", and in fact recruitment from Dominion universities for the tropical administrative service does not seem to have exceeded an average of one a year.

The older generation of Empire-builders, of whom

Lord Lugard is perhaps the most eminent representative, held a firm faith that, in dealing with native races, to have an administrative staff of officers and gentlemen was half the battle. It is evident that this faith still lives and works in high places. The public-school spirit is highly valued in the colonial service, and it is a matter of conscious policy to ensure that the supplies of it shall be constantly replenished. The Report goes so far as to say this: Vision, high ideals of service, fearless devotion to duty born of a sense of responsibility, tolerance, and above all the team spirit are what are wanted in a colonial administrator. Such qualities are not the monopoly of the products of the public schools and Oxford and Cambridge. But recruits drawn from these sources are more certain to possess them than are candidates of different antecedents.

There are those who resent this attitude as a slight on the collective character of that great majority of students who are educated outside the public-school system. They see it as an attempt to maintain a class barrier which equity demands should be overturned. Others, again, welcome it on the grounds that the Empire is in any case a class interest, whose chief social effect in this country is to consolidate class divisions and to strengthen the position of the owners *vis-à-vis* the workers. That being so, it is fitting in itself, and better for the prospects of the social reconstruction the country needs, that the running of the Empire should be left to the only class which can and does benefit from it.

The foregoing outline should make it plain enough that the candidates who find admittance into the colonial service to-day are men of good intelligence and general ability. Given our present social, economic, and educational systems, we are unlikely to be able to produce human material appreciably better in these respects. But are they equally suitably equipped in what may be called social outlook for the complex problems of race, culture contact, applied anthropology, economics, politics, and administration which their official life is devoted to handling?

§ 3. THE OFFICIAL AT WORK

The position of an administrative official in a mixed colonial community is by no means easy. By a mixed community I mean one where a small, but sentimentally compact and race-conscious, group of Europeans lives in the midst of a large coloured majority. In Africa such a majority consists mainly of Africans, together with groups of non-European immigrants—e.g., Indians and Arabs. The evidence as to relations between officials and settler groups falls under three heads, and may be briefly summarised as follows.

Outside observers convey the impression that, if an official desires to expedite his advancement in the service, he will be well advised to identify himself directly with the general standpoint of the settlers. " Knowledge of African life and readiness to defend the rights and interests of Africans are not the qualities that mark men for promotion ", was the verdict of Norman Leys in regard to Kenya twelve years ago.*

Most independent writers since his book was published seem to confirm this view and to accept it as applicable generally to areas where white settlement has established itself. Not inconsistently with it, spokesmen of the settlers treat of the principle of " trusteeship ", on which native policy in British Africa is said to be based, as though it split the white community in two, " putting officials in a class by themselves as the natural protectors of the natives against the settlers, who by implication at any rate are expected to exploit them ".† The consequent tendency is for settlers to look on the administrative service at large as a form of political opposition to be overcome—an attitude

* " Kenya ", Dr. Norman Leys, p. 155.
† Lt.-Col. S. Gore-Browne, *Journal of Royal African Society*, October 1935, p. 384.

which perhaps bears witness to the genuineness of official endeavours to fulfil the " sacred trust ".

Opinion among the official element itself on these matters, being seldom, if ever, published, is harder to come at. But it is no rare thing to hear the presence of a settler community privately spoken of as something which complicates and hampers the proper work of the white man in Africa. It is probably safe to say that when the grosser injustices are perpetrated on subject peoples for the benefit of a settler class, or of British commercial and industrial interests, this happens at the instance of Governors and Secretaries of State, not at that of the body of the administrative service.

As for the dealings of British officials with native populations, one generalisation may fairly be made. They run more smoothly, and show more of friendliness and mutual confidence, when they touch the tribal ʿpeople than when they touch the African intelligentsia. The educated African, isolated from the day-to-day workings and often also from the traditions of the tribe, and at least half-Europeanised, is a type-African of the next few generations, who has great need of us, as we too have of him. But little is done to fit him into the British scheme of rule or into colonial social life, and he and his wife in European clothes are often ignored, ridiculed, and made bitter.

In this the British official stands in marked contrast with the French, who is apt to get on well with educated Africans and badly with " raw natives ". One recalls T. E. Lawrence's penetrating summary of these differences of national temperament in the " Seven Pillars of Wisdom ".* Since God has not given it to Africans to become English, their duty, we hold, is not to ape the Englishmen, but to be good of their own type. Consequently we admire native custom; study the language; write books about its folklore and dying industries.

* p. 347.

D

"The French, though they started with a similar doctrine of the Frenchman as the perfection of mankind, went on contrarily to encourage their subjects to imitate them; since, even if they could never attain the true level, yet their virtue would be greater as they approached it ". The British look on imitation as a parody; the French look on it as a compliment.

Relations with the tribes are undergoing a process of change, owing partly to the disintegration, here quicker, there slower, of tribal society, partly to the spread of nationalist, liberationist, and anti-European feeling among subject races everywhere, and partly to the extension of the method of indirect rule—a method to which the French have given the witty title of " administration à parapluie ". Indirect rule has the consequence of obliging the European administrator to deal more and more with native notables in official positions, and less and less with other elements in the native population. He tends to leave direct contact with the masses to his native subordinates, and at the same time to regard those subordinates rather as cogs in the governmental machine than as mouthpieces of African public opinion.

This latter point is illustrated by two specific cases which happened to come recently to my notice. Promotion was withheld from two African civil servants in deference to reports from European district officers. One report stated that " this chief is too apt to push his people's ideas "; and the other that " this man tends to concern himself with general matters not confined to his sub-division ". Such decisions argue a certain want of flexibility and imagination in those who make them.

To sum up, the personnel of the colonial service is drawn in the main from types of young men who, in the circumstances for example of a general strike, would be apt to be overcome by patriotic emotion. They would see the strike as a disorderly attempt to hold the nation to ransom, and therefore as a movement to be forcibly suppressed.

If anyone were to put to them the view that, while in such a case strike-breakers fight on behalf of a social actuality which is not a community, strikers fight for a real community which is not yet actual, it would probably be unintelligible to them. Owing to this kind of limitation of perspective and sympathy, combined with a fragmentary acquaintance with sociology, even the best colonial officials are given to supposing that there is little need to study and draw out the aspirations of the native rank and file, provided a European sense of orderliness and justice is approximately satisfied.

On the other hand, the modern official is remarkably free from jingo sentiment, and views with wholesome scepticism the old clap-trap about Empires being designed to spread European enlightenment in the dark places of the earth. He sees himself not as an Empire-builder, but as a builder and decorator of native societies. His strength lies in his courage, his endurance, his capacity for hard work in exacting conditions, and his loyalty in honouring his bond by disinterested service in return for the remuneration he has accepted. His weakness is that he seldom grasps how that service is frustrated by the economic framework within which it is performed. But obviously it is unreasonable to expect a civil servant to be a rebel into the bargain; or even to understand the case for rebellion.

CHAPTER IX

EMPIRES A CLASS INTEREST

§ I. A BUTTRESS OF PRIVILEGE

THE facts relating to investment, trade, and employment in the Empire drive it home to us that, though it may be both true and fair to say that the Empire is of value to Britain, when Britain is understood as a national unit distinct from and in contrast with other national units such as Germany and Italy, it is none the less false to assume that inside Britain there exists a single homogeneous community to all of whose members the maintenance of the imperial system is of equal benefit.

The people who gain directly from the Empire are certain numerically small groups embodying particular commercial, manufacturing, investing, and professional interests; the people who gain indirectly are all those who are concerned to preserve the existing economic and social order. To those numerically much larger classes whose interests are bound up with the radical reconstruction of that order the Empire is, on the other hand, a grave disadvantage.

It is essential, therefore, to understand the Empire as fundamentally a class interest, strengthening and consolidating the power and privileges of the groups which are already dominant in the economic and political life of the country. The Empire, in its present structure, constitutes an immense obstacle to British progress in the only valid meaning of the term—namely, the reorganisation of British society in the interests of the unprivileged. Not only that. Its very economic advantage to the limited groups of which I have spoken, so far from being a national advantage in the true sense of the word national, constitutes a national danger, and an international danger too, since, as we shall see in Chapter XIX, it makes a collective system impossible.

The analysis of imperialism must await a later chapter. But it is desirable here to anticipate to the extent of reminding ourselves of the main findings of J. A. Hobson, who states the matter thus: *

" The chief economic source of imperialism has been found in the inequality of industrial opportunities by which a favoured class accumulates superfluous elements of income which, in their search for profitable investments, press ever farther afield: the influence on State policy of these investors and their financial managers secures a national alliance of other vested interests which are threatened by movements of social reform: the adoption of imperialism thus serves the double purpose of securing private material benefits for favoured classes of investors and traders at the public cost, while sustaining the general cause of conservatism by diverting public energy and interest from domestic agitation to external employment.

" The ability of a nation to shake off this dangerous usurpation of its power, and to employ the national resources in the national interest, depends upon the education of a national intelligence and a national will, which shall make democracy a political and economic reality."

§ 2. THE CONJURING TRICK

All this may be true, some readers will reply; but how do you account for the curious circumstance that most people in England, even among those whose interest it is to believe what you say, in fact believe something quite different, and indeed quite contradictory?

People in Britain are brought up to believe that the British Empire is (a) essential to their well-being and indeed their

* Op. cit., p. 361.

life, and (*b*) a triumphant expression of their political genius.* These beliefs are a variant and expansion of the old idea that unless Britain either enjoys peace or exercises naval supremacy, the people of these islands cannot be fed. The uninterrupted flying of the Union Jack over all those territories which are conventionally coloured pink on the map comes to be identified with naval supremacy; and by a further confusion the preservation of the British Empire in its present structure comes to be identified with the maintenance of the food supply for Britain.

If one looks at these conceptions in the light of the facts, two things at once strike the mind. First, that in modern conditions there is no such thing as naval supremacy in any general sense. Japan may be said to be supreme in the Western Pacific, the United States in the Eastern Pacific, and Britain perhaps in the North Sea and Eastern Atlantic. That is about all the naval supremacy there is in the world, and very restricted and localised it is. The proper inference is not that British policy should aim at restoring a world-wide naval supremacy which geography and history alike render impossible, but rather that the trade routes on which these islands depend can be kept open only by means of a co-operative international system of mutual security.

In the second place, the notion that there is any close connection between maintaining Britain's food supply and maintaining a policy of imperialism in the meaning of the term as used in this book, is wholly fallacious. The imperialism here criticised is not the patriotic infantilism which amuses itself by saying that Britain and the great self-governing Dominions are indissolubly bound together in a royal league of nations by the unifying link of the Crown. It is the imperialism which exerts a repressive and purposeful political and economic domination

* This is precisely what Hitler invites Germans to believe about the colonies whose retrocession he is demanding.

over the people of India and Africa. Of course it is true that Britain imports two-thirds of her total food supply. It is true that rather more than one of those thirds comes from the Dominions and colonies. It is also true that anything like full self-sufficiency is impracticable for this country within any period that need now be taken into account. It may even be true that if self-sufficiency were suddenly forced upon it, it would mean " ruin, starvation, a complete reconstruction of the entire way of living—and a population cut down by at least one half ".

These things are undoubtedly evidence of a certain weakness in Britain's position as viewed from a military angle. All I am concerned to ask is how that weakness is strengthened by holding India and Africa in subjection? If we are really safer by making our suppliers our subjects, why stop at India and Africa? The Dominions, the Argentine, and Denmark are much more important as suppliers. Yet even our imperialists do not suggest we should send troops and a viceroy to bring Denmark and the Argentine under the Union Jack: they actually insist that the independence the Dominions enjoy is a fine feather in the cap of British statesmanship. Why, then, do they suppose that independence for India and Africa would mean the cutting off of supplies for Britain from those sources? The basic fallacy is the fallacy entertained by the industrial, financial, and professional interests who in fact benefit from Empire—namely, that what benefits their group as a group thereby benefits the nation as a nation. The linking of the idea of vital food supplies, favourable standards of living and so on, with the idea of imperial control of colonial territories is the conjuring trick by which they pass off their sectional advantage as an apparent general advantage.

§ 3. MASS SELF-DECEPTION

In performing the trick these groups commonly deceive themselves as successfully as they mislead the main body of the nation; it is a condition of the trick's success that it should be done in a kind of unconscious automatism. In the main it is honestly held among such groups that " biology and sociology weave thin convenient theories of a race struggle for the subjugation of the inferior peoples " in order that the white man may take their lands and live on their labours. Economics reinforces the argument by representing the white man's task of conquering and ruling as his share in the international division of labour. History thinks up reasons why the lessons of empire in the past do not apply to this empire in the present. Social ethics portrays the impulse of imperialism as embodying the desire to shoulder the burden of educating and elevating " the child races ".*

Thus are the cultured or semi-cultured classes indoctrinated with the intellectual and moral grandeur of imperialism. Thus also are the real facts and forces persistently misrepresented, " chiefly through a most refined process of selection, exaggeration, and attenuation, directed by interested cliques and persons so as to distort the face of history ".

The controlling and directing agent of the whole process, Hobson urges again and again, is the pressure of financial and industrial motives, operated for the direct, short-range, material interests of small, able, well-organised groups in the nation. These groups secure the active co-operation of statesmen and political cliques who wield the power of party organisations, now by associating them directly in their business schemes, now by appealing to the conservative instincts of the possessing classes, whose

* For all this topic see Hobson, op. cit., Part II, Chapter 3.

vested interests and class dominance are best preserved by diverting the currents of political energy from domestic to external politics.

" The acquiescence, even the active and enthusiastic support, of the body of a nation in a course of policy fatal to its own true interests is secured partly by appeals to the mission of civilisation, but chiefly by playing upon the primitive instincts of the race." Towards the masses is directed a crude call to hero-worship and sensational glory, adventure and the sporting spirit. For their sake current history is falsified in loud glaring colours to stimulate the combative self-regarding impulses.*

The instruments of such stimulation are the party, the press, the church, the school, the film, and above all the Crown, which by a *tour de force* of crooked idealisation has been laboriously built up into the most evocative of all symbols of the beneficence of empire. There is pathos in the careless gusto with which great crowds of the common people will, on occasions of regal pomp, line the streets and cheer and bow down before that emblem which more than any other is used to blind them to the reality of their danger and their servitude.

Hobson in a further memorable passage has expressed the view that even the universities, which might perhaps have been expected to muster enough independence of mind to offer some resistance to the strange process of mass self-deception, have, on the contrary, lent themselves to it. " The price which universities pay ", he says, " for preferring money and social position to intellectual distinction in the choice of chancellors and for touting among millionaires for the equipment of new scientific schools is subservience to the political and business interests of their patrons: their philosophy, their history, their economics, even their biology must reflect in doctrine and method the consideration that is due to patronage, and the

---

* Question. Account for the difference between the reputations in England of (*a*) Cecil Rhodes and (*b*) King Leopold II of Belgium.

D 2

fact that this deference is unconscious enhances the damage done to the cause of intellectual freedom ".

Whatever happens or does not happen in the universities, there can be no question about the continual barrage of propaganda by insinuation to which the man in the street is subjected. The old influences of press, school, Empire day celebrations, and the rest are supplemented to-day by the radio and the cinema. The news-reel, indeed, has become the most telling of them all. There are indications too that full-length entertainment films are now being prepared with official backing for purposes of imperial propaganda.

" The Drum ", produced by Alexander Korda from a story by A. E. W. Mason, is a recent example. This work of art expressed the received assumption that Britain had fared forth to the ends of the earth, conferring gratuitous benefits on all and sundry, and that the proudest moment in the life of a brown-skinned oriental is when he catches sight of a Union Jack unfurling above him. " Bengal Lancer ", " Elephant Boy ", " Sanders of the River " are other instances of the same trend. No efforts were spared to make " The Drum " glamorous and technically perfect. To lend the picture verisimilitude, it was photographed on the North-West Frontier, where previously no such photography had been allowed. Films of this type are thus coming to form a definite part of the ordinary citizen's political education. The tragedy is that many good artists, actors, and photographers and producers allow themselves to be made use of for such work. Occasionally they see the game that is being played and break away, as Paul Robeson did after " Sanders of the River ". But the rebels are few and far between.

Such are some of the means by which the people of Britain at large are brought to assent to a depraved choice of national life, and to support imperialist policies which defeat the true social interests of the nation that countenances them. Hobson's eloquent and cogent denunciations were originally delivered nearly forty years ago. The social psychologist will be fascinated and perhaps puzzled at finding they have remained unheeded through two generations, while world events have incessantly been shouting their justification from the house-tops. The reformer will lament that the need for emphasising them should be as great to-day as when they were first uttered.

PART III

WHAT IT FEELS LIKE TO BE A COLONY

(a) HOW ACQUIRED

CHAPTER X

ZULULAND

THE Colonial Secretary in Disraeli's last Cabinet was a gentleman whom Queen Victoria, with her fondness for adjectives, called "good but nervous and somewhat weak and sentimental Lord Carnarvon". His colleagues had a shorter name for him—"Twitters". Now, Twitters in the year 1877 had one great preoccupation in colonial policy, and that was to bring the whole of Africa south of the Zambesi into a single confederation under the dear old Union Jack.

He had various reasons for wanting to do this. One of the most important was what he called the "native peril". He thought that the various European settlements in southern Africa would have to unite if they were to establish a permanent race-domination over the African tribes among which they were living. Another reason, perhaps more important still, was that the scramble for Africa was beginning, and he was anxious to keep foreign powers out of this part of the Continent.

Twitters started the unification ball rolling in April by annexing the Transvaal, at that time an independent Dutch republic. Disraeli concurred in the high-handed step. "Paul Kruger", he wrote, "is an ugly customer." That sentiment was to be solemnly re-echoed by many another British statesman in the years to come.

After collaring the Transvaal, Twitters sent out to South Africa a special High Commissioner to complete the work of union. This was Sir Bartle Frere, a thruster from the North-West Frontier of India, ruthless, self-reliant, full of " patriotic ambitions "—the very man for a forward policy.

Less than a year in South Africa seems to have convinced Frere that the native peril centred in the great Zulu tribe. It was a period of widespread native unrest and resentment at European penetration and aggression. Frere made up his mind that Cetshwayo, the Zulu king, was at the bottom of these native movements everywhere. The view was unfounded, but at the same time convenient. Resolved, in his own words, " to bring the Zulu nation into such shape as was compatible with the safety of Natal and the Transvaal ", Frere proceeded to justify in advance the war he meant to wage by blackening the Zulu character and customs as inhuman, disgraceful, and barbarous.

The Zulus had always been on good terms with the British. But their kingdom had been much torn by civil strife, and they had long been at feud with the Transvaal Dutch. In 1878 a perennial boundary dispute with the latter came to a head. Frere appointed a Commission to make an award. Although the Zulus had no spokesman on it, the Commission, greatly to Frere's surprise and embarrassment, rejected the Transvaal claim and reported in the Zulus' favour.

Frere dared not set the award aside; yet it was difficult to squeeze out of it a pretext for fighting Cetshwayo. However, Frere's ingenuity was equal to the emergency. He gave the Zulu king the empty name of sovereignty over the territory in question, and at the same time guaranteed to the Boers who had illegally settled there the private ownership of the land they had occupied. Not content with this sharp practice, he linked it with a formal ultimatum to Cetshwayo, requiring him to break up the entire Zulu military organisation and to accept a British Resident to tell him how to govern his country.

Cetshwayo, as Frere expected and intended, made no reply to these demands within the stipulated time. So in

January 1879 British troops marched into Zululand, and the shooting began.

The Cabinet at home went through the motions of reprimanding Frere for starting the war without telling them what he was up to. But they let him keep his job. And they made it clear that their objection was not to the war as such, but to its outbreak at a time of " imperial difficulties in other continents ".

*   *   *   *   *

Who was this Cetshwayo, whom Frere represented to the British Government as a bloodthirsty tyrant given over to methods of rule so savage that even his savage subjects found them unendurable?

It is a curious coincidence that the name Cetshwayo in Zulu means " He who is slandered ". There is not the least doubt that Frere, for reasons of policy, made the king out to be a monster from whom it would be a kindness to deliver the poor Zulu people. He used every kind of libel he could lay tongue or pen to for the purpose. As far as we know, no section of Zulu opinion ever thought Cetshwayo a harsh ruler. And the Europeans who knew him as a personality formed a view very different from Frere's.

Colenso, the Bishop of Natal, met him twenty years before the war began, and described him as " a fine handsome young fellow of about thirty years of age, tall and stout-limbed, with a good-humoured face and strong, deep voice. . . . Our men, one and all, commended him as a pleasing young prince." And when Cetshwayo came to the throne in 1873, the head of the Natal Native Affairs Department, whose business it was to conduct the colony's official relations with the Zulu kingdom, said, " Cetshwayo is a man of considerate ability and much force of character. . . . He ranks in every respect far above any native chief I have ever had to do with."

This, then, was the man whose person and authority the British now methodically set out to smite down, as they ravaged his lands and slaughtered his people. High policy called for his destruction. And the call of high policy is like a royal invitation: it may not be refused.

The war, like most British wars, opened with a serious reverse for British arms. But by July the British had killed 10,000 Zulus, as against the Zulu's bag of 2,500 British. This being considered a satisfactory restoration of the balance sheet, the Cease Fire was sounded. Eight weeks later Cetshwayo was betrayed into the hands of the British and dragged off, a prisoner to Capetown.

By the peace terms the Zulu kingdom was broken up into thirteen fragments, and Zulu nationhood laid in the dust. Cetshwayo, the British spokesman declared, would never again be allowed inside his own country.

*　　*　　*　　*　　*

The settlement which terminated the war was known as the Kilkenny Cat settlement. The Zulus had been defeated but not crushed, and Frere thought it simpler on the whole to complete the process by egging them on to destroy one another than to shoulder the donkey-work of destruction himself. He therefore set out to provide all the conditions for an epidemic of civil strife in Zululand. This part of his policy was a great success.

Meanwhile, Bishop Colenso began his heroic and almost single-handed fight for Cetshwayo's restoration. He travelled down to the Cape and visited the captive in gaol. "What would your feeling be", Colenso asked, "if you were sent for to England to see the Queen?"

Cetshwayo looked distressed and said, "The sea would kill me".

"You need not fear the sea," replied Colenso. "And if you were to go, you would not return to Africa just as you now are, a prisoner."

"Do you really think that?" asked Cetshwayo excitedly. "And you wish me to go? I will agree then at once, if I am asked, although I have a great horror of the sea."

By this time Zululand was in chaos. The Zulus were

petitioning hard for the restoration of Cetshwayo as the only man who could calm the fighting factions. The British dared not publicly admit this popular demand. Their excuse for the war was that it had freed such Zulus as survived it from the clutches of a cruel tyrant. It would never do for the world to learn that these rescued savages were clamorous to have their despot back again.

The bout between Colenso and the British authorities now waxed fast and furious. The British stopped at nothing in their efforts to hide the truth about the Zulus wanting Cetshwayo's return. They developed an intense hatred for Colenso, because his activities made ten evasions or falsehoods necessary, where but for him one might have sufficed.

Colenso, from his side, began an encircling movement. He got the Boer Government in the Transvaal, which had just recovered its own independence, to cable Downing Street asking for Cetshwayo's release and restoration. The Cape Ministry and the Governor of the Cape did the same thing. Gladstone's Government had succeeded Disraeli's, and eventually allowed Cetshwayo to make the journey to England. Queen Victoria saw him and said " I respect you as a brave enemy. Now I trust you as a future friend."

Cetshwayo returned to Zululand on January 10th, 1883, after three and a half years of exile and imprisonment. Colenso had triumphed over the serried ranks of officialdom.

*   *   *   *   *

But officialdom still had a shot or two in its locker. In spite of solemn pledges repeatedly given that no part of Zululand should be annexed, Cetshwayo found that in fact more than half of it had passed out of his hands. The Transvaal Boers had seized the old disputed territory along the north-western border. In the north the Natal Government had given an independent command to a chief called Zibebu, who was bitterly disaffected towards Cetshwayo. And now in the south another third of Cetshwayo's whole country was taken by the British, nominally as a refuge

for " those chiefs and people who were unwilling to be
Cetshwayo's subjects ". The people inhabiting this
territory, so far from being grateful for such kind consideration, protested strongly that they should be allowed
to remain under their king.

Colenso foresaw clearly the strife to which this dismember-
ment and disorganisation would lead. He implored the
authorities to stay their hand; but without avail. The
troubles he prophesied followed swiftly. They hastened the
close of his own life (he was now in his seventieth year and
wearied out by the unceasing fight) and they involved the
death of Cetshwayo.

Within two months of the restoration, fighting broke out
between the king's men and Zibebu's. The British had
allowed the latter to drill soldiers and provide them with
firearms, although Cetshwayo, in name and in law Zibebu's
paramount, was forbidden to maintain any military system
at all. Zibebu was also egged on and assisted, with
Government connivance, by a band of European freebooters,
who, besides influencing his policy, acted as a kind of
cavalry arm in his forces.

The renewed disturbances were blamed on Cetshwayo
by the Government, but were actually started by Zibebu
at the instigation of white officials and freebooters. An
educated Zulu eye-witness wrote to Colenso at this time,
" Now you know that the Zulus are set at loggerheads by
the cunning of white men, who want to eat up their land.
My heart is full of grief, I cannot find words to express it,
for this splendid old Zulu people."

The Government would not allow Colenso to keep in
touch with Cetshwayo himself. But in a last desperate
attempt to ward off the impending doom, the Bishop sent
up (at his own expense) a European adviser called Grant to
be with Cetshwayo at his headquarters and to assist him
in his dealings with the Government. This effort made, the
gallant Colenso died (June 20th, 1883).

In July Zibebu made a surprise attack on Cetshwayo's

kraal. The king was wounded, and driven out, a fugitive once more. His family was slaughtered. After six months of wandering through the African forest, friendless, deserted, and broken in spirit at last, Cetshwayo died.

*   *   *   *   *

The mother of Parliaments found in Cetshwayo's story a little comic relief from the end-of-session tedium.

Mr. P. Yorke. Can the Under-Secretary for the Colonies say whether Cetshwayo is dead or alive?

Mr. Ashley. Yes, sir. Information has been received that Cetshwayo is now in the Reserve. (Loud laughter.) A reliable witness says he has seen him alive. I think we may argue from that that Cetshwayo is still with us. (Laughter.)

(Hansard, August 10th, 1883.)

CHAPTER XI

RHODESIA

THE tragedy of Lobengula, king of the Matabele, is a drama in five acts. On the stage of history it took a little more than five years to play.

In 1887 England was celebrating Queen Victoria's first Jubilee. Colonial statesmen being gathered together in London, opportunity was taken to hold an Imperial Conference. Cecil Rhodes, the Cape financial magnate, was not a delegate to the Conference, but he had enough influence to interest British statesmen in his big Empire-building schemes. Among these was the idea of a solid economic block of British territory running the whole length of Africa from Egypt to the Cape.

In carrying out this Cape-to-Cairo plan, the first danger Rhodes had to meet was that of being forestalled by some foreign power. The scramble for Africa had already begun, and agents of most European countries were bustling about and grabbing land when and where they could. Rhodes feared that the Germans moving in from the West Coast and the Portuguese moving in from the East Coast might meet on the middle Zambesi, thus closing the north–south line to the British.

Now, in the heart of this middle Zambesi region lay the kingdom of the Matabele. Lobengula, their ruler, was therefore a key-man from the standpoint of Rhodes' plan. If Rhodes could square Loben to keep the Germans and the Portuguese out, the first Cape-to-Cairo hurdle would be cleared.

So the British authorities sent an official to Loben'

118

headquarters at Bulawayo " to safeguard British interests ".
The official was the Rev. J. S. Moffat, who had spent some
years in Matabeleland as a missionary, and was a son of
the pioneer missionary Robert Moffat. It was a shrewd
choice. Loben and his people knew Moffat, respected
him, and were prepared to trust him. The Matabele
seldom felt this way about white men; there had been
too high a proportion of scallywags among such Europeans
as they had had dealings with.

But if they could not trust Moffat, whom could they
trust? The king did not like signing documents, especially
documents drafted by white men, but Moffat persuaded
him to put his mark to a letter in which he agreed not to
cede any of his territory without the consent of the British
Government. As Loben had no intention of ceding any
territory to anybody, surely there could be no danger in
saying so. From the Matabele point of view the declaration
was unnecessary but harmless.

Moffat saw things in a different light. For him his
" treaty " was a warning to all the world that Britain had
secured an option on Loben's dominions. And, as he
knew, one day the option would be exercised. He had
tapped in the thin end of the wedge. " The days of the
Matabele ", he wrote, " are now numbered."

          *   *   *   *   *

The Moffat treaty rang down the curtain on Act I.
That was in February 1888.

The second Act opens in October of the same year.
Two more agents of Rhodes, called Rudd and Thompson,
visit the king's kraal at Bulawayo, and pester the king into
secretly signing another paper. This is the famous Rudd
Concession, which purports to give Rhodes the monopoly
of all minerals in all Loben's kingdom; in consideration
of which Rhodes pays Loben 1,000 rifles with 100 rounds
of ammunition each, a steamboat to ply on the Zambesi,
and a pension of £100 a month. Loben was very worried
lest in granting the concession he might be opening the

door to white aggression. The rifles were intended to put
his mind at rest on this point, for, as Thompson impressed
upon him, " Who gives a man arms, if he expects them
later to be used against himself? " Besides, in this instance
too, Loben had the benefit of missionary advice in favour
of signing. Rudd had seen to that.

The moment the concession was signed, Rudd dashed
off with it to Rhodes in Capetown, and Rhodes, as though
running a relay race, dashed on with it to Queen Victoria
at Balmoral. After much wire-pulling, the British Government upheld the concession and made it the basis on which
Rhodes' company, the British South Africa Company,
obtained its royal charter. The Chartered Company
became the final instrument of Loben's destruction.

Meanwhile, news of the concession had leaked out into
the Capetown press and trickled through to Bulawayo.
This put the fat properly in the fire. Loben's was a limited
monarchy, and he had no constitutional right to grant
concessions over tribal property by his own secret diplomacy.
His councillors, whom he was bound by tribal law to have
consulted, were wild with rage. To save himself Loben
had to repudiate the concession, and, for good measure, he
ordered the execution of Lotjie, his Prime Minister, who
alone of the Matabele had been privy to the concession
scheme. And with Lotjie went the whole clan that shared
his kraal. One long night through the killing continued
—three hundred men, women, and children. All night
Thompson listened to it with a sick heart. At the first
streak of light, he jumped on a horse and fled southwards
for dear life.

*　　*　　*　　*　　*

In Act III the main body of his enemies begin to advance
against the king. Rhodes sends in the first batch of settlers
to occupy part of the king's lands. The Rhodesian pioneers,
as they came to be called, are a formidable column,
accompanied by 500 Bechuanaland Police and a body of
native labourers and troops. Loben, who had been led to

expect a peaceful party consisting of a few mining pros-
pectors, becomes alarmed at the size of this force, and
orders it back from his frontier. But the British Government moves up a further body of troops, and thus provides
the pioneer column with safe passage. Within three
months (September 1890) Salisbury, the present capital of
Southern Rhodesia, has been founded.

Every pioneer was allowed by Rhodes to stake out a
farm of 3,000 acres. Unfortunately, the Rudd concession
conferred no rights in land, and Rhodes therefore could
grant no legal title in respect of such farms. While he
was wondering in what precise way this little difficulty was
to be overcome, Rhodes learnt, to his extreme annoyance,
that Loben had recenty granted land rights to someone
else, a gentleman of the name of Lippert. The poor king,
hoping to divide the alien forces which were closing in on
him, was taking to the old game of playing one group off
against another.

Rhodes handled the position in a characteristic way.
Having satisfied himself that the Lippert concession was
genuine and that its terms would be approved by the
British Government, he offered to buy it. This would
torpedo Loben's policy of dividing the enemy, but it
meant practising some deceit, for Loben must not discover
that both the Lippert and the Rudd concessions were going
to end up in the same hands.

Here the supple Mr. Moffat came in useful once again.
He successfully drew the wool over Loben's eyes, and
induced him to confirm the land concession to Lippert.
Moffat knew that Lippert had now become Rhodes' secret
agent; Loben supposed Lippert to be still representing a
group opposed to Rhodes.

Moffat had a painful moment in May 1892, when it
became his official duty to inform Loben that the Chartered Company had acquired the Lippert concession.
Loben gave no outward sign of the flaming resentment he
felt. But he saw at once that his whole plan for upsetting

Rhodes' apple-cart had come to grief and would recoil upon himself. The Rhodesians had crossed his border claiming the right to dig for gold. Now, it was clear, it was his country and his people they meant to seize. " All white men ", he cried bitterly, " are liars."

*   *   *   *   *

Act IV. Rhodes had now got all the scraps of paper he wanted. But his anxieties were not at an end. Rhodesia was hardly proving an Eldorado; the fabulous gold reef which was supposed to run through it had not been located; the settlers were finding settlement very hard. The country seemed to be gravitating towards bankruptcy.

Trouble was brewing too on the financial front. When the news reached London that the pioneers had founded Salisbury, the shares of the Chartered Company were placed on the open market and began to change hands at high prices; for the public innocently supposed not merely that Rhodesia was full of gold, but also that the mineral rights belonged to the Chartered Company.

This was not so. The Rudd concession, it appeared, was in effect the private property of Rhodes and certain of his co-directors on the board of the Chartered Company. These gentlemen were willing to part with it to the Company for a million specially created Chartered shares, but not otherwise. As Chartered shares at this time (1890) stood around £4, the arrangement wore an attractive air for Rhodes and his friends. But members of the outside public who had bought their Chartered shares dear, were impressed by the fact that it would depreciate their holdings and halve any dividends. They spoke of it with some warmth as a common swindle, and threatened legal proceedings.

In view of their outcry, " capitalisation " was postponed, first till the end of 1891, then till the end of 1892, then again, in spite of all Rhodes' efforts to carry it through, till the end of 1893. Throughout all this delay, the

Chartered Company seemed to be crumbling. Its cash and reserves were almost exhausted. Sinking steadily into debt, it just survived on a monthly dole from Rhodes' great diamond concern, the De Beers Company.

Something drastic had to be done. If the Chartered Company were to pull through, there must be some dramatic improvement in its prospects. Along what line did maximum improvement and maximum drama lie? Evidently that of unrestricted possession of Loben's whole domain. Thus Rhodes reasoned with himself. From that moment it was Loben's head or the Company's.

*   *   *   *   *

The fifth and last Act is a short one. Rhodes gets his agents-provocateurs to work along the Matabele border, and cuts direct communication between Loben and the British authorities. A quarrel is picked between some of Loben's men and some of the Company's. Loben's men, though they deny it, are said to have fired first.

The fighting started in October 1893. The Company's machine-guns worked wonders in two skirmishes. These weapons were a novelty in warfare in those days, and no mention had been made of them when Rhodes was supplying Loben with rifles. By November the Union Jack was flying over the smoking ruins of Bulawayo. Loben was a fugitive, his kingdom torn to shreds, his people decimated. When Christmas came, Loben himself, the tall, stout, well-built Lobengula, who weighed twenty stone and looked every inch a king, lay dead.

Chartered shares had risen at the mere rumour of war. After the conquest they went on rising, until in 1895 the £1 shares touched £9½. The previously disgruntled shareholders agreed to Rhodes's capitalisation scheme, and the Company had no difficulty in raising £750,000 on debenture to pay its creditors and the cost of the campaign. Rhodes had weathered his storm. The Cape-to-Cairo route was open.

Ten years later Thompson met one of Loben's councillors on the platform at Bulawayo station. " O Tomosong," said the African, " how have you treated us, after all your promises, which we believed? " Thompson had no answer.

CHAPTER XII

GOLD COAST

THE Ashanti, whose country lies inland from the Gold Coast in West Africa, were long known as an intelligent people, great traders, yet well organised for war, and notably courageous. Their social cohesion proved tough enough to withstand five separate wars, extending over three-quarters of a century, with the British. Not many native African societies have shown such resilience.

In 1874 the British decided that the organised power of Ashanti was incompatible with the purposes of the British Empire. General Wolseley, in a six months' campaign, destroyed the military strength of the Ashanti kingdom, burnt its capital to ashes, and imposed a fabulous indemnity (payable in gold). This figures in the history books as the 6th Ashanti war.

Wolseley, however, attempted no constructive work. Having pulled the old order to pieces, he left Ashanti to stew in its own juice. The juice took the form of fourteen years of civil war, during which the suffering and loss of life were, it is said, greater even than those occasioned by Wolseley's campaign. The civilisation and arts of the country began to decay. Communications were so unsafe that trade languished.

It was in these depressing circumstances that King Prempeh came to the Ashanti throne in 1888. The country was in such straits that he had to borrow £300 from his British enemies to pay for his coronation. Still, in the early days of his reign, Prempeh managed to pull things round a little; peace returned, and with it the beginnings of prosperity.

In 1893 the British called on Prempeh to hoist the dear old Union Jack and to bring his country inside the Empire fold. As an inducement, a British Resident would be sent to Kumasi (the Ashanti capital) to tell Prempeh how to govern.

Prempeh came of a long line of kings who were commonly thought in Ashanti to have governed with great success. He wanted no outside help, least of all from the very people who had recently laid his whole land waste. He said as much. Thereupon the British moved another military expedition on Kumasi, and the 7th Ashanti war began.

But this time the Ashanti, for what reason we shall see in a moment, decided not to fight. During 1896 Prempeh surrendered without a shot fired. The British promised not to depose him so long as he paid another indemnity of £250,000 in gold. To a king who not long before had been obliged to do his own coronation on credit, this seemed a raw offer. However, Prempeh turned out his pockets, and announced that he could only pay £2,720 on the nail. The balance, he said, he would pay in instalments.

At this, the Governor of the Gold Coast, who was conducting the negotiations on the British side, ordered King Prempeh, the king's mother and father, his two uncles, his brother, and several others—in fact, practically the whole of the royal family—to be flung into jail. The people of Ashanti, in their quaint African fashion, took the Governor's act to be one of deliberate treachery.

Prempeh, now an exile as well as a prisoner, was shifted first to the coast, and then to the Seychelles Islands, where he remained captive for nearly thirty years.

*   *   *   *   *

Two hundred years before Prempeh's banishment a famous magician called Anotchi came to the Ashanti king at Kumasi. Anotchi proclaimed that the sky-god had sent him to make Ashanti a great and powerful kingdom. As the king registered some interest in this news, Anotchi, in the royal presence and that of a large gathering of tribes-people, summoned down out of a black thunder-cloud a wooden Stool heavily adorned with gold. The Stool sank slowly through the air and came to rest on the king's knees. Anotchi bowed to his audience, and impressed on them that the Golden Stool contained the soul of the Ashanti people. " With it ", he cried, " is bound up your life, your honour, and your welfare. If ever it should be captured or destroyed, this people will surely perish."

From that time forward the Ashanti tribes cherished the Golden Stool as their most sacred possession. It was their Ark of the Covenant. Once a year they carried it in solemn procession under its own ceremonial umbrella and with its own servitors in attendance. The king himself played second fiddle to it. His place in procession was behind it, not in front, and the royal pomp was altogether of a lower order of magnificence than the Golden Stool's.

The reputation of the Stool, at least in the eyes of the Ashanti people, steadily increased throughout five genera-tions—in fact right up to 1874. But Wolseley's campaign and the destruction of Kumasi gave the Ashanti what Wolseley delighted to call a thorough lesson. The Stool's stock slumped. We now know that Prempeh refused to fight in 1896 because his people were scared of taking the Golden Stool into a war they were certain to lose.

When Prempeh vanished into exile, the Stool was the only linch-pin left to hold Ashanti together. Consequently, the custodians of the Stool took the greatest precautions to hide it away in a safe place.

The Governor, a certain Sir Frederick Hodgson, deter-mined to unearth the Stool and seize it in the name of the Great White Queen Victoria. For he supposed that the Ashanti would never be suitably submissive while this national emblem remained in their possession.

After several unsuccessful attempts to discover the where-abouts of the Stool and to abstract it by guile, Hodgson swaggered into Kumasi in March 1900 and tried pulling out the rough stuff. " Where is the Golden Stool? ", he blustered to an assembly of the chiefs and people. " Why have you not given it to me to sit on at this moment? I represent the paramount power: why have you relegated me to this chair? "

To the Ashanti this speech seemed the wildest sacrilege. No king had ever sat on the Golden Stool. It was never thought of, let alone used, as a royal throne. It was not an appurtenance of the kingly office at all, nor even a symbol of national sovereignty.

But the Governor, with his head full of Union Jacks, Royal Ensigns, crowns, orbs, sceptres, thrones, dominations, princedoms, powers, was confident the Stool must correspond to one of these. He was a plain man. How should he recognise this precious piece of furniture as the pledge and seal of a divine promise, the holy receptacle of the very soul of a people?

The Ashanti listened to Hodgson in outward silence and inward rage. As soon as he stopped, they went home to prepare for the 8th Ashanti war.

The Ashanti willingness to fight on this occasion is very instructive. They knew they would lose, just as they had known they would lose when Prempeh refused to fight four years earlier. But the difference was this. In 1896 the dispute with the British had nothing to do with the Golden Stool. The Stool was only involved in so far as the defeat of Ashanti, if war came, would damage its prestige. Better, therefore, to give the British a walkover, no matter what the material cost might be, and maintain the prestige of the Stool intact. But Hodgson in 1900 made the ownership of the Stool itself the direct issue. To admit his claim and part with the Stool would be more destructive of Ashanti even than war with Europeans. Therefore better fight. Such was the working of Ashanti logic.

And the Ashanti logic was confirmed by events. They lost the war. The last shred of independence was stripped from them, and their country formally annexed to the British crown. But in the settlement nothing was said about the Golden Stool.

*   *   *   *   *

Twenty years went by. The Stool was moved by its guardians from one secret lair to another in order to prevent the British from laying hands on it. Finally, they had to bury it in the ground. And then one day its hiding-place was accidentally discovered—not by the British, but by a road-making party. Four native scallywags managed to get hold of it, and under the leadership of one of their number who had been converted to Christianity, they looted all the gold from it and sold it. The game of Hunt-the-Stool was over, and the British had not won it.

When the desecration became publicly known, the country was in an uproar. The British Government, which had at last taken the trouble to find out the true nature of the reverence in which the Ashanti held their Golden Stool, calmed things down by sensibly announcing that it regarded the Stool as the property of the people, and that the Kumasi Council of chiefs would be allowed to try the culprits.

The Government added that there was no longer any need to conceal the Stool. In future it would not attempt to interfere with the Stool, so long as it was not made use of for seditious purposes (i.e., for making the Ashanti a free people again).

The chiefs condemned the thieves and their " fences " to death. The Government, however, always ready to show clemency towards offences which did not touch the British raj, commuted the sentence to perpetual banishment.

The concluding note is one of pathos rather than tragedy. In 1923 the Government sanctioned Prempeh's return from exile. He came back just a private citizen, a poor old man without rank, or honour, or pomp; but not forgotten. His former subjects gave him a tremendous, a formidable welcome. For three more years the Government watched

E

how things went. Then, satisfied at last of Prempeh's abiding harmlessness, they put him back again upon a nominal throne from which all authority and all power to advance his people had been meticulously extracted.

You might think that Prempeh would have been broken by age and suffering and the loss of half his life marooned in the Indian Ocean. If he was, he did not show it. At his restoration, he struck observers as a very dignified, self-contained, quiet, but powerful person, rather like Lord Baldwin in appearance and manner, but with more reserves of strength and no pipe.

With the massive commonsense and the fine self-command of the African, he said no bitter word and gave no sign of the inner wounds inflicted on him by the desecration he had so strangely shared with the Golden Stool. The British had confiscated most of the royal revenues, and Prempeh found himself deeply impoverished. But he appeared to be on the best of terms with his overlords. Having no power but his personality, he set himself to use that. Without fuss and without advertisement, he quietly obliged the British Government to consult him and to work through him in their dealings with Ashanti. Then he died.

CHAPTER XIII

UGANDA

In the heart of Africa, along the northern shores of Lake Victoria, lies Uganda, a small country about the size of Britain. The people who inhabit it are called Baganda. Fifty years ago they represented the most advanced and prosperous stage which African civilisation had reached. Uganda is now part of the British Empire.

Like Rhodesia, Uganda straddled the Cape-to-Cairo route. Like Rhodesia, it had to be brought under British control, if that all-British route was to be completed. Cecil Rhodes in his handling of Lobengula was consciously reaching out towards a certain Captain Lugard, who was at that time engaged in carrying the Union Jack into Uganda. This is the story of how the flag was planted there.

In 1884 a new king came to the throne of Uganda. His name was Mwanga. It was a time of fierce political strife among his subjects. Three different sets of missionaries were at work in Mwanga's domain, Moslem, Protestant, and Catholic. All these missions had political as well as religious stakes in the country. The Protestants were Englishmen, and wanted to see Uganda brought under the British flag. The Catholics were Frenchmen, and wanted to see Uganda brought under the French flag. And the Moslems were Arabs, and wanted to bring Mwanga under their political influence in order that the Arab slave trade might continue without interruption.

Each mission had secured large numbers of adherents from among the Baganda. Their conflicting aims and ambitions, at the time of Mwanga's accession, were splitting the whole people into groups so keenly hostile to one another that the king found it difficult to maintain even an armed truce between them.

Alarmed for the very survival of royal authority, Mwanga called his council together. "What is best", he asked them, "for the monarchy and for the country as a whole? I wish to choose one of these religions as the true one, and to reject the others. Then all our people shall cleave to the true, and there will be peace in the land." But the Councillors could not agree upon which was the true religion. "The best religion will outlast the others, O King," was their reply. This was little help. Mwanga was king enough to know that in a crisis the issue cannot be left to time to settle.

While the king was racking his brains for a policy, a deputation from the Moslem party asked for an audience with him. "Your Majesty," they said, "news has just come to us from Zanzibar that a great white man is on his way from England to Uganda to drive you from your throne and make himself king in your place."

The great white man was Bishop Hannington. The Arabs had invented the part about his wanting to seize the throne, because they thought it would damage their Protestant enemies. It did. The king was greatly perturbed by the report, and gave instructions that Hannington should be killed as he entered Uganda.

So a party of spearmen met Hannington near the frontier. "Why do you want to kill me?" the bishop asked; "I come to preach the gospel of peace." The leader of the spearmen replied, "The matter does not rest with us. The king's orders have to be obeyed." Coolly, in the short grass under an umbrella-topped thorn tree, shaded from the harsh African sunlight, Hannington knelt down and began to pray. A soldier, walking up to him, drove a spear through his heart.

* * * * *

Hannington's death (1885) served only to intensify the

dissensions among Mwanga's subjects. There followed a period of intermittent civil war, the waves of which threatened to overwhelm the king and his throne. Politics and religion became indistinguishably confused.

In 1888, Moslems and Christians for once banded together. They drove the king out and chose his brother to rule in his stead. A year later Christians and Moslems were fighting one another. This time it was the Christians' turn to be driven from the country. These exiles made approaches to the king they had exiled, and promised to reinstate him. The king joined them, and after several Christian failures, the Moslems were finally defeated in October 1889. Mwanga re-ascended the throne, and the two Christian parties, the Protestants and the Catholics, were free to fight among themselves. In the language of the country the Protestants were known as Wa-Ingleza (the English) and the Catholics as Wa-Fransa (the French).

Many times in these years the banana groves of Uganda rang with the armed strife of Wa-Fransa and Wa-Ingleza. The men fought with spears and guns and knobkerries. Converts to the gospel of peace fell with smashed skulls and twisted bodies in the grass. Shots cracked and hissed among the trees, and smoke rose. The tiny white-breasted birds that haunt banana trees fluttered to and fro in terror. A scent of decay hung in the air. The black-and-gold coloured birds stopped their singing.

The dead came in the end to be numbered by thousands. They died for France or England, as the case might be. But there was not one Englishman or Frenchman among them.

*   *   *   *   *

Into this strange Uganda atmosphere there now strode an Englishman with an armed force of his own—Captain Lugard. He was in touch with Cecil Rhodes, and happened to start from the coast of Mwanga's country in August 1890, just as Rhodes' pioneers were invading the Kingdom of Lobengula.

Lugard, however, was not acting directly as Rhodes'

agent. He was employed by another Chartered Company,
the Imperial British East Africa Company, which was
trying to do for its own part of the continent what Rhodes
was doing for his. Lugard's instructions were to impress
Mwanga with a sense of the Company's power, to secure
control of all white affairs in the country, and, while
assuring everybody of religious freedom and toleration, to
consolidate the Protestant party. As I have said, this
party, the Wa-Ingleza, wanted Uganda to come under the
British flag.

Lugard treated Mwanga with much less respect than
Rhodes' agents showed to Lobengula. He marched his
troops straight to the king's capital without asking permission, and there insisted on his signing a treaty.

The King demurred. "I fear the English, Chief
Lugard," he explained, "because of the vengeance they
may exact for the killing of Hannington. I would rather
sign treaties with the Germans or the French."

"I seek no vengeance," Lugard replied. "I offer you
pledges of peace in your kingdom."

Mwanga tried playing for time. But when he found
Lugard would give nothing away, he fell into great fear
and excitement. "It is my country and my people you
are after," he cried despairingly.

Lugard gave him a front-bench official answer. "I
shall not be deterred by your opposition, Chief Mwanga,
from the course I have set myself to follow."

"But," came Mwanga's final remonstrance, "if I sign
your fly-blown paper, my proud Baganda will be no better
than slaves."

Lugard drove him into a corner. "They will meet a
worse fate if you do not sign. For I shall go to your enemy,
Kabarega of Unyozo, and join with him in making war
upon you."

Threatened thus, and having exhausted the armoury of
evasion with which Africans are richly equipped, Mwanga
muttered angrily, "What choice is left me but to sign?"

At this there was a tremendous clamour from the assembled tribespeople, who threatened to shoot the white men and those who signed. Lugard thought it prudent to adjourn the meeting.

This all happened on Christmas Eve 1890. On Boxing day, out of sight of the protesting populace and with the worst possible grace, Mwanga signed.

The treaty gave the British East Africa Company complete monopolist power over the government, trade, and land of Uganda.

* * * * *

The treaty may, as Lugard hoped, have restored the British prestige which the Hannington affair was thought to have compromised. It did nothing to establish the internal peace Lugard had promised. Mwanga identified himself more and more with the Wa-Fransa, and eventually embraced the Catholic faith. He and his supporters refused to fly the Company's flag; the Wa-Ingleza accepted it. Once again the bitter rivalry of the factions was daily threatening civil war.

However, by March 1891 Lugard felt the situation at the capital to be so far in hand that his subordinates could take charge of it. He himself set forth on an expedition of conquest westwards in the direction of the Belgian Congo. He fought a battle with the Moslem party, which was now raising its head and raiding some of Mwanga's villages. Then he continued his march for a further nine months, building forts and annexing territory as he went.

At the end of 1891 he was back in the capital at the head not only of his own troops, but also of 1,000 well-armed Sudanese whom he had picked up in the course of his wanderings and enlisted in the Company's service. On the grounds that a fresh outbreak of civil war was imminent, he issued arms to the Wa-Ingleza and lent them the support of the Company's resources against Mwanga and the Wa-Fransa.

Mwanga's forces were driven on to an island in Lake

Victoria and soon defeated, with considerable loss of life; the new weapon, the machine-gun, proving just as useful in Uganda as Rhodes's men were to find it in Matabeleland. Mwanga had to sign another treaty, by which the Catholics were confined to one corner of his kingdom. The Wa-Ingleza took the opportunity to burn many of the stations and villages of the French missionaries. Lugard also showed his skill in inducing a Moslem pretender to the throne to surrender.

A year later (April 1893) the British Government took over from the British East Africa Company, Uganda came under the control of Parliament at Westminster, and the dear old Union Jack serenely unfurled itself by the waters of Victoria Nyanza. This arrangement, said the Church Missionary Society's report, " must be regarded as an answer to the Church's prayer ".

Even that was not the end. For some time it seemed doubtful whether the Union Jack was after all what the Baganda wanted. There was never-ending trouble with the Sudanese soldiers whom Lugard had introduced into the country and then left rather untidily lying about without any provision for maintenance or control. In 1894 the British authorities were fighting Mwanga's old enemy Kabarega. In 1899 these two lifelong foes joined forces with one another and with the Sudanese to free the country from British rule. They were defeated, captured, and deported.

Mwanga was taken, a prisoner, to the islands of Seychelles in the Indian Ocean. In this remote exile he soon ate his heart out, and died in May 1903.

PART III *(Continued)*

WHAT IT FEELS LIKE TO BE
A COLONY

(*b*) HOW GOVERNED

CHAPTER XIV

HEALTH AND SOCIAL SERVICES *

§ I. EDUCATION

THE African colonies, for the most part acquired in the kind of way just described, comprise to-day about three-quarters of the total population and nearly nine-tenths of the total territory of the Empire, excluding the Dominions and India.

Their reception into the imperial fold was not, the reader may agree, of the happiest. But how do matters stand with them now that they have had fifty years or so of British care and protection? What kind of perspective will give us a true view of our relations as British citizens with the peoples of these colonies for which we are still responsible? We have to remember that they are politically subordinate to Parliament at Westminster, and therefore in the last resort to the British electorate, and economically subordinate to the industrial system which we in Britain have built up for ourselves.

Let us, provisionally at least, put the case thus. The task of the nineteenth century, so far as concerned the relations between Europe and the so-called subject races, was a task of liberation. The old slave-trading and slave-owning imperialism was transformed into what is fashionably called trusteeship. True, European imperial rule was extended over great areas and great populations which had not previously been subject to it. But throughout, the sustained interest of statesmen, administrators, and mission-

* The only social services in black Africa are medical and educational. There are no schemes for health or unemployment insurance or pensions, etc.

139

aries was increasingly towards the human, or humanitarian, side of the problem. The nineteenth century set a term to the era of crude atrocities, and recorded a general heightening of the sense of moral responsibility on the part of imperial powers for native welfare.

The twentieth-century task, on the other hand, is a task of co-ordination. It involves planning the satisfaction of international economic needs, and coupling the colonies to this process, while avoiding exploitation in the bad sense, and at the same time accelerating the completion of the process of colonial liberation.

What progress has been made with these two tasks? How much still remains to do? Is the rate of progress to-day quicker or slower than it has been in the past? Are there any sectors of the front where ground, once gained, has had to be surrendered?

There are many who, taking a bird's-eye view of the last twenty-five years of colonial history, find material for a ready and confident answer. Since 1913, they inform us, the external trade of the colonies has been multiplied by 3 and the aggregate revenue of colonial governments by $3\frac{1}{2}$. Expenditure on the administrative services has been multiplied by $4\frac{1}{2}$, on health services by $5\frac{1}{2}$, and on education by 8. Famine and disease have consequently been checked—I quote from a publication of the Royal Institute of International Affairs *—" slavery and the slave-trade, intertribal wars, human sacrifices, and the ordeals of witchcraft have been suppressed. The natives are being taught to conduct their own affairs with justice and humanity, and they are being educated in letters and in industry."

The implication behind this kind of account is that internal peace and economic development have brought about a rise in native standards of life, and this in turn has provided the source of revenue for extending governmental activity along many lines. Again, it is suggested that the rise in living standards has been commensurate

* " The British Empire ", p. 143.

with the increase in overseas trade, and has averaged as much as 100% for every eight-year period since 1913. And finally it is implied that in every part of the field things are going on very nicely, and that all we have to do is to continue as we are. There may be a few black spots here and there, of course; but they are gradually being erased, and provided we do not let ourselves be carried away by enthusiasm or impatience, we shall reach the millennium without undue difficulty or delay.

If there is more optimism than accuracy in such a picture, the form of expression is partly to blame. Take, for example, the reference to an eight-fold increase in educational expenditure, and see how it applies to a relatively advanced colony such as the Gold Coast. In 1913 education there cost £25,000: in 1931, the peak year, it cost just over a quarter of a million. This is ten times as much, and there can be no objection to calling it such, or to calling it an increase of 900%, if you prefer. The same fact can be stated, though less impressively, by saying that educational expenditure took eighteen years to rise from 3% to 7% of Government revenue. Both forms of statement omit another fact, which is equally relevant—namely, that even in 1931 four Gold-Coast children out of five were receiving no schooling of any kind, and less than $\frac{1}{2}$% got past the primary stage. Some experts, indeed, make calculations more unfavourable than these, as the diagram on page 143 bears witness.

In none of our tropical African colonies is the proportion of children who get any kind of schooling above 20%, and it sinks to 8% in Sierra Leone, where British rule has been established for a century and a half. (Education is nowhere free.) Authorities have calculated that at our present rate of progress it will be 700 years before the natives of even the Gold Coast can read and write their own language.* In East Africa the time required to achieve a

* Or 3,500 years, if the natural increase of population is taken into account. See the careful statistical article in *Africa*, April 1938.

similar result will be well over 1,000 years. Moreover, our customary rate of progress appears to be slowing down, for the percentage of expenditure on education not only in the Gold Coast, but in the other territories of British tropical Africa, has been falling or stationary since 1913 or earlier. The one exception to this statement is Nyasaland, where the percentage has risen from 2.8 to 3.2.

§ 2. HEALTH AND WORK

When we turn to the question of health and health services, we find again that the pretty picture needs touching up in ways which rather spoil its prettiness. No doubt it is true that we spend on health services to-day more than five times as much as we did in 1913. But it is not of great significance, since in 1913 expenditure for this purpose was almost non-existent. What is significant is that almost every African native is infested with hookworm or similar parasites; that to say that two-thirds of the African population is infected with malaria would be an under-estimate; that in many areas there is insufficiency · of food; and that infant mortality stands at a level which must be described as appalling. Only in a few favoured spots does the infant mortality figure fall as low as 150 per 1,000; for Nigeria as a whole it is said to be 300, for Northern Uganda 350, and for Kenya as a whole 400. The corresponding figure for the United Kingdom is 59. These facts are not the worst that can truthfully be said about the situation; they are taken from official sources and represent what the defenders of our imperial rule feel obliged to acknowledge.

In any case, they are sufficiently disturbing to prompt the question whether among societies subsisting in such conditions extensive depopulation may not be taking place. They demonstrate the falsity of the vulgar notion that British rule is synonymous with automatic social progress for native races fortunate enough to fall under it.

We know, moreover, that the above conditions are

SUMMARY OF FACILITIES AVAILABLE

PERCENTAGE SCALE

BASUTOLAND

SOUTHERN RHODESIA

UNION OF SOUTH AFRICA

BECHUANALAND

SWAZILAND

NYASALAND

NORTHERN RHODESIA

SOUTH WEST AFRICA

UGANDA

KENYA

ZANZIBAR

GOLD COAST

THE GAMBIA

SIERRA LEONE

ANGLO-EGYPTIAN SUDAN

TANGANYIKA

NIGERIA

SOMALILAND

THESE BLANK COLUMNS REPRESENT THE PROPORT-ION OF CHILDREN FOR WHOM FACILITIES HAVE YET TO BE ARRANGED

PERCENTAGE SCALE

■ GOVT & AIDED   ▨ UNAIDED

[By courtesy of *Africa*.

Educational Provision in British Africa

reinforced by a crazy system of labour recruiting which involves the absence from their villages for months, and even years at a stretch, of half the adult male population; this large-scale migration, among a multitude of dis-integrating social effects, must have some bearing on the birth-rate, though that bearing has nowhere yet been satisfactorily measured.

A Government-appointed committee in Nyasaland in 1936 uttered the warning that local Africans driven abroad by economic circumstances might " acquire a complete loathing for and distrust of administration by white men " if present tendencies were not checked.

Administrators between the Limpopo and the Nile have been exercised about the problem ever since the labour question in the Congo was investigated by a Belgian Com-mission in 1924. The Hilton Young Commission, which reported in 1929, had some sound observations on policy. But in practice little progress has been made towards bringing the situation under control. The finding of the Belgian Commission was that it would be unsafe to with-draw more than 5% of the able-bodied adult males for employment at a distance from their homes. In a number of rural areas in British Africa to-day more than 50% of such males are permanently absent from their homes in wage-service with white employers. Not only tribal organisations, but family life itself is being undermined. In developing Africa's material resources we are destroying her human resources.

One does not have to be a mystic or even a humanitarian to regard this as unsound. Nor does it apparently do much to meet the total demands of employers of labour. All territories in this part of the continent are importers as well as exporters of labour, and in all of them complaints of labour shortage never cease. Everywhere employers' organisations spend money on recruiting labour from some-one else's territory because someone else has spent money on recruiting labour from theirs.

Into a tropical Africa already reduced to social chaos by these means, the Union of South Africa entered in 1937 as a competitor for the labour which had been proved inadequate even for local needs. Theoretically this competition should be welcome, in so far as the Transvaal gold-mines and some other Union employers pay higher rates of wages than are to be found in the tropical zone. But two practical considerations are decisive against it. First, the compound system, under which the Rand mine labour is controlled, is wholly intolerable; * and, second, the social life of tropical Africa cannot support the strain of an increased percentage of exiled males.

Nevertheless, the South African Parliament passed in 1937 an Act permitting the entry into the Union of indentured native labour from British tropical areas. This had previously been illegal, since experience has shown an alarmingly high death-rate among tropical mine workers. Medical science has, according to Union Government spokesmen, now surmounted this difficulty. The gold boom involved an increase between 1932 and 1936 of nearly 100,000 in the numbers of Africans employed on the mines. The Union Government has estimated that by 1946 a further 140,000 will be required, bringing the total mine-labour force up to 450,000. If the mines expand like this there will, of course, be a corresponding expansion of employment in other forms of industry. The effect of such re-duplicated demands on the fabric of native society can easily be imagined. Scarcely an African village between Johannesburg and the equator but would feel it.

§ 3. POPULATION QUESTIONS

The attempt to measure the consequences of developments like these from the standpoint of vital statistics comes up at once against one of the great obstacles to the study of African affairs—absence of reliable records. But let us

* See Leonard Barnes, " The Duty of Empire ", Chapter XVI.

see what material is available. The Chatham House publication entitled "The Colonial Problem" states that the total population of Africa is estimated to have risen from 135 millions in 1913 to 145 millions in 1935. "The rate of increase", the same authority adds, rather surprisingly, "is considerable." In fact, it is not considerable, in the usual sense, at all; on the contrary, it is alarmingly low. It represents an increase of only 7.4% in twenty-two years, an average of 0.33% per annum. In Britain in the same period the increase was 10.4% or 0.47% per annum—this in spite of the fact that, as is well known, we have been dropping towards an actual decline in numbers after 1940.

However, the figure of 135 millions for all Africa in 1913 may be largely guess-work, and the figure for 1935 is perhaps in little better case. Let us discard them both and try another line of attack. Kuczynski, in his book on Colonial Population already mentioned, gives the official estimates of population for all African territories in each year from 1931 to 1935. From his tables it appears that between these years there were increases in six out of the twelve British tropical dependencies, and decreases in the other six. The increases outbalanced the decreases, and there was consequently a net over-all increase of 1.2% for the four years—in other words, an average annual increase of 0.3%.

In the same period the increase in Britain has been higher (1.8% or 0.45% per annum), although we know that gross reproduction rate has been below unity, and that therefore our future numbers can no longer be stabilised, let alone increased, by any fall in mortality.

It may be, and probably is, mere coincidence that the figure for Africa corresponds with our previous result. I do not suggest that either of them is anything but inconclusive, especially as an independent study by S. J. K. Baker indicates that over some large part of Eastern Africa population is actually increasing by more than 1% per annum, even in districts where the infant mortality rate is as high as 400.* On the other hand, I do suggest that predictions made by so eminent an authority as Lord Lugard of a rapid general increase seem to be unwarranted by the evidence.†

§ 4. NUTRITION

Of all the factors we have been considering, malnutrition may be taken to be the basic one. Its consequences are, first, diminished reproductive vitality, tending to lower the birth rate; next, high infant mortality and greater frequency of epidemics; and last, weakened resistance to every kind of infection. Two square meals a day and two pairs of shoes a year are the African's prime need. The one would give him strength to fight disease, and the other would give him full protection from the life-draining plague of hookworm. Both together would mean a revolution in his physique. With their aid he would soon pluck up heart to tackle his last and worst natural enemy, the mosquito.

Some examples to illustrate the nutrition situation may be chosen at random. G. St. J. Orde Browne, Labour Adviser to the Colonial Office, reporting on Labour conditions in Northern Rhodesia,‡ says, " Considering now the actual conditions of life in the village two sinister elements are conspicuous—under-nourishment and disease. The view is occasionally expressed that the native is well and happy in his own surroundings and that it is a mistake to introduce him to modern ideas as to sanitation, diet, and so forth. Even a superficial investigation of conditions will show this to be a disastrous fallacy; birth-rate, infant mortality, physique, and general health all indicate a population subjected to a perpetual drain only partially

* See " Africa ", Vol. X. No. 1.
† See *International Affairs*, January 1936. The conclusion reached by Lord Hailey in his " African Survey " is that " in the present state of our knowledge it is only possible to say that the African population is probably now either stationary or subject to a very slow increase ".
‡ Report published by Stationery Office, September 1938.

offset by sun, fresh air, and the African's natural vitality." Describing the meagre dietary of the villages, it is mentioned that caterpillars, ants, and other insects, with fungi, roots, and nuts, serve to add variety when available—" though by no means all tribes appreciate the more unusual of these delicacies ". Meat hunger and the desire for salt are said to be almost universal. In Barotseland, once again, " the spectacle is presented of an underfed weakly population, with the best of its elements drained away by the distant lure of high wages ". The " high wages ", as we shall see in a moment, sometimes rise to the sumptuous level of 32*s*. a month.

Meanwhile, let us turn to the annual report of the Medical Director in Southern Rhodesia. We there find that during the year ending November 1935, for instance, some 75,000 Africans were employed in the mines of the colony. In this labour force the total casualties from disease during the year amount to 41,620, or about 55%. The percentage, we are told, " could have been greatly reduced by a more generous ration scale, and still more by a correct one, for it is perfectly obvious that most of the illness among these natives was the direct outcome of improper feeding and lack of protective foods. But there appears to be no incentive to furnish the working native with his physiological requirements." *

Why is this incentive absent? Why do Africans lack their square meals and their shoes? These are not extravagant requirements. If the standard of living has really been mounting step for step with the trebled external trade, how comes it that such rudimentary needs still cannot be met?

§ 5. WASTAGE OF ENERGY

The fact is that rising imports and exports are, in African conditions, no direct index of changes in native living

* See *United Empire*, October 1938, p. 440.

standards. As regards the food supply, the main reasons for its general insufficiency seem to be these. Much of the agricultural labour force is wasted because it lacks the tools and the organisation modern science could give it. In Africa it takes about forty men to do the work that one can do under modern systems of cultivation. In many places, also, the alienation of tribal land to European immigrants has thrown the traditional farming economy out of gear, without introducing any counter-balancing modernisation of native methods. The consequence has been the exhaustion and over-stocking, followed often by the actual phsyical erosion, of much of such land as has remained available for native use. This particular phenomenon, being an accompaniment of white settlement, hardly occurs in West Africa, but is common in the East and South.

Again, in some places it has happened that colonial governments, relying, as they often do, on customs duties for a large part of their revenue, have encouraged export crops at the expense of the local food supply. Indeed, one of the strangest commentaries on imperial rule is that the importance of local food-supplies for general colonial development is only now beginning to be understood. Finally, the labour migration mentioned above has lowered the productivity of tribal agriculture by withdrawing from it the most active part of the male population, and putting them to work either on mining or on the production of plantation crops for which Africans do not form, and are not expected to form, a market.

That is the short answer why the African is undernourished. Turning now to the question why he goes about barefoot and picks up hookworm, the short answer is that he cannot afford shoes. This is partly because our own industrialists do not always remember that in a poor market like the native African market, price is generally much more important than quality. There may be a wide sale for second-rate rubber-soled canvas shoes at 2s. a pair, but no sale at all for the first-rate article at 3s. a pair. The African, whose social tradition prompts him to walk about unshod, may make a concession to vanity or comfort or even the representations of the health authorities and buy shoes, provided he can get them at some particular price. If he cannot get them at that price, he may prefer simply to revert to the habits of his ancestors. So when the British Government claps a virtual embargo on the entry of Japanese goods into our colonies, what happens is that Japan is injured, the British manufacturer very little benefited, and the African native condemned to the continued loss of half his life-energy, owing to the attentions of the nimble hookworm. From such a policy the hookworm is the only gainer.

CHAPTER XV

WEALTH AND NATURAL RESOURCES

I. AFRICAN POVERTY

WE are still left with the question why Africans cannot afford, or think they cannot afford, to pay 3s. for a pair of shoes. In order to answer it, we must recall something of the conditions under which colonial production and development take place. Firstly, the purchase of shoes involves the possession of cash, and cash is a thing with which the traditional African society does not provide its members. Broadly speaking, there is little in the way of a cash market for African agriculture, except when it is engaged in producing export crops. The normal African family being engaged in subsistence farming, very little exchange occurs. The food requirements of African labour employed in mines and on plantations are supplied in the main by European settlers or by the employing enterprise itself. Wage-service is therefore the chief source of such cash income as comes the African's way. Most of the cash thus earned is earmarked for the personal expenses of the earner, and for the payment of his tax and that of non-earning members of his family.

In other words, the African generally earns cash from those natural resources which have been withdrawn from his ownership, and not from those which remain in it. There is irony in this. It also means that the cash he earns is very little, since, if colonial governments had wanted the development of minerals and plantations to enrich Africans, they would clearly not have taken them out of African ownership in the first place.

No adequate study has yet been made of the social income of colonies and its distribution. But we know that an African family with cash resources totalling £5 a year is considered, and considers itself, well-to-do. We know that a labourer will undertake on his bare feet a journey of several days to reach employment whose remuneration is 10s. a month, a journey of weeks for 15s. a month, and a journey of months for the 23s. 6d. a month,* which he can get at the Eldorado of the Northern Rhodesian copper-mines. Incidentally, the mine authorities have found that it takes from six weeks to two months of special feeding to bring these recruits to a condition of physical fitness for a normal day's work in the mine.

The belief that the economic development of Africa necessarily enriches Africans ignores all these conditions. There may, of course, be such enrichment; cotton-growing in Uganda and cocoa-growing in the Gold Coast are, or have been, examples of it. But extensive African impoverishment can also accompany what from the European standpoint appears as the winning of fabulous new wealth.

A classic example of this process is described by the late Rev. James Henderson of Lovedale in a memorandum published as an appendix to the Select Committee Report on General Hertzog's Native Bills in 1927.† Dr. Henderson shows that in the fifty years which followed 1875, the years of the large-scale exploitation of South Africa's diamond and gold resources, the consuming power of one characteristic native area (the Ciskei) fell by more than 50% per head. Anyone who had inferred from the soaring figures of South Africa's overseas trade between 1875 and 1925 that the standard of living of South African natives had universally risen during the period, would have been mistaken.

In general (the remark will bear repetition), overseas

* This is a general average for all kinds of African labour, whether surface or underground. The separate averages are: Surface 18s. a month, underground 32s. a month.

† S.C. 10, 1927.

trade is a fallacious index of the wealth of a colony so long as any attempt is made to equate wealth with social well-being.* It is not hard to see why. Take as an example the case of copper in Northern Rhodesia.

§ 2. COPPER AND TOBACCO

The output of copper, all of which is sold outside the colony, was worth some £12 million in 1937. Of the £12 million, £5 million went in dividends to shareholders (all non-residents). Half a million was paid as royalties to the British South Africa Company, which is quite functionless so far as the copper industry is concerned, but which happens to own all the minerals in the colony by virtue of a so-called treaty made forty years ago with Lewanika, King of the Barotse.

An approximate income and expenditure account for the industry for 1937 reads as follows:—

By copper exported . £12,000,000	To dividends . .	£5,000,000
	,, royalties . .	500,000
	,, Income-tax .	700,000
	,, salaries of 1,690 Europeans .	800,000
	,, wages of 17,000 Africans .	244,000
	,, Balance (other costs of operation, maintenance, stores, freight, insurance, etc.) .	4,756,000
£12,000,000		£12,000,000

Of the above figures,† the £12 millions appear in the Customs returns, and may be taken, if you like, as an index of " the economic development of Northern Rhodesia ". But to speak as though copper-mining had made that sum available for increasing the social welfare of Africans

* On this point cf. W. M. Macmillan, " Africa Emergent ", p. 71.
† For a fuller account of them and their meaning, see *Empire*, July 1938, p. 22.

in the colony shows either too much ingenuousness or too little. In point of fact, African consuming power is directly raised only by what is paid in miners' wages and by that part of European salaries which is spent on hiring domestic servants—say £350,000 in all. Even when all indirect benefits to Africans are taken into account, their gross gain can hardly be put higher than £1 million. And in order to arrive at a net figure expressive of welfare economics, we have to set against the gross figure (a) whatever is injurious in the impact of the new economic order on the minds and bodies of the African tribespeople, and (b) any net diminution of the food supply of Africans that may be occasioned by the diversion of tribal man-power from agriculture to mining.

This account of the copper situation gives the typical pattern of our behaviour wherever mineral production is concerned. Broadly, we appropriate the natural resources, develop them in our own ways and for our own purposes (ways and purposes which wholly ignore the preexisting structure and function of African society), and of the wealth so produced carry out of the country £11 for every £1 we leave behind. Many English people like to call the procedure trusteeship, but when they do so, they are perhaps using the term a little loosely.

Results nearly as advantageous to Europeans and hardly less unfavourable to Africans can be obtained without any complete alienation of natural resources. The Nyasaland tobacco industry furnishes an example of this alternative process. Two tables will indicate the position.

A. *Persons Employed in the Industry and Deriving their Livelihood Therefrom.*

Europeans. Growers, Supervisors, buyers, transporters, graders, packers, etc.		240
Africans. Growers on Native Trust land and private estates	90,000	
Labourers	30,000	
		120,000
		120,240

B. *Incomes Derived from the Tobacco Industry.*

Europeans	£241,405
Africans	198,150
Government	106,500
Railway	105,000
	£651,055

These figures * do not include profits accruing from the sale of the exported tobacco, except in so far as they are returned to and circulated in Nyasaland.

It is worth noting:—

(1) that the railway is privately owned (by Europeans), though the Government has a contingent liability in respect of loan interest commitments;

(2) that the annual income per head from tobacco is £1,000 for Europeans, and 33s. for Africans.

§ 3. THE TECHNIQUE OF MONOPOLY

A new technique has been developed for securing this apportionment of the wealth the industry produces. Europeans are given by statute the monopoly of the marketing of the crop, and even in some cases powers of compulsion over its producers. Nyasaland tobacco is an instance of the new system in a pretty complete form. Every phase of the industry—growing, processing, grading, marketing— is under the control of a Board with full statutory powers. Africans are not represented on the Board.

In late years the systematic creation of trading and marketing monopolies of this kind has become more and more a matter of British official policy. Commodities to which the policy has already been fully or partly applied in Africa alone are tobacco, cotton, cloves, coffee, and cocoa. It is intensely unpopular among the colonial peoples

* They are taken from a report (T.N. 40) dated March 5th, 1938, published by the Nyasaland Tobacco Association, and signed by the Director of Agriculture and the Comptroller of Customs, among others.

affected, and is at least in part responsible for recent dis-
orders in more than one dependency.

Something of the African feeling in the matter was
brought out in the evidence given to the Cocoa Commission which investigated the cocoa strike on the Gold
Coast during 1938.

Sir Ofori Atta, one of the chief African witnesses,
emphasised the following points:

(1) What has all along seemed odd to the African
farmer is that, while the European merchants fix the
price of their merchandise, he himself is at the mercy
of the European buyers (who are the same merchants
acting in another capacity) in regard to the price of his
own product.

(2) The farmer gets a fixed price irrespective of quality,
since grading is done at a later stage, so that the higher
returns from cocoa of the better qualities go to merchants.

(3) The same firms are organised as a ring both for
buying African produce and for selling European manufactures. When, therefore, the world price of cocoa rises,
the merchants increase (irrespective of cost prices) the
price of some staple goods which are most in demand,
thus depriving the farmer, who spends almost all his
earnings in purchasing imported goods, of the benefit
of the increase in the price of cocoa.

(4) By controlling produce prices and the prices of
trade goods, the merchants have turned the farmer's
ability to work into a commodity, and have reduced
him to full economic dependence.

Most readers of this book probably do not come of
pheasant-shooting stock. I cannot claim to do so myself.
But some people do; and Gerard Clauson, of the Colonial
Office, is one of them. He has amusingly explained the
economics of pheasant-rearing in this way, quoting, I
believe, from his grandfather: " Up goes a guinea, bang

goes a penny, and down comes half a crown ".* You have only to stand this image on its head, and you get an almost exact picture of the economics of mining and plantation industry in the colonies.   Half a crown to Royalty owners and Government taxation, a penny to native wages, and away flies a guinea's worth of gold, copper, tin, tea, rubber, sisal, or whatever it may be.

It is the guinea that figures in the Customs return and only the penny that goes to swell the purchasing power of the native population.   The rest of the guinea, apart from wages and local taxation, does nothing to enrich the colony or its inhabitants, but is distributed among various residents in Europe and America, who are either mere shareholders, or manufacturers supplying the mines with machinery and stores.   And that explains why the external trade of a colony can be multiplied three times without being accompanied by any appreciable rise in the standard of living of Africans who do the actual work of wealth production.

The point that calls for emphasis is that colonial economic development, whether in the form of mining, plantation-farming, or native agriculture, is still regarded primarily as an extension of British industry at home.   We are imposing on Africa a kind of industrial revolution, the direction, speed, and amplitude of which are determined in the main by what we take to be the needs, not of African society, but of our own economic system.   In the exercise of what some call our trusteeship, our efforts are given not to altering that basic relation, but to mitigating a few of its most obvious ill-effects.   The mitigations may serve to quiet our own uneasy consciences, but as objective factors they operate on too small a scale, and in too localised a sphere, to be of much importance in the total African situation.

* See "Some Uses of Statistics in Colonial Administration " (*Journal of the Royal African Society*, October 1937).

§ 4. SOME ECONOMIC SUGGESTIONS

The fundamental problem in tropical Africa is to develop the internal market, or in other words, to raise the colonial standard of living. Africans will have to command a much larger share than they get at present of the wealth their country produces.

How is this to be done? This is not the place for any detailed answer to so large a question. All that can be attempted here is to outline certain general considerations that may be relevant.

First, post-war experience has finally disposed of the old hypothesis that African consuming power could best be increased by increasing Africa's output of primary products for export. In general, supply now exceeds effective demand for tropical products, and, in view of the population trends in Europe and America, is likely to continue to do so, unless social changes on a grand scale lead rapidly to the more equal distribution of income and property in those continents. The terms on which tropical countries were originally drawn into the international division of labour have, in fact, radically altered.

Second, since an expanding demand for African exports is improbable, and since African wealth obviously cannot be increased by the mere restriction of African output, some third means of adjusting demand and supply needs to be discovered. In principle, such a *tertium quid* will be bound to involve encouraging (*a*) the increased production and exchange of subsistence crops in the colonies, and (*b*) the development of local manufactures.

Third, the experience of India and the Dominions suggests that the growth of secondary industry in colonial countries is both desirable and, on a long-range view, inevitable. From the standpoint of Britain, however, such a growth in Africa would mean an expansion of the market for certain capital goods and a decline in the market for certain consumption goods, followed, if the colonial industries were successful, by a rising demand for other and generally more complicated types of consumption goods.

Fourth, the possible hardships likely to arise from such a shift in British industry could be foreseen and neutralised by appropriate Government action. But on a short-range view the shift might well imply a conflict between the interests of Africa and those of British employers, and even of British workers. This being so, it is probably Utopian to expect British policy ever to identify itself with the requirements of a sincere and energetic trusteeship. Indeed, trusteeship and African interests only meet at the infinity of colonial independence, where the status of ward and that of guardian alike disappear. Unfortunately the same forces which make genuine trusteeship Utopian also preclude Africa's self-determination. The economic and the political issues are bound up together beyond all disentangling.

Fifth, it is in any case impossible to say at present what economic policy ought to be followed by any given colony, since we lack essential information about its economic structure and potentialities. A series of detailed studies designed to supply this want is urgently needed.

Sixth, we may be sure that there will be little economic advance for the African so long as his trustees begin their duties by removing the natural resources of African territories from African ownership, and until the trading and marketing monopolies that dispose of Africa's exported wealth are transferred to democratic African control based on the principles of co-operation.

CHAPTER XVI

CIVIL AND POLITICAL LIBERTIES

§ 1. DESTRUCTIVE LIBERATION

WE can now put our finger on the heart of the colonial problem. It is this. European economic penetration of Africa has set up conditions to which the clan-bond, the tribal structure, the old unity of African life, is no longer relevant. We are destroying the solidarity of blood-related societies in which all members were productively active and of whose co-operative character and significance all members were fully and directly aware. We have split the whole basis of social relationship, and are putting in its place a society which is no society, a society divided against itself and riven by the conflict of opposed group-interests. We are, in a word, introducing into African life our own type of class-society with all our own unhealed social wounds.

In the material sphere the process is accompanied by those social evils with which the history of the early industrial revolution in Britain has made us familiar. In the psychological sphere it is involving the gradual disappearance of the animistic terrors and magical beliefs which characterise the primitive, and which reflect his want of control over the material environment. In their place are emerging the disintegrated faculties of the citizen in class-society, together with his idealistic thinking and his fantasy—projections of recovered social unity in a millennial world or in a life beyond death. These, in turn, reflect that citizen's despair at the perilous slope down which his own civilisation is leading him, and his sense of the impossibility of establishing real human community within the prison of his own social structure.

In a sense, of course, the whole process represents liberation for the African, just as the period between the first and third Reform Acts represented liberation for the common people of Britain. But we should not forget that the same period of liberation spanned perhaps the worst years of economic misery that the common people of Britain had known since the reign of Stephen. Birth, we know, is a painful business, both for the mother and the child. The new African society, which is no society, but which yet is the source from which knowledge and freedom and equality will ultimately spring, is being wrenched feet foremost from the womb into the cheerless light of day, while its infant mind is cleft by the same psychological trauma which separation from their mother's blood-stream is said to inflict on individual children.

Social unity is a precious thing. Even when seen in its primitive tribal form, it exerts a strange fascination over us " civilised " Europeans who have never directly experienced it in any form at all. Hence it happens that some anthropologists and colonial officials seek to postpone the break-up of the tribal structure by applying an administrative and educational technique known as indirect rule. But this is merely screwing down the stopper of a bottle which is already cracked at the base. What has snapped the clan-bond is not this or that administrative method, but the broad fact of economic penetration; the break cannot be repaired by a smooth dovetailing of the administrative mechanism with native social institutions, when productive relations in general are such as to render those institutions more and more unworkable.

In any case, the problem of Africa in the modern world is not to preserve the unity of the tribe, but to find a new social unity, a final emancipation at a far higher productive level than tribalism can ever reach, on the farther side of

F

class-divided society. The tribe must go, and it is well that
it should; for in no other way can the ground for that
final emancipation be prepared. What is important is
the order of the tribe's going. Are we to repeat in-
definitely the process of hacking it to pieces by means of
an uncontrolled and indiscriminate industrial revolution?
Or can a scientific sociology, even now, lead Africans
quietly to the new communal life, without dragging them
through all the sufferings which in the last 150 years the
labouring masses of Europe have had to endure? Are we,
to whom it is still open to be the navigators of the African
ship—are we ourselves sufficiently educated to grasp the
meaning of our own past social blunders and misfortunes,
and to apply in our colonial world the lessons they teach?

Mutatis mutandis, similar considerations apply to India.
The problem there is not to find a short cut from tribalism
to industrialisation, which will by-pass capitalism. Rather
it is whether we are to hand over India to Indians on terms
which will leave the Indian people the victims of their own
entrenched reactionaries, or on terms of another kind.

We may sum up, then, by noting that the nineteenth-
century task of liberation is still incomplete and has not
yet proceeded beyond the destructive stage. The imperialists have in the main, though not entirely, destroyed
slavery and the slave trade. They have carried far the
disruption of the tribe. Both these demolitions were
necessary in order that the foundations of freedom and
scientific knowledge might be laid. But they have left
Africans without any present bond of social unity. Africans
themselves are groping round for a unifying principle,
and are experimenting more or less at random with religion, communism, and bare anti-European feeling.
Europeans for their part seem for the moment to have no
further choices to offer them. And as the economic
bases of African society are in so transitional and insecure
a state, little headway has been made with the construction
of liberty in the civil and political spheres.

§ 2. WANT OF CONSTRUCTIVE PLANNING

As for what we called the twentieth-century task of planning and co-ordinating the material and social development of the " backward " or " primitive " areas of the world, it is not merely incomplete; it has scarcely been begun.* So far as the British Empire is concerned, the little that has been attempted can be briefly summarised under five heads.

(1) There has been some research into scientific agriculture with a view to increasing maximum yields. Marketing problems and the possibility of introducing alternative crops in various areas have also been given some attention.

(2) Arrangements have been set up for a pool of commercial and scientific information, to which all dependencies may contribute and from which they can all draw.

(3) By international agreement schemes have been brought into force for controlling the output of various materials—e.g., rubber, tin, copper. They are sometimes called valorisation schemes.

(4) In general the tendency has been since 1931 to treat the whole colonial Empire as a single economic unit, and not a mere " scatter " of unrelated territories.

(5) There was the decision at Ottawa (1932) to establish preferential markets for colonial produce throughout the Empire, and for Empire produce in the colonies.

These conceptions vary in importance. The scale of them cannot be called grandiose. (1) and (3) are mutually contradictory. All are very young and ill-developed. Clauson reports that as late as 1931, when the

* Except in those territories which form part of the Soviet Union. But with them we are not here concerned.

Secretary of State asked the Colonial Office staff " What are the most important products of the colonial Empire? ", nobody could tell him, because nobody knew.* It was in fact only the fright given to the Colonial Office by the great slump that brought forth even these weakly ideas. The Colonial Office, we may say, was their mother, and the slump was their father. They bear all the marks of their ancestry.

Quite clearly their aim is to bring the colonial Empire as a whole into more and more intimate economic relations with the self-governing parts of the Empire, regardless of the effect either on the colonial peoples or on those of foreign countries. Perhaps what impresses one most about them is their little-mindedness, their character of scared and fussy selfishness. Viewed from the international standpoint what they embody beyond this notion of privilege and exclusion is little enough, except an effort to create scarcity, wherever the resultant shift of price level is thought likely to benefit the producer.

§ 3. DWINDLING LIBERTY

To return to the matter of colonial liberties. There is nothing surprising, of course, in the absence of political enfranchisement. A colony is by definition politically dependent. But it has been generally assumed, indeed often officially declared, that the colonies will be granted self-government as and when they become fitted to exercise it.† The further assumption is that their constitutional development will follow broadly the lines laid down by the precedent of the Dominions. Now, Dominion status has been achieved by a steady progress from colonial dependence through four main stages: first, autonomy in internal affairs; next, fiscal autonomy, or self-determination

* Op. cit.

† Cf. " An African Survey ", by Lord Hailey, p. 1639: " The political future which British policy has assigned to the African colonies must be understood to be that of self-government based on representative institutions ".

in the matter of external trade; then, autonomy in the matter of military defence; and finally, autonomy in the conduct of foreign relations. The mere recital of this outline history shows how long is the journey still ahead of even the most advanced of the dependencies. In none of them has so much as the first of the four stages been fully attained. The constitutional colour bar is still very much of a reality in the British Empire.

We shall discuss the general problem of colonial emancipation in Part V. Meanwhile, it is necessary to emphasise the point that during the present century the movement of events in the colonies has on the whole been away from, not towards, self-government. Malta, Cyprus, British Guiana are only outstanding examples of the trend. Even in advanced colonies natives on legislative councils get no administrative, but only critical experience. The Donoughmore constitution in Ceylon, partly modelled on an English borough council, was an attempt to overcome this difficulty. But the experiment has so far been defeated by the efforts of Governors to limit the powers handed over to responsible elected Ministers and to increase their own.

The record of what may be called the common law liberties of colonial peoples is very similar. As the traditional social cohesion of Africa weakens, it becomes necessary in the view of colonial governments to replace it by statutory restrictions. There thus springs up, within the broad movement of destructive liberation, a markedly authoritarian tendency. Since the last war, and hand in hand with the closing of the economic door to foreign nations, the common law liberties of Africans have been trenched upon so far that very little of them remains. The new penal codes relate to personal movement, to the right of association and combination, to freedom of speech and writing, including the importation of literature, gramophone records, &c.; and in practice they widen in a remarkable way the legal meaning given to the term sedition. Indeed, the whole field of colonial legislation dealing with sedition and allied offences has been worked over afresh, and the authorities have assumed new and extensive powers. New offences have been created, and in many cases penalties for old offences have been increased. By anyone who troubles to study these laws as they now operate, the boast of British democratic rule in colonial territories can at once be seen to be empty.*

Colonial governments have been given unfettered discretion to intern or deport natives without trial and without bringing specific charges; to break up and confiscate the funds of any political or industrial organisation; and to prohibit or disperse summarily any gathering of natives. Any native association, for example, whose members undertake not to accept wages below a certain level may be declared illegal. And in some dependencies it may be punishable for a native to say publicly that employers pay low wages. Some years ago, a Nyasaland native was sentenced to three years' hard labour for importing copies of the *Worker's Herald*, which circulated freely in the Union of South Africa, a country little enough disposed to grant extravagant licence to native political activities. In 1937, a Gold Coast native was convicted of sedition for writing a newspaper article expressing the view that the Europeans believed in a God whose name spelt Deceit, and referring in bitter terms to recent legislation in the colony.

Some of the practical consequences of this trend are shown by the fact that according to a recent Howard League report, of the four countries with the highest prison population in the world, two are in British Africa, and one is in British India. Clearly in such conditions there is no hope of the free and independent trade-union movement which increasing industrialisation makes necessary and for which a recent Colonial Secretary expressed a desire.†

* See Hansard, December 20th, 1935.
† Hansard, February 28th, 1938.

The gaols of the West Indies are thronged with men who have been heavily sentenced for sedition—the substance of their offences being that, perhaps in strong or crude language, they urged their compatriots to organise in trade unions for the purpose of resisting the very types of exploitation we described in the last section.

The old liberal imperialism, whose conceptions gave shape to the trusteeship principle, took it for granted that political and civil liberty would be open to Africans, and that education and the direct example of white men would then mean their automatic advance to the level of civilisation reached by their conquerors. This assumption—and it is a vital one for those who speak of trusteeship—is being more and more falsified throughout the dependent Empire to-day. The economic subordination in which African life is being increasingly held necessitates in turn a methodical encroachment on the democratic rights of Africans.

But civil liberties do not depend only on the state of the law. They depend also, perhaps mainly, on the relatively impartial administration of justice. This in turn depends mainly on three factors: an independent judiciary, an alert body of public opinion, and a free press. None of these three factors is present in British colonies.

Colonial judges are members of the Colonial Service whose personnel and conditions of employment we inquired into in a previous chapter. They are subject to its regulations. Their prospects of promotion—and promotion or transfer from one colony to another is a regular routine—depend on satisfactory personal reports and other impalpable factors. There is notoriously a certain friction in most colonies between the executive and the judicial branches of the administration, owing to occasional independence displayed by judges.

In the atmosphere of a colony, where the white man's prestige must be maintained at all costs, one can hardly expect the law relating to, say, sedition to be interpreted in a liberal spirit. It is not that the actual provisions of the law differ so much from those in force in England. The British Government possesses legal powers which could make short work of every liberty enjoyed by Englishmen, if they were exercised with the full permitted rigour. In the Colonies such powers are rigidly enforced and literally interpreted in a manner which, as Dicey said fifty years ago, would make political discussion impossible in England if the same rigidity were applied. Recent prosecutions in West Africa and in the West Indies amply illustrate this view.

Again, once a man is convicted, a successful appeal is very difficult to secure. Judges equally affected by the colonial atmosphere hear the appeal. An obvious reform would be a right of appeal to a Court in England on much wider grounds than the very narrow ones on which the Judicial Committee of the Privy Council sometimes, though very rarely, hears an appeal.

In all except the highest branches of the Colonial Service, administrative officers, usually men without legal training, do all the judicial as well as the administrative work. One man is in the position, all over British Africa, of being the prosecutor, counsel for defence, jury, and judge, as well as chief constable responsible for the order and welfare of his district. In these circumstances it is not surprising that pressure is brought to bear on administrative officers acting as magistrates not to give decisions or pass sentences or even make observations from the bench that may be found politically inconvenient by the Governor or his advisers.*

Finally, native courts all over British Africa exercise a large jurisdiction, hear thousands of cases, and have wide powers of punishment. These courts observe none of the safeguards normal in courts of law; in fact cases that come

* Examples of such pressure are afforded by the experiences of S. V. Cooke in Tanganyika and of Maurice Collis in Burma. For the latter see " Trials in Burma ", by Maurice Collis.

to notice from time to time show that they are free to disregard every elementary principle of justice. We are making no attempt to explain and enforce the principles of British justice which are our pride at home.*

§ 4. MASS UNREST

Empires are always and everywhere maintained by periodic violence. The British Empire is no exception to the rule, and its costs of maintenance, expressed in terms of repressive force, are continually rising.

Look back over the last year or two and recall merely the cases that found their way into the headlines. There has been bloodshed, sometimes quite extensive, in Northern Rhodesia, South Africa, Zanzibar, Mauritius, Tanganyika, St. Lucia, Trinidad, Barbados, Jamaica. In India and Burma repression by shooting is endemic. There has been the great strike and boycott movement in the Gold Coast; in Cyprus large-scale arrests of working-class leaders and dismissals of officials with liberationist views. In Burma a few years earlier (1932) there was widespread rebellion. In August 1938 the Rangoon riots resulted in 150 killed and over 500 injured. In Palestine the British have been for years at open war with the inhabitants. More significant still, India has seen a great growth of the peasant movement in political consciousness, taking the form of mass demonstrations of peasants and mass strikes in the jute and cotton industries.

All this mass unrest, springing up simultaneously in so many scattered places between which there is little direct intercommunication, cannot be accidental. It is clearly a product of certain social forces which are operating on a world-wide scale. Sometimes they express themselves

* It is impossible here to give the detailed evidence which forms the basis of these comments on the administration of justice in the colonies. Cf. Julius Lewin's article on " The Recognition of Native Law and Custom in British Africa " (*Journal of Comparative Legislation and International Law*, February 1938).

as claims to self-determination, either in the political sphere, as in Palestine, or in the economic sphere, as in the Gold Coast; at other times they are more or less instinctive reactions against material conditions which have become intolerable for the hardships they inflict (e.g., the West Indies).

But whatever form they take, they always have one thing in common—their anti-imperialism. They are the work of people who ask to be left alone, who want to serve their own purposes and not those of alien overlords, who crave to be granted a glimpse of hope, " sweet hope which is mightiest to sway the restless soul of man ".

In some places, such as Northern Rhodesia, Trinidad, and Gold Coast, full official inquiries have laid bare the roots of working-class grievances. The Trinidad report was sensational news even in the daily press at home. As to the report on Northern Rhodesia, one need only quote the mild comment of the *Economist*, that " it is disquieting to those who believed that the principle of native trusteeship was being generously carried out in the colonial Empire ". This report was supplemented in September 1938 by a further special report on labour conditions, which, as the *Manchester Guardian* put it, " gives the customary distressing picture of undernourishment and disease ".

§ 5. A COLONIAL MAGNA CARTA

All these reports serve to confirm what we noticed above—namely, that in the industrial revolution which they have forcibly imposed on the colonies, the British are repeating nearly all the blunders of the early industrial era in this country. Under this stimulus a native Chartist movement is slowly and often almost blindly beginning to take shape.

One of the most important forms which the colonial question assumes is " What help can democrats in Britain lend to this struggling colonial Chartism? "

First and foremost, they can themselves stand for and agitate for the Charter, the immediate points of which are:

(1) *Compulsory Free Education.*—No one, of course, supposes that so great a reform can be carried through in a flash and simultaneously in every part of the colonial Empire. But here is the first principle of policy to be recommended for acceptance to those in control of public and private education. In India the Congress, as soon as its Ministries assumed office in various provinces, committed itself to the principle of a seven years' compulsory education which should be provided free on a nation-wide scale. There is every reason to suppose that Africa, if it were politically developed enough to have a Congress of its own, would do the same. Those who speak of themselves either as guardians or as allies of colonial peoples seem therefore to be under an obligation to make good by their own efforts this present deficiency of colonial organisational strength.

(2) *Freedom of Speech, Movement and Association.*—The growing restrictions on these basic liberties, which we noticed above, often take the form of applying to this or that colony, with modifications to suit local conditions, the provisions of the Indian Penal Code. From the legal point of view the Indian Penal Code is the British model of repression. It appears to be the sanction for all manner of abuses on the part of the police, to whom excessive powers have been granted, and it necessitates constant challenge by those subjected to it in order to preserve any political life at all.

If colonial peoples are really to move towards democracy by the development of their own political life and their own political leadership, it is essential to establish the principle that no Government has the right to treat as seditious anything short of the direct advocacy of public violence. Many of the things now done with impunity in the name of colonial government constitute a challenge to all of us who call ourselves democrats. Do we regard the democratic principle of civil liberty as universal in application, or merely as a privilege of people who inhabit the United Kingdom? Is it, in our view, an article of export? To call for its application to the colonies is to call for a liberal revolution there. Do we, as democrats, want to further that revolution? Or do we, as fascists, want to suppress it? Or, again, do we suppose we can be democrats at home and fascists overseas? (If so, let us hear no more of the British Empire as the great bulwark of democracy.)

(3) *A Minimum Level of Labour and Social Legislation.*—A certain amount of colonial legislation already exists on conditions of work in industry and the " protection of labour ". Much of it is unsatisfactory, as anyone who is familiar with the position of child labour and female labour in Ceylon and Kenya, for example, will realise. Much of it, again, just remains a dead letter. Minimum Wages Acts, for example, are on the statute books of many colonies, but I know of no colony in which a minimum wage has actually been fixed. It is broadly true that what we in Britain understand by social insurance is not found in the colonies at all. These are questions for the trade unions of colonial workers, when such unions have been formed and have found their feet. In some colonies unions are still illegal; in others they are legal only if they are tame company unions or, worse still, unions formed and supported by the colonial Government. The present policy of the Colonial Office is to handle colonial labour questions either by means of such tame unions or by the creation of a new Government service of labour officers or by both.*

---

* Colonial Office policy is brightly illuminated by the following report of the proceedings of the Royal Commission on the West Indies. Sir Walter Citrine, a member of the Commission, is examining a witness, A. W. Grantham, the Colonial Secretary of Jamaica (*Manchester Guardian*, November 24th, 1938):

" Now, there is another kind of protection the worker could have, a voluntary organisation called a trade union?—Yes.

These methods are undesirable, and indeed dangerous. At any rate the clear task of those who believe in the people's power in Britain is to give all the help they can

---

"It is the policy of the Home Government to encourage in these colonies the formation of trade unions?—Yes.

"Now can you tell me anything that has been done by this present Government or its immediate predecessors to encourage the formation of trade unions or to help them in any way?—This Government is proposing to introduce at the coming autumn session a short preliminary trade unions law.

"But at the moment nothing has been done to encourage trade unions?

Mr. Grantham: "There is the Trade Unions Law of 1919. . . .

"Now I suppose that what you really want to find in this island are trade unions operating something like the trade unions in England? —To begin with, we must have a fairly simple law and develop by degrees.

"But at the beginning you want to have in Jamaica what I might call for convenience bona fide trade unions?—Yes.

"I have tried to show you that there is no protection in your law offered to working people. And I have tried now to develop a point as to the extent to which a real and effective organisation can do that. Now, your law was passed in 1919. Do you realise that in that law a very important section of British trade-union law was omitted?— Which section was that?

Sir Walter explained that it omitted the provision of the 1906 Act designed to overcome the difficulties of the Taff Vale decision. Sir Walter's questioning went on:—

"Isn't it a fact that this special provision which was put in the Act of 1906 after the Taff trouble was deliberately cut out of the bill in the Legislature here by the act of the Government? Isn't that true?—I am not in a position to answer that question.

"If I tell you this provision is vital to the operation of trade unions, would you accept that?—I would accept it, yes.

"There is not much use, is there, setting up trade unions to protect the interest of members and giving them power to withhold their labour, and at the same time draft the law in such a way that if they did withhold their labour the union could be sued for damages and consequences? —No.

"There is another provision, picketing. . . . Are you aware that that provision, too, is absent and was deliberately omitted from your law?—I know it is absent.

"The Acting Attorney-General moved that this clause should be struck out, so that we are to take it as a deliberate omission. . . . It is very important we should have trade unions here using legitimate powers?—Yes.

"Trying as best they can to regulate the relations in industry and protect their members?—Very important.

"It is important that the Government should give them that help. Up to now not much help has been given?—No, that is true.

to the common people in the colonies in the organisation of free unions and the building up of an independent trade-union movement. The most urgent need of all is a reasoned faith in the capacity of colonial workers to conduct their own struggle, provided they are given proofs of solidarity and some technical assistance from our side.

Why, for example, should not the Miners' Federation of Great Britain invite to this country a few selected organisers from among the African miners of the Northern Rhodesia copper-belt, or the workers in the oil-fields of Trinidad and Burma, and give them a course of instruction in trade-union methods and procedure? Some of the larger unions here might " adopt " a child from among the new struggling industrial organisations of colonial workers. By such means permanent and fruitful contact would be maintained between the two movements (more accurately, the two sections of the one movement), and the colonial working class in the hour of its crying need would be relieved of the sheer sense of isolation that it is bound to find so crippling at its present stage of development and in the present condition of the world.

CHAPTER XVII

TAXATION*

§ 1. " MONEY ECONOMY "

WHEREVER and whenever British government was set up over African tribes, the first preoccupation of the Governor was to make the Africans concerned pay the cost. The Chancellor of the Exchequer in London insisted on that. Other parts of the state machine—the good offices of royalty and the whole apparatus of diplomacy—were freely used to advance the private interests of the empire-builders. British taxpayers' money was often poured out in profusion to meet the military expenses of conquering new colonial territory. But once the conquest was complete, the understanding has always been that the conquered should be made to foot the bill—for the conquest if possible, and at the very least for the trouble of holding them down afterwards.

What was more, these newly established colonial governments wanted to make their collections and exactions in cash. It is rather embarrassing, if you are a new government, to have taxation paid to you in goats and cattle, and tax payment in kind, though occasionally permitted, is always discouraged at the earliest opportunity. But the use of coined money was nowhere known in tropical Africa before the coming of the Europeans. So, if Governments were going to stipulate for payment in cash, there was only one thing they could do. That was to put money into the hands of Africans, and then take it away again.

---

* Much of the substance of this chapter is derived from articles contributed by Norman Leys to *Empire* in October, November, and December 1938.

It is true that in some colonies the earliest tax was paid in the form of a month's labour on public works of one sort or another. But so inflexible a kind of revenue had very limited uses, and it was soon found that both labour and money could be got best and quickest by one particular dodge. The dodge was in three parts: (1) displaying for sale various alluring products of civilisation with which the tribes-people were previously unacquainted; (2) making a simultaneous offer of work for money wages; (3) recovering a proportion of such wages by direct taxation.

The imposition of a cash tax in effect made work for wages compulsory except for such few tribes-people as possessed or could acquire saleable products for which an accessible market existed. In former times this kind of produce consisted of slaves; later of ivory, gold, and skins of animals, etc.; and later still of vegetable produce such as palm oil, copra, cocoa, cotton, coffee, tobacco, and so on.

Wage labour was naturally a factor which bulked larger in the economy of those areas which were given over to white settlement than in areas which the white man penetrated only as a visitor. There were two reasons. First, that the settlers themselves set up a demand for wage labour; and second, that the fact of white settlement involved an alienation of most or all land except the actual ancestral holdings of the tribesmen, and sometimes even parts of these also. These holdings were traditionally intended only for growing the food supply of the people. Hence the capacity of Africans to grow export crops is limited in white settlement areas both by the fact that most of their time is spent in wage-service under the whites, and also by the fact that the land available for their use is only enough to provide their own food, and sometimes less than enough for that.

§ 2. HUT TAX AND POLL TAX

Only in the southern Gold Coast has direct taxation of Africans been dispensed with. There the money economy was introduced slowly by the gradual growth of trade through several centuries. The name Gold Coast suggests another reason why the transition there was easier than in other parts of Africa. Gold was worked in some quantities, and gold is a commodity that always finds a ready market. Thus governments were able to rely for their revenue on customs duties rather than on direct taxes.

Everywhere else in British Africa there exists a poll tax or a hut tax or both. In Nigeria the practice is to make a lump-sum assessment on a whole village or similar unit. In a few places the hut or poll tax is graded according to local circumstances, but generally is a fixed flat rate over a whole territory. Nowhere is there any direct relation between taxation and personal income. Perhaps the lump-sum assessment is the nearest approach to such a relation, because it is possible for the village heads to take individual circumstances into account in distributing the assessment's incidence on individuals. On the other hand, it may equally be said that the distribution of the assessment is open to corrupt manipulation by village heads.

In Britain a rich man may pay as much as one third of his income in direct taxation (millionaires, indeed, even more, unless they have reduced tax-evasion to a very fine art). In the colonies the highest incomes are nowhere taxed more than one tenth, possibly because in the colonies the rich men are always white men.

While colonial taxation is lighter for the rich, it is also heavier for the poor. In Britain the scheme of indirect taxation is notoriously regressive. The total tax-burden on incomes of £500 a year is, according to some authorities, approximately 7%, while on incomes below £200 it is approximately 11.5%.* Other authorities state that direct and indirect taxation together take 13.5% of the incomes under £250, 9.3% of incomes of £300, and 8.6%

* See " Report of the Colwyn Commission on Taxation "; also D. M. Sandrall in the *Journal of the Royal Statistical Society*, 1931. These figures assume a married man with three children.

of incomes of £500.* It is impossible to defend this discrimination. But what are we to say of British Eastern Africa, where the average cash income per family is estimated to be £3 a year, of which one third is paid to the Government in direct taxation alone (hut tax and poll tax)?

The rate of poll tax is fixed for each locality. In some it is as low as 5s., in others as high as 20s. a year. It has to be paid by every male African when he reaches the age of fourteen, sixteen, or eighteen, according to the colony he happens to be born in. The hut tax is a sum of similar amount levied on every inhabited hut. African families live in single-room huts, the number of which varies according to the size of the household. Extra huts are demanded by decency, not normally for extra wives, since polygamy is increasingly uncommon everywhere, but for adolescent or aged dependants. The system therefore has this result, that the larger the circle of a man's dependants, the larger the total tax he has to pay. The law acknowledges that hardship may be caused, and it accordingly provides for exemptions. Indeed, in Tanganyika since 1935 the system itself has been altered. There the hut tax has been given up in favour of a house tax, the definition of a house including any number of huts grouped together in such a way as to constitute the dwelling of one family. The house tax thus ceases to discourage—what is always discouraged under the hut-tax system—the building of separate huts where a family cannot live in one hut without unhealthy overcrowding.†

§ 3. INCREASING INEQUALITY

We can see, then, that when Africans first began to pay tax for the benefit of being ruled by the British, people whose incomes were roughly equal paid a tax roughly equivalent to a month's labour. When, however, govern-

* See Colin Clark, " A Socialist Budget ".
† See " African Survey ", p. 568.

ments found that people would pay the equivalent of a month's wages without resistance, they soon went on to demand the equivalent of two. " Everywhere in fact ", as Norman Leys puts it, " the tax was raised step by step, until in at least three countries bloodshed resulted, when it was somewhat reduced."

Moreover, at the same time as taxation was being increased in this way, the conditions in which most African incomes had been roughly equal were being subjected to rapid change. To-day if we glance at the territories lying between the Zambesi and the Nile we find that the standard wage rates vary very widely indeed. They are from 5s. to 15s. a month for the great majority, 20s. to 40s. a month for a semi-skilled minority, and run up to as much as £5 per month for a few literate clerks in certain colonies where the colour bar does not prevent Africans from doing such work.

The Report on Northern Rhodesia by Sir Alan Pim gives the results of an inquiry into the budgets of fifty families in that colony. The cash income of the families surveyed (income, that is, excluding food grown at home) was 28s. a year. Sales of produce brought in 18% of that sum; work in the family's own district, within a radius of perhaps fifty miles from home, 12.5%; and work outside the district 68.5%. Average expenditure was 30% on taxation, 48% on clothing, and 22% on everything else. The Report adds, " It is obvious that over large areas the local resources of the country are entirely inadequate to provide the taxpayer with the means to pay 7s. 6d. a year "—which was the rate of tax in that particular district.*

A generation ago it was openly admitted that the direct taxation of Africans was intended not only to raise revenue for governments, but also to bring Africans into the labour market. In Nyasaland for many years a rebate of half the

* See " Report on the Financial and Economic Position of Northern Rhodesia ", Colonial 145, 1938.

tax was given to a man who could prove that he had worked for wages. In Rhodesia and Kenya the circuit of compulsion was closed by deliberately stopping up alternative ways of earning money. How complete the stoppage sometimes became is shown by the fact that of the exports from Kenya nearly 90% is the produce of European farms and plantations. European farmers in Kenya number less than 2,000 out of a total population of 4 million.

In times of slump, when the volume of employment dwindles, some curious consequences come to light. In Northern Rhodesia direct taxation of Africans brings in only one eighth of the total revenue. Yet there in one recent year taxes equal to the yield of the tax for eighteen months were in arrears. In Kenya, on the other hand, the tax brings in one third of the total tax revenue, and there more than 9,000 men every year are punished for failure to pay tax, either by imprisonment with hard labour or by a term in a " detention camp ". The Kenya Report says that sentences in detention camps " practically mean from one to three months' idleness at the expense of the Government ". One of the reasons given why men are not allowed, as they once were, to do work in lieu of tax is " the possibility of affecting adversely the labour supply to farms and other private undertakings ".

§ 4. OTHER TAXES

Nor is direct taxation the whole story of the tax burden on Africans. Heavy duties are also payable on most of the imported goods which they consume. In British Eastern Africa the chief weight of the tariff falls on articles for which there is a big native demand, such as clothing, hardware, and bicycles. The rate of duty on these is approximately 50% *ad valorem*. There is, it is true, a free list that comprises articles valued at about a third of the total importations. The list is almost wholly composed of goods which European landowners and employers use, machinery, fencing materials, motor lorries, and so forth.

The only items in the free list of the East African tariff that are even partly for Africans' use amount to less than one sixteenth of the whole, and are mainly books and medicines.

Again, Africans may be liable to a local " cess " or levy. This is simply an extra hut tax on males, and varies in amount between colony and colony and between tribe and tribe. In some few tribes there is no levy at all; in the rest it may be anything between one tenth and one third of the main tax. The yield is used chiefly for what we call local government purposes, such as road-making, water supply, sanitation, schools, etc. It is interesting to observe that in the districts where land is owned by Europeans there is no local levy or local rate. The work that in the tribal areas is paid for out of local cesses is in the European areas paid for out of central government funds.

The upshot of all this is that tens of thousands of Africans go to gaol every year for the crime of having heads, or huts to sleep in, but no money. Now, no taxation can have any claim to be scientific or equitable that is not a proportion of some amount that people earn or spend. If therefore Africans living in areas whose local resources are inadequate to provide them with the means of paying 7s. 6d. a year should be taxed at all, we should at least cease to tax their heads and their huts, and tax instead what they buy or what they sell. As we have seen, they are already taxed on what they buy. Tariff and freight charges double, or more than double, the cost of imported goods bought by Africans.

If that is not enough, there are still earnings, the proceeds of the labour or the crops that Africans sell. The earnings they derive from the crops they are allowed to grow for sale are so small that it would be a meagre source of revenue. Nothing, then, is left but wages. A tax on wages would, so Norman Leys suggests, have every advantage in all the countries of British Africa over the hut or poll tax. It would be far easier to collect. It would put an end to sending people to gaol for being penniless. It would not have the same effect in forcing men into wage-service. It would be less unpopular than the present system. It could be easily graded so that a man earning say 8s. a month paid 6d. in the £, while a man earning £5 a month paid 4s. in the £. Sir Alan Pim, in the Report already quoted, makes for Northern Rhodesia a similar recommendation of a general minimum tax plus a percentage of wages above a fixed rate.*

§ 5. WHAT THE TAXPAYER GETS IN RETURN

The taxes Africans pay are applied mainly to the general expenses of administration—that is to say, to what is called justice, the maintenance of law and order, and the tax-collecting system. Some part of them goes on the social services whose scope we have already examined. And some part, again, goes in indirect subsidies to various forms of private European enterprise. These three heads are exhaustive.

We have already seen in what circumstances the Union Jack was hoisted in Lobengula's country. Let us just glance, for the sake of illustration, at what has happened to it since. Under the name of Southern Rhodesia it now has 55,000 European and 1,100,000 African inhabitants. It is governed by a Parliament. The Europeans have adult suffrage, the Africans, though legally eligible to vote, are in practice not allowed to qualify, except in infinitesimal numbers.†

The Dominions Office in theory represents the interests of the African majority by vetoing discrimination against them, but in practice prefers to shelve the responsibility. Gold was what led to the British occupation fifty years ago. It had been mined for centuries by Africans. But when the

---

* Pp. 127–8.

† This result is achieved by setting up a property qualification of £150 and an income qualification of £100. These qualifications are such as to disfranchise very few whites and to enfranchise even fewer blacks.

British occupied the country, they seized the best of the land and all the minerals.

That is why the " Native Reserves ", though extensive, contain only 10% of the railway mileage. Since the occupation no African has been allowed to mine gold. The law does not explicitly prohibit Africans from mining, any more than from voting. The desired result is got by refusing them licences to mine. They are, however, required to work as servants for European miners at from 6d. to 8d. a day.

The most important agricultural produce of Southern Rhodesia is maize. Maize has been the staple food of the people for three centuries. To-day it is grown for export as well, mainly by Europeans employing African labourers at about 6d. a day or less, on land that once belonged to those labourers.

Since 1931 a Maize Control scheme has been in operation which provides that the price of maize inside Southern Rhodesia shall be much higher than the world price. It works out in this way, that about two thirds of the whole maize crop is sold for internal consumption at about double the price the other third fetches in the export market. With such an arrangement the vital question clearly is which of the people with maize to sell are to get the higher price, and which the lower.

The short answer is that the law makes two provisions on this point. First, that the bulk of the maize grown by the handful of European farmers shall get the higher price. Second, that Africans must sell at least 75% of their output at the lower price. The Colonial Office has recently extended the same type of scheme to Northern Rhodesia.

A similar picture of the status of Africans in their own country is presented by the policy followed in Kenya. The Estimates of government revenue and expenditure in that colony show, for example, that more than two thirds of the expenditure on roads is spent in the areas where the land is owned by Europeans.

Notoriously the great bulk of the hundreds of thousands of pounds spent by the Agricultural and other technical Departments is spent on the Europeans' behalf. In 1931 the Government lent them over £250,000 as " advances " on their maize and other crops. During 1938, when just over half the money had been repaid, an Ordinance was passed remitting all future payments of interest on the balance outstanding, most of which is irrecoverable.

In March 1938, it was announced that the Government would remit for two years the 5% royalty on the gold mined in Kenya.

Such are but some of the proofs that white settlement survives only by being lavishly subsidised at Africans' expense. The black man's burden is not only the mining companies that spirit his gold and his copper away like conjurors; not only the trading combines that manipulate against him the price of the cocoa he sells and the price of the cotton goods he buys; but also the white sahibs who take up residence in his country and live on and off his land. Less lucky than Sinbad, he carries three old men of the sea upon his back.

PART IV

THE ISSUE DEFINED

CHAPTER XVIII

ANALYSIS OF IMPERIALISM

§ 1. EXPAND OR EXPLODE

No one who knows anything of human nature or human history is surprised when men behave like wolves to their fellows. The Athenian envoys said to the Melians in 416 B.C., " You know and we know that right is considered in men's discussions only when both parties are of equal strength. What he *can* do is the only standard of the stronger; the weaker suffers what he must." And in proof of their words, they proceeded to put all the Melians of military age to death.

Hitler and Chamberlain were saying and doing very similar things to the people of Czechoslovakia in A.D. 1938. India and Africa have had centuries of experience of the same kind of treatment at the hands of the white sahibs.

To many men the sense of domination is sweet; and to have other men working as your servants and producing wealth which you can at once appropriate and enjoy is, to say the least, convenient. These things need no explaining to anyone who is, or has been, a human being himself. The paradox of imperialism is not that men prefer the status of master to that of slave; it is rather that the masters come to believe, often quite genuinely, that their mastery is beneficial to the slaves. More curious still, the same belief can be readily insinuated into the minds of many of the slaves themselves.* And most

* Cf. Karl Mannheim (in " The Social Sciences ", 1937): " In a society which has reached a certain balance there will always be some élites the standards of which will become representative, and will be silently accepted even by those groups which are subjugated and essen-

curious of all, to neither slaves nor masters does it often
occur that things might be better for everyone if the
difference of status between them were abolished.

The group impulse to domination which we call imperialism is rationalised in various ways.

It may be represented as a matter of life and death from
the economic point of view. Defending French colonial
expansion in 1885, Jules Ferry pleaded in the Chamber of
Deputies, " It was a question of having outlets for our
industries, exports and capital. That was an absolute
necessity; that was why France had to expand in West
Africa, on the Congo, in Madagascar." This is the doctrine of the " expand-or-explode " school, of which
Mussolini in his time has declared himself an adherent.
Dr. Goebbels, also, has affinities with it, to judge from a
speech of his at the end of 1935, when he observed, " We
are beggars. We are confronted with difficulties which
we cannot overcome by interior methods. It is dangerous
for the world not to concede such demands, because some
day the bomb will explode." Such a reading of the
situation is, for obvious reasons, popular among nations
which are expanding or which hope shortly to expand.

§ 2. IMPERIAL MYSTICISM

There is, however, another approach to the question
which is commonly used by spokesmen of countries that
already possess empires of their own. It is now fashionable
among them to discuss in a detached way how far colonies
are of value to their owners, and how far the general
interests of international peace require a modification of
the colonial *status quo* in favour of the countries which do
not own colonies. These discussions normally lead to the

---

tially frustrated by these valuations ". Mussolini, taking a leaf out of
the book of the British in India, conquered Ethiopia with African
troops. The hall porter at the Carlton Club is a more jealous guardian
of certain standards of conservatism than the members themselves.
Jay Gould said he could always hire half the working class to shoot
down the other half. And he knew what he was talking about.

conclusion that colonies are of no particular economic value; and the usual further inference is, not that colonies are not worth keeping, but that they are not worth giving away. This is broadly the position taken up by Norman Angell in this country and by O. Louwers in Belgium.

It is not unusual for members of this school of thought to make shipwreck, as Louwers himself does, in a kind of imperialistic mysticism.* In spite of their economic worthlessness, colonies do of themselves bring political prestige with them, but their real value is seen in the spiritual sphere. Colony-owning countries enjoy a sense of self-perpetuation outside themselves; "it is one of the great laws of life ". What is to become of countries to which this sacramental ecstasy is not open, Louwers does not consider.

An extreme example of such mysticism among English writers is afforded by John Coatman. For him the British Empire is an organic whole, the life-blood of which is a spiritual unity. The Empire therefore provides a working model of the world organisation of the future; it sketches the true foundations of a world state. It is a priceless asset not merely for all the peoples in it, but also for the entire residue of humanity outside it. The Empire has this inestimable advantage over the League of Nations—that the League is a piece of lifeless machinery which the nations, as external operators, work as best they may, while the Empire is moulded from within by the consubstantial general will of its members to unite. It thus figures as the guide and inspiration of an admiring world which has no other designs in regard to it than to contemplate its steady realisation of the moral ideals of mankind.†

Alternatively again, the established imperialists may embrace the now somewhat discredited myth of the white

---

* See "Le Problème Colonial du Point de Vue International", 1936.
† " Magna Britannia ", by John Coatman.

man's burden, and translate it into the relative refinements of the dual mandate and trusteeship. Typical of this school are De Kat Angelino in Holland, Lugard in England, Gaston Pelletier and Louis Roubaud in France. With such enthusiasts the imperialism of their dreams has nothing to do with monopoly or exploitation; its aims and its methods alike are assistance, education, production, and co-operation. All the same, as Pelletier and Roubaud insist, " notre prestige en dépend et aussi notre securité ".*

The general outlook of this school is fairly displayed by the following passage taken from the same source : " There is a pitfall against which the native intelligentsia should be on its guard, for Moscow, in trying to foment colonial revolution, must logically be seeking to extend social revolution as well. That being understood, we must none the less recognise that certain native claims when they are reasonable and do not imply independence or even autonomy, cannot be rejected *en bloc*, and deserve to be examined with some goodwill."

§ 3. TRUSTEESHIP

The position indicated by the terms " dual mandate " and " trusteeship " is the official position of the British Government and also of the League of Nations in its relation to the mandate system. It is, in fact, Article 22 of the League Covenant which speaks of " the well-being and development " of certain colonial peoples as forming " a sacred trust of civilisation ". The mandate system, whose working the League Council supervises, seeks to carry out under a form of international guarantee this principle of trusteeship.

When politicians introduce the conception of the holy into their day-to-day activities, it is a safe guess that they do so as cover for a more than usually bad conscience. So the question at once crops up whether " trusteeship " is more than a vague and decorative notion to which anyone

* " Empire ou Colonies? ", 1936.

can attach any meaning he pleases—one of those " masked words " of which Ruskin spoke in " Sesame and Lilies ", and which J. A. Hobson in " Imperialism " brilliantly examined, and found to be the means whereby we endow ourselves with an almost preternatural power of self-deceit.

The conception of the ruler as trustee naturally did not make its first appearance in the League Covenant. Locke, in his " Essay on Civil Government ", expresses the view that the legislature does not possess arbitrary power, rather it acts pursuant to a trust, which is violated by all that does the people harm. An even better-known passage is in Burke's speech on Fox's India Bill in 1782, where he submitted to Parliament the proposition that " rights and privileges derived from political power are all in the strictest sense a trust ". Burke also insisted that in regard to India it was the British people who were in the last resort responsible for the trust's execution.

Such an attitude was certainly then a novelty in British colonial history. In the normal eighteenth-century view, the function of a colony was to produce the maximum wealth for representatives (not always, or pre-eminently, official representatives) of the colonising power. Burke's humaner idea was taken up, developed, and in the end built into the structure of British colonial policy by Wilberforce, Fowell Buxton, and the philanthropic school, until to-day every cadet in the colonial service believes that he is responsible before all else for the material and moral protection and advancement of the colonial people under his charge.

What those seem to mean, then, who talk of trusteeship is this. We have abandoned the eighteenth century conception of a colony, and propose to conduct our relations with colonial peoples with a view to their social progress rather than to our material gain. We need not strive officiously to avoid gain if it comes our way, and we are entitled to use our colonies as an instrument of policy for injuring other industrialised countries with whom we happen to be in commercial rivalry. But we are pledged, as trustees, not to compel colonial peoples to produce wealth for us instead of for themselves.

"We claim, in a word, that our imperial economics are welfare economics, involving the development of peoples rather than of territories, and estimating costs and utilities, not as saleable goods and services or mere monetary values, but as experiences, injurious and beneficial respectively to the ordered social growth of our wards."

§ 4. THE COMMONWEALTH OF GOD

There thus arises, the conception of the British Empire, including the colonial empire, as constituting in a real sense a single Commonwealth. The term British Commonwealth of Nations was originally invented as a composite title for those autonomous, equal, and freely associated countries which are known also as the self-governing Dominions. Britain, too, was commonly suffered by courtesy to include herself in this sacred band. But India and the colonies were not—at least, to begin with. Their existing status was too obviously subordinate. They might not be without the law; they were lesser breeds none the less. And, what was more unfortunate still, their inhabitants had dark skins.

The term British Commonwealth, like the term Dominions, was intended, among other things, to mark the fact that those to whom it was applied had emerged from the twilight of colonial dependence into the full noon of sovereign nationhood. It would defeat its object, and offend the very Dominion susceptibilities it was designed to flatter, if the coloured dependencies were indiscriminately lumped together with White Australia and White South Africa under its banner.

In recent years, however, the tendency has been more and more to use British Commonwealth as though it were co-extensive with British Empire, and even to substitute the former for the latter, on the grounds that " Empire " carries with it connotations which are disparaging and therefore inapplicable. For, after all, if we do genuinely act in accordance with our professions in this matter of trusteeship, is it not literally true that Britain has no colonies? A colony is a territory which is obliged to produce wealth for others than its own inhabitants. But this vicarious money-making is precisely what our imperialists claim to have eliminated not only from relations with the Dominions, but also from those with India, tropical Africa and the rest. If these premises are well grounded, John Coatman has logic on his side when he says: " Thus we see that from end to end of the British Empire there is no essential difference anywhere between any of its parts, and therefore in a real sense the whole Empire is one Commonwealth ".* The British Empire family consists of majors and minors certainly, of trustees and wards if you like, but not, on your life, of parasites and hosts.

Surprisingly large numbers of people in Britain still accept some such picture as representing the facts. The help which masked words like " Commonwealth " and " trusteeship " lend to this mass self-deception is very powerful—so much so that the self-deceivers are enabled to ignore a great volume of material and now readily accessible evidence, much of which we have summarised in previous chapters, because it happens not to harmonise with the sentimental logic for which the masked words clamour in their minds.

§ 5. THE GENETIC APPROACH

Clearly, if we are ever to grasp what imperialism really is, we must cut through the tangle of shibboleths, conditioned reflexes, and patriotic sentiments by which the British public, like the public of all colony-owning countries, masks or rationalises its customary lust of domination. We can

* Op cit., p. 72.

G

make the cut most easily and effectively if we glance back for a moment at the earliest imperialist methods.

The Greek historian Thucydides explains that as soon as coastal peoples gain some command of the sea, they " turn to piracy under the lead of their most powerful men, whose motive is their own private gain and the support of their weaker followers; and falling upon cities unprovided with walls, they pillage them and get most of their living from that source ". And he goes on to add, in his dry way, " This occupation did not as yet involve disgrace, but rather conferred something even of glory." * This account still covers all the main features of imperialism. It has been re-stated most clearly in modern times and in terms appropriate to them by J. A. Hobson,† who presents his thesis in the form of the following propositions:

(a) A country acquires colonies primarily because its exporting and financial classes demand new markets and fields of investment.

(b) This demand arises because home production tends to outrun home consumption.

(c) Surplus production arises because we tend to save a larger proportion of the national income than can usefully find expression in new capital.

(d) Over-saving in this sense means simply that too large a share of the general income is put into the hands of the employing and owning class, and too small a share into those of the working class.

(e) Political democracy has educated the working class up to the point where it now understands that a democratic system cannot work without substantial economic equality in income and ownership of property.

(f) The defence of capitalism is thenceforward bound up with the destruction or enfeeblement of civil liberty, popular franchise and representative government both at home and in the colonies.

* Book I, Chap. 5.   † " Imperialism ", 3rd Edition, 1938.

The great strength of Hobson's work is the overwhelming proof he gives that imperialism is not an isolated phenomenon, but an integral part of the social disasters which are shaking contemporary civilisation to its foundations. The cruelties of imperial rule, the horrors of war, and the miseries of slump and artificially restricted production all proceed from one cause. And what is that cause? The fact that you and I do not get a big enough share of the national income. Such is Hobson's shorter catechism, over-simplified of course, but not substantially falsified.

In this way he drives home a vital but neglected truth. We must rectify the disordered balance between production and consumption at home, and so utilise fully the productive resources of the nation, if we wish to reduce that pressure for external markets alike for trade and investment which seems to be the main stimulus to imperialism and international rivalry. A better and more equitable use of the national income is thus the most valuable of peace policies, and the one sure antidote to imperial aggression.*

§ 6. MARX AND LENIN

Hobson's formulation of the Empire problem is well in line with Marxist doctrine. For Marxism our profit-seeking economic order tends increasingly to defeat itself by producing more than it allows society the means of consuming. And it tends, also, by filling up the world with rival imperialist groups, to destroy its power to get rid abroad of the surplus products which cannot be consumed at home.†

So it happened that Lenin, who had a sharp eye for the truth even in bourgeois and reformist shape, came to rate Hobson's book highly, and he wrote in 1916 a careful supplement to it. This was published as a booklet under

* See J. A. Hobson, " Confessions of an Economic Heretic ", p. 137.
† See G. D. H. Cole and R. Postgate, " The Common People ", p. 406.

the same title of " Imperialism ". In it Lenin described the particular type of imperialism which had been rampant in the last years of the nineteenth century, and which led up to the great war. He defined it in these terms:

> Imperialism is capitalism in that stage of development in which the domination of monopolies and finance capital has taken shape; in which the export of capital has acquired pronounced importance; in which the division of the world by the international trusts has begun, and in which the partition of all the territory of the earth by the greatest imperialist countries has been completed.

The definition implies a valuable distinction. The last pre-war stage of imperialism (the stage which Lenin was studying) was one in which the interests of the investor had become the main driving force behind the imperial process. This fact differentiated it from, say, the eighteenth-century stage when the main driving force was supplied by the interests of the merchant; or from the nineteenth-century stage (up to about 1870), when it was supplied by the interests of the industrial manufacturer.* It also differentiates it from the totalitarian stage on which imperialism entered during the 1930's.

§ 7. THE TOTALITARIAN PHASE

It is too early yet to attempt a scientific definition of the totalitarian stage of imperialism. But a number of new tendencies can already be distinguished. The mercantile, industrial, and financial elements of the earlier stages obviously persist, and would have to be given their proper weight in any definition that might be attempted. When we speak of a new stage, we do not mean something sharply separated from or fully supplanting those earlier stages.

---

* These three stages of imperialism are strikingly illustrated by the main phases through which British-Indian relations have passed. See L. Barnes, " Skeleton of Empire ", pp. 16 ff.

We mean something in which the earlier survive and are included, while being at the same time overlaid and modified by the intrusive factors.

The new tendencies in imperialism arise, needless to say, from the changing character of capitalism in the advanced capitalist countries. Before the war the main driving force behind the imperial process was a search by a jostling, undisciplined rabble of private interests for markets for goods or for capital. These interests continually fought one another, and except on the rarest occasions seemed incapable of concerted action; when they did succeed in co-operating uneasily for a brief space, it was in order to fight another similar rabble flying another national flag. It was part of the technique of these interests to use the state machine and the public power for the advancement of their private plans. But they did so spasmodically, after an unsystematic and *ad hoc* fashion, and always by the time-honoured method of lobbying and log-rolling.

From the procedure of Japan, Italy and Germany one may judge that in the new struggle for colonies initiative in policy and action will be provided by the state itself. This does not necessarily imply that the profit motive and capitalist requirements will cease to guide the process. But the profits and the requirements will not be those of isolated and unco-ordinated owners of capital, all of whom are individually free to exert what pressure they can on the state machine in their own several interests. They will be the requirements of certain particular capitalist interests which have succeeded in establishing a dictatorship over finance capital as a whole, and which use the state machine, not spasmodically, but continuously as the sole co-ordinated weapon of capitalist expansion.

The body of interests to which it has been customary to attach the label " finance capital " were until the great slump casually grouped together on what was from their own internal point of view a remarkably democratic basis. To-day in the fascist countries they are regimented almost as ruthlessly as the workers, the peasants, and the middle class. But they are regimented by one of themselves, as it were: by their own most reactionary elements. For the moment those elements find it convenient to express themselves through the armament industry in the broadest sense. It is therefore permissible to say that contemporary fascism takes the form of government by and for armament monopolism.

The connection between the arms industry and fascism is not of course accidental. On the other hand, it would be a mistake to suppose that armament monopolism is the only form fascism can take. In the 1880's capitalism turned to empire-building as a means of marketing surplus value, and temporarily solved its crisis in that way. Fifty years later, when the crisis has greatly deepened, capitalism turns to armament-building as a not dissimilar means to the same end.

As Brailsford puts it, " The firms that make capital goods, and especially machinery, are always the first to suffer in a slump and the last to recover. To these firms rearmament spells prosperity and their gains stimulate the whole market. A gun is, moreover, a machine of a very unusual type. It has the merit of producing nothing. It will not glut warehouses and barns with unsaleable goods and surplus crops, as looms and ploughs may do. It may be manufactured profitably without creating the plenty that capitalism dreads." *

In a word, armaments are among those rare kinds of goods for which production and consumption are, so to speak, a single process. They are sold at a profit as soon as they are made; and that without any need for an increase in the purchasing capacity, and therefore in the political and economic power, of the common people.

But it is unlikely that capitalism can pause at the point of armament monopolism for very long. From the nature of the case, the gigantic military machines now being

* " Why Capitalism Means War ", p. 12.

constructed will have to be either used or largely dismantled. In the latter event, the search for profit by monopolism of the fascist type may become deflected along the line of industrial exploitation of cheap colonial labour.*

As Palmer has suggested,† the *mise en valeur* of colonies (particularly those of tropical Africa, *which contain by far the largest water power resources in the world*) ‡ will in many cases depend on the simultaneous development of water power and manufacturing industry. The process will involve very large and carefully planned capital expenditures—investment on a scale and in a concerted way possible only to vast monopolies or to totalitarian states. This phase of totalitarian industrial parasitism battening on cheap coloured labour has yet to be brought into being by the European states. The Japanese make no bones about their determination to achieve it in the east.

Developments of this kind may be accompanied in the usual way by economic war between parasite powers. Or again such powers, recognising the joint threat directed at rulers' privileges by the democratic movements at home and the liberationist movements in the colonies, may combine together for the joint repression of both movements, and for the planned and co-ordinated exploitation of colonial labour and resources. Whatever the outcome may be, the evidence already available warrants the judgement that a totalitarian phase of imperialism is rapidly developing.

* See Chapter IV, § 7.
† " Science and World Resources."
‡ See " Transactions of 2nd World Power Conference ", 1930.

CHAPTER XIX

EMPIRE AND PEACE

§ 1. THE ROOT AND THE FLOWER

PEACE, as a positive idea, and not as a mere abstention from mass-slaughter, must always be the final aim of civilised society. Peace is, in fact, a synonym for society in its fullest meaning. It is social order, social harmony, a proud collective humility in which all turbulent egoisms, whether of individuals or of groups, have been laid to rest— the supreme temperance that crowns and completes human culture. Peace is the free intercourse of free men subject to the law and the discipline of freedom.

The considerations advanced in the preceding chapter suggest that the possibility of general peace is a problem of social organisation. That is to say, peace depends in the last resort on the inner social structure of those local groups which make up what we so ironically term the comity of nations. Some types of social organisation are compatible with international peace, and some are not. Unfortunately, most of those actually existing to-day, our own among them, belong to the latter class.

Many people will think this a partial and biased observation. Now, all good qualities have their due season and their proper spheres of exercise. If impartiality means a suspension of judgement on points on which certainty is for the moment out of reach, then clearly no effective thinking can be done without it. But we do not spend our whole lives on the bench or in the laboratory. There are times when life inexorably summons us to leave the weighing of evidence and to act—to make a practical choice not from some unattainable basis of intellectual certainty, but according to such lights as we have. In these crises, as the word itself implies, we do and must decide and choose, however much we may try to postpone or avoid doing so. It becomes, quite simply, a case of " Who is not for me is against me ". Neutrality at such a time is a sheer impossibility. For the man who declares, " I shall do nothing, and I shall not take sides ", throws the weight of his inertia effectively over on to the side of negation, of conservatism, of resistance to change.

Our world, I believe, stands at a crisis of this kind to-day. If we refuse to range ourselves openly and actively with one or other of the opposed forces, we none the less act objectively as a buttress of those classes and institutions whose alteration or future or position is in dispute. What is more, in seeking, however vainly, to escape partiality we abdicate from the responsibility which belongs to us as human beings; which is only another way of saying that we testify to our indifference to the very distinction between the respective values of good and evil, truth and falsehood. That indifference is what Plato meant by the lie in the soul.

And Dante, you will remember, somewhat severely records that it is unfair to Hell to expect it to harbour the would-be neutrals, the trimmers, and the non-interventionists, who " were not rebellious nor were faithful to God. Heaven chases them forth ", he says, " to keep its beauty from impair; and the deep Hell receives them not, for the wicked would have some glory over them." Accordingly, a place of special torture and ignominy was prepared for them in the shadow of Hell Gate, but outside it. There Dante saw, and wept to see, the dreary souls of men and women who had lived without blame and without praise— " the crew of caitiffs," he calls them, " hateful to God and to his enemies ".

§ 2. " TELL ME WHERE IS BATTLE BRED ? "

The opponents of our present social organisation bring many grave charges against it, and gravest of all, perhaps, the charge that it breeds war. How are we to assess this charge? History appears to support it. If I look back over only my own lifetime, and take account only of major wars, I can recall the Spanish–American War, the South African war, the Russo–Japanese war, a series of Balkan wars, the Great War, the wars of intervention against Bolshevik Russia, the Græco–Turkish war, the war of France and Spain against Abdel Krim in Morocco, the Gran Chaco war, the Manchurian war, the Abyssinian war, the present wars in Spain and China.

The total casualties in these wars and in the various famines and pestilences which directly arose out of them do not fall short of 100 millions. And the reckoning omits a whole multitude of colonial wars, punitive expeditions, and the like. The stupendous tale of destruction is the work of the European, the white man, aided by the aptest of all the white man's pupils, the Japanese. I suppose most people in this country still habitually think of the white man as constituting the moral and intellectual leadership of the world, the highest product of human civilisation. This view is not shared by the awakened minds of Asia and Africa, who, on the contrary, have come to regard us and our culture as organisms stricken with loathsome disease.

Who could candidly deny that the history of the last forty years affords at least a *prima facie* warrant for their attitude? But let us not beg the question. Indians, Africans, and our revolutionaries at home may be wrong. Europeans may merely have been unlucky. The above catalogue of almost continuous major wars may be nothing but a chapter of accidents, what the insurance companies with light-hearted blasphemy call Acts of God, unconnected with the ways in which mortal men arrange their social relations.

But suppose, just for the sake of argument, that the critics are right. Suppose this scourge of war does infect the very tissue of our social order. Suppose war is not only an extension of policy and diplomacy, but an extension too of our domestic social forces. Then, surely, the white man has a duty to isolate himself in quarantine. Empire, involving as it does the Europeanisation of primitive peoples, becomes a crime. Every political and sociological idea which has occupied our mental field comes up at once against a staggering challenge. The whole direction of our thinking abruptly shifts.

Beliefs and institutions which are proved and tried, as the phrase goes, and which are therefore identified with our present state, fall under instant suspicion. Unless we are prepared to go on living limply as the patients of a world of destruction till it destroys us as well as its agents, we have to acknowledge a tremendous presumption in favour of the new. At such an organic turning-point of history, the real treason is to defend the *status quo*.

§ 3. THE WAR AGAINST WAR

Concerted efforts have, of course, often been made, generally on an international basis, to control whatever elements in our social constitution make for war. Holy Alliances, Concerts of Europe, Leagues of Nations, came and were and are not. Undeniably some of the work they accomplished had value. But in their main object of rendering the curse of war a thing of the past, all alike made shipwreck.

Many of us, who saw at close quarters the most brutal aspects of the great war, wondered what victory could be worth that intolerable price, and believed for a time that we had found the answer in the League of Nations. We allowed ourselves, with the rashness of desperation, to hope that in the League there had been invented a machine which might secure the outlawry of war. In some of us the bitterness with which we think of those who have betrayed the League is proportionate to the height of that hope.   But in the dark time when grief pours freezing over us, bitterness serves only to deepen the gloom.   It is more profitable to gather together what remains of our strength, and to draw what instruction we may from the grounds of failure.

Those liberal idealist lawyers who drafted the League Covenant worked from a base of five assumptions : first, that so far as the organisation of peace was concerned, national states were the only relevant social groupings; second, that the League membership would soon include all the most powerful national states, as well as a great majority of the less powerful; third, that all national armaments would soon be reduced, and limited to the reduced level; fourth, that political democracy would become the pre- vailing form of government in the world; and fifth, that the economic system would, broadly speaking, continue to operate on the accustomed pre-war lines, with the breaking-in of savage Germany completed, and with widening ripples of social reform spreading outwards from a centre of private profit-seeking enterprise.

From our vantage-point of time, we may be ready enough to sneer at such an outlook as characteristic of people who had never reflected critically on the foundations of the social order they had been brought up in.   But in fact these five assumptions retained at any rate a partial validity for ten years—right up to the onset of the great depression in 1930.   In view of history's refusal to observe any kind of speed-limit in the post-war period, ten years must be considered a creditable run.   True, the stresses of the war itself had brought to very difficult birth and life in Russia an entirely new kind of civilisation, in spite of frenzied attempts by Britain and France first to procure abortion and later to commit infanticide.   Furthermore, in the first slump after the war, fascism arose in Italy, soon to be followed by other examples of popular preference for dictatorship over democracy.   But in spite of some failures and some dishonest compromises, the assumptions of the Covenant were not, it seemed, being comprehensively falsified by experience, and the League was growing both in membership and authority.

The great depression sent history skidding round a hairpin bend. In the last eight years the vision of a universal League of disarmed democracies has broken into fragments, and is now so manifestly delusive that even the most sentimental of us have given up dreaming of it. Instead, we see the menacing reality—a fragmented League set in the midst of an arms race of unparalleled intensity, face to face with heavily armed and openly hostile dictatorships, in a world where, so far from nations being the only relevant forms of social grouping, it is conflicts of economic class that ultimately determine both the internal and the foreign policies of all states.

If the designers of the League had recalled to mind the history of tyranny in the city-states of ancient Greece, they might have foreseen how extremely unlikely it was that the great war and the peace settlement which continued that war in another form could lead to any flow of the democratic tide in a devastated and war-maddened Europe. But they could hardly have foreseen, and certainly in fact they never dreamed, that democracy would soon come near failure in the very countries where victory had crowned it, the very countries which for generations had been its foremost champions. What has happened in the western democracies since 1930 is not merely a progressive trenching upon old-established civil liberties; nor merely that these democracies have shown, by comparison with the dictatorships, an almost ludicrous ineffectiveness in the diplomatic field. Much more than this, the democracies have become incapable of providing any channel through which the deepest political aspirations of the people they claim to represent, can be realised.

Here, in particular, come to mind the related questions of peace and world trade. Since 1930 world trade has been strangled by narrowly nationalist and imperialist economic policies, and in consequence the world has been sliding rapidy towards catastrophe. This has happened against the will of the people, and in the main against the conscious intentions of their elected governments. Partly, no doubt, it has happened because of public ignorance of what the price of peace was, and in what coin it must be paid; partly, because of reluctance to pay a price as high as circumstances were stipulating for. But the main reason is one which has been described by the Economic Committee of the League (Report published September 1935) in the following terms: " In the sphere of commercial policy Governments have to reckon with the resistance of individuals and groups who, while they are quite ready to talk of the interdependence of peoples, are naturally not concerned with anything but the interests of their own particular branch of production. It is from this necessarily one-sided standpoint that these individuals and groups continually demand the enforcement of measures the paralysing effect of which on international economic relations we have seen."

Thus the League report. And we may add that, once international economic relations are paralysed, the demand for intensified programmes of national defence swiftly follows, and war itself becomes merely a question of time. We are left, then, with the ironic conclusion that the forces which drive the nation against its will towards war are embodied in those great industrial enterprises which most people are accustomed to think of as constituting the foundation of national prosperity and well-being.

§ 4. THE LIBERAL FALLACY

If this is so, the framers of the Covenant gravely miscalculated when they assumed that political democracy would in practice afford fair representation to all interests within the nation, and that therefore domestic economic and social issues would have little effect on foreign policy.

The framers of the Covenant compared their projected League with the system of periodical Congresses for the settlement of international disputes which Castlereagh, Metternich, and the Tsar Alexander had tried to work in the years following Waterloo. They took the view that the Congressional system broke down, because then the governments did not represent the peoples, and the states did not represent the races. And they further concluded that the League Covenant plus political democracy in the member states would circumvent this source of failure.

Here they did much more than mistake the measures of political organisation appropriate to their given situation. They revealed a root-defect of liberal thought. No doubt it was natural that they should see the Covenant as what in fact it is, a form of social contract between independent sovereign states. But it was a cardinal error to follow further in Rousseau's footsteps, and to conceive the domestic social order of the several nations as a social contract between individual units, who in their relations with one another corresponded to independent sovereign states. This, of course, was the conception which placed them in a position to argue that, given universal political franchise, all interests comprised within a national society could and would secure fair and proportionate representation in a sovereign parliament.

The whole notion that society is a voluntary coming together of independent individuals makes it impossible to understand the social forces actually at work. When we study social relations, we are dealing with mankind from what may be called a statistical standpoint. The substantial factors are the groups which arise and undergo differentiation in the social activity of finding and using the material means of life. To this process individuals, whatever they may be from the standpoint of art, or religion, or morality, are incidental. The error of liberal democracy has been to carry over into the sphere of social relations ideas which directly apply only to the sphere of personal relations. The tissue of events and forces which form the life of a society is not a network of the free activities of separate individuals. On the contrary, it is made up of the objective interests of the several groups into which the human herd divides itself for the purposes of production and consumption.

When we accept this position, two important inferences follow. One is that the relative strength or weakness of opposed groups is determined, not by political representation, but primarily by economic power, that is to say, by the degree of control exercised over the processes of production. The other inference is that such values as justice, freedom, and reason in the social sense cannot be realised directly by mere goodwill and intelligence operating in abstraction from the problem of economic power. In other words, such values can never manifest themselves except as intrinsic attributes of a substance which consists in a particular form of *economic* organisation of society.

We can now see some of the main reasons why the League has not managed to prevent war. We can say, for example, that the failure of the League of Nations is a failure not of the League, but of the nations. We have learnt that peace depends on something more fundamental than adjustment, or even organisation, of international relations. The roots of war reach deep down into the social structure of national societies. Before a lasting peace system can be set up, the inward character of nationhood must change.

Liberal thinkers often express this need by pointing to the difficulties caused by the tradition of absolute national sovereignty. No collective security scheme, they explain, can succeed in practice unless it really establishes a fresh and untainted source of international authority. And no such source can be tapped while nations remain obstinately unwilling to devolve upon the central organ of the League any fragment whatever of their sovereign powers. This formulation, valuable for its recognition of the existence of the problem, seems inadequate as a definition of the problem's nature, since it omits all account of why sovereignty is so jealously guarded as in fact it is.

§ 5. STATE POWER AND VESTED INTEREST

To this latter question many answers might be given. But the most significant of them is the one we have already seen hinted at by the Economic Committee of the League—namely, that even in so-called democratic states the state power is effectively wielded, and national policy effectively determined, not by a majority of the electorate, but by certain minority interests of great economic influence, which depend on their concealed management of the state power for the maintenance both of their competitive strength against foreign rivals and of their privileged status in the social order at home. It was, I believe, the late Lord Balfour who remarked, in what some of his democratic supporters must have felt to be an unguarded moment, that no matter what party was in office, the conservatives would always rule the country.*

The partition of Africa, which preoccupied European statesmanship during the last quarter of the nineteenth century, is an admirable example of what is politely termed the outward thrust of private capital; or, in other words, of the strategy of group interests, consisting mainly of industrialists and investors, who were able to enlist in their support the whole diplomatic and military power of the modern civilised state. Time and again Governments themselves exhibited extreme reluctance to intervene in Africa; but time and again, against their better judgement, they were swung round by the pressure of the strong minority interests which stood to gain by intervention. It would be a simple matter to multiply instances of the

---

* Cf. also Hilaire Belloc's lines On a Great Election :—

The accursed Power which stands on Privilege
    (And goes with Women, and Champagne, and Bridge)
Broke—and Democracy resumed her reign:
    (Which goes with Bridge, and Women, and Champagne.)

same kind of process from the history of pre-war and post-war diplomacy and domestic policy.

All this is, of course, an old story. But many people still laugh off Balfour's dictum as a playful cynicism, instead of accepting it as a strictly accurate account of how the combination of political democracy with a profit-system of production and distribution works in practice.

Balfour had in mind something which is actually a dominant feature of our present-day society. The oligarchs who direct and control, but do not necessarily own, our vast accumulations of investment capital and our great producing plants, have become powerful enough to tow the state with its organised apparatus of coercion in the wake of their own economic needs. These private economic needs, operating through the state power in this way, gradually conduct the country to a point where its internal equilibrium depends, or appears to depend, on foreign markets and fields of investment. And when that point is reached, the same private economic needs naturally appear to assume the character of a national interest. Here we may refer again to the League Economic Committee, which observes that whenever any attempt is made to get away from economic nationalism and imperialism, producers and vested interests of all kinds at once leap up to prove beyond refuting that utter ruin would result for the whole nation.

From the standpoint now reached, it is easy to see why national sovereignty is a weapon far too precious for the dominant groups who wield it to forgo in the interests of world order, or any other cause involving a measure of altruism. It is easy, too, to see why its preservation and active use may appear, although falsely, a vital concern of the nation at large, and not merely of certain privileged groups within it. Sovereignty has been erected into a totem of national honour and prestige, yet it remains objectively the embodiment of a class interest, valued less on constitutional or political grounds than as an instrument of economic power, and for its recalcitrance to forms of control which might benefit the unprivileged.

Finally, it is easy to see why the hard core of national sovereignty, in whose recalcitrance liberal thought has detected the main stumbling-block to the organisation of world peace, cannot be excised until after the community has applied surgical treatment to those strongly entrenched groups who employ their economic power to convert sovereignty to their own ends, and employ sovereignty to consolidate their economic power.

National sovereignty, like the sanctity of private property, once stood for methods of organising human life which, whatever their drawbacks, were then a step forward. Both, with all their immense ramifications and consequences, have survived into an age when, as R. H. Tawney puts it,* " they are about as relevant to practical realities as chain-armour in a modern battle. Both still pay handsome dividends to those in a position to pull the right strings, and are an intolerable nuisance to everyone else.

" From the state of inflamed exasperation which such absurdities produce, there are two possible exits. One is to alter the institutions to fit the facts; the other is to keep the institutions and silence anyone who calls attention to their inconveniences. The fascist states do the second, with the aid of concentration camps and torture. Those which call themselves democracies would, if wise, do the first. Since most of them, however, are governed by oligarchies of property-owners, who hold power subject to popular acquiescence, but hold it all the same, they are at present too deeply divided against themselves to act with decision either in social or international affairs. What will happen when that acquiescence ceases it is impossible to say. At present it is a fact; the task of the moment is to destroy it."

Any reading of the peace problem, then, which ignores the special relevance of group divisions within the national

* *New Statesman*, November 26th, 1938.

society, is hopelessly inadequate to the facts. Indeed, in some aspects divisions between classes are more fundamental to that problem than divisions between nations. Or, perhaps better, national divisions are tending to coincide with class divisions. Germany, for example, is identified with the owning class in the same sense in which the Soviet Union is identified with the working class. In this way national hatreds become reinforced by class hatreds.

§ 6. THE DEMOCRATIC PRINCIPLE

All the same, our class-divided society does show a surprising organic stubbornness. It resembles a prize-fighter, battered time after time to his knees, who as often drags himself, blind and spent, to his feet again, as though supplicating his opponent to deal the knock-out blow. In a word, it keeps going somehow. But at what a price! Were there a referee, he must for pity's sake have stopped the fight long ago. Dispensing with metaphor, are we not obliged to say that the productive potential of our time has risen to a point where the old forms and relations of property, and the boundaries of nationality, are no longer capable of accommodating it? Those forms and relations and boundaries have become, in the context of the present turning-point of history, mere obstructions.

True, they survive. With them, or in spite of them, the world continues for the moment, however shakily, to revolve. It is customary for British patriots to look back over the last thirty years and to conclude that the condition of our unprivileged masses has notably improved in that time. They even infer that, apart from a few black spots, things are moving in the right direction.

Let us assume—what is a debatable point—that their estimate, as distinct from their inference, is correct. They still do not realise to how large an extent any relative improvement in this country has been gained at the expense of other populations less fortunately placed—at the expense mainly perhaps of Indians and Africans, but of Germans,

Italians, and Japanese too. Extend the purview to take in the world arena as a whole. Force emotional comprehension to include the vast areas of central and southern Europe, of India, of China, and of Africa, where more than half the population of the world pays year by year with its own deepening distress for the comparative comfort of ourselves and a few other most-favoured nations. The moment this imaginative effort is made, is it any longer possible to evade the judgement that our social-economic structure has, on any showing, ceased to justify its costs of maintenance?

Involved in those costs are not merely militarism, imperialism, continuous crises, and almost continuous wars. There are also such things as competitive currency devaluations, extravagantly high tariff duties, foreign exchange control, trade quotas, and embargoes. The two groups of costs together swallow up and squander so much creative energy that no scope is left for further growth of generally diffused prosperity and culture. The advances which science and technology are ready and waiting to make are either perverted or held up. The rank and file of humanity is driven deeper either into actual poverty and distress, or into frustration, apathy, and bewilderment, or into all at once. The very flame of the spirit of man gutters and smokes for want of its proper fuel.

It is impossible, no matter how the mind is spent in searching, to discover any general means but one to the righting of these basic maladjustments. That one means is implicit in much that has already been said. It lies in the bold extension of the democratic principle. The battle for peace has to be fought and won on the home front, even more directly than in the chancelleries. Economic democracy needs to be called in to make employees their own employers in a manner comparable with that in which political democracy professes to have made the governed their own governors. Self-employment in industry and trade is the essential complement of self-government in politics. Responsibility for production and distribution must vest in the community at large in order that responsibility for domestic and foreign policy may vest in the community at large.

Only so can a term be set to those conflicts of economic class which are the true germs of imperialism and of international war. Only so can the great industrial and investing interests, which blindly and sometimes unconsciously push governments into war, be brought under a popular control whose real prime care is for equality and freedom, and therefore for peace. Only so can democracy itself be made a reality. If we want to save the life of democracy from the multitude of aggressive enemies which now threaten it, we must offer proof that it is a living and active principle. We have to widen the field in which it effectively operates, and give it nourishment and room for growth. For democracy is not yet a possession to be defended. It is a prize still to be won.

CHAPTER XX

SNUGGLING UP TO HITLER

§ 1. CAPITALIST COLD FEET

By 1900 the supply of undeveloped (and unappropriated) territories and peoples was running very short. Of powers hungry for colonies there was, however, no corresponding shortage. Thus began to take shape a problem which some people quaintly call that of the unsatisfied powers, but which would be more reasonably described as that of the exhausted colonies.

The scramble fizzled out for the quite simple reason that there were no more worlds to colonise. One consequence was that thenceforward new empires could be built only by means of the re-distribution of old empires, and that such re-distribution was likely to involve war between great powers. How far official German and official Britain during the great war were animated by the desire to destroy each other's empires for the sake of strengthening their own we have already seen.* The glad springtime of imperialism when Rhodes, Lugard, Karl Peters, and the rest were swaggering up and down Africa with a hey and a ho and a hey nonny no, the only pretty ringtime when vast provinces could be snapped up by presenting a case of gin and a few rifles to some illiterate chief—all this was yielding place to a somewhat bleak autumn in which it seemed doubtful whether empire-building was any longer a game for a gentleman to play. The stakes were rising so unconscionably. Even Lloyd George flinched when he saw that the true price of imperialism included " the horrors of such a war ".

* Chap. II, § 1.

There was a second consequence also—the rise of an active movement against imperialism among the subject or colonial peoples themselves. Some say that these peoples have learnt from their conquerors the ideas of nationalism and democracy; others more simply leave it that they resented, and therefore resisted, the fraud and violence with which they were reduced to subjection and were being held in it. In time their demand for freedom from foreign control and exploitation grew into a force with which their masters had seriously to reckon. Throughout the middle east, India and China, the revolt has met with appreciable success. The ferment is now powerfully at work in Africa and the West Indies.

Worse still, imperialism as a strenuous missionary creed was losing its appeal to the masses in the owning countries. The rulers and the statesmen of course continued to stamp with the brand of shame all impulse to domination in their rivals, while adoring the beneficence of their own over-lordship. But the common people were beginning to apprehend the incongruity of vast empires being ruled by so-called democracies. They were beginning to wonder whether highly exclusive and highly armed commercial empires really formed the best foundation on which to build a stable system of international peace and disarmament. They were beginning to ask whether such empires might not be morally wrong.

The rulers began to hear the sound which of all sounds is the most dreadful to their ears—the common people murmuring, " It don't seem right to me ". That common voice, once it is raised and knows its own meaning, can plough down palaces and thrones and towers. There were even some among the common people who dared to suggest that colonies were only maintained, to the injury of the people's interests, because it paid a few powerful financial concerns to secure the use of the national apparatus of coercion for the purpose.

Even among the rulers and the powerful financial

concerns for whom they spoke and acted, a certain lassitude prevailed.* The great war, the black-and-tan period in Ireland, the long-drawn-out manhandling of the liberationist movements in India and Palestine, had all sickened even the imperialists themselves. Violence as an instrument of policy fell into some discredit, even by those whose position could not long be maintained without it. They still used it, of course, but spasmodically and, as it were, guiltily. The will and the strength of British rulers to hold the dependent empire intact have been on the wane throughout the post-war period; while at the same time the period's economic difficulties have increased their desire to exploit exclusively that Empire's economic possibilities.† The two tendencies are insuperably discrepant, for you cannot be exclusive unless you are also prepared to be violent if and when your exclusiveness is challenged.

§ 2. FADING PRESTIGE

The sad truth is that large sections of the ruling class were losing their nerve. As early as 1919, the perception of J. M. Keynes ‡ had noticed the growing debility of the great capitalist class which had emerged from the industrial triumphs of the nineteenth century as the acknowledged master of the world. In 1900 capitalists believed in themselves, " in their value to society, in the propriety of their continued existence in the full enjoyment of their riches and the unlimited exercise of their power ". The war changed all that. It knocked the *Herrschaft* out of them. As they watched the endless carnage, their eyes turned horror-struck away. In their hearts they knew the war was their war; the child of their cutting, thrusting,

---

* Cf. the Nazi writer B. von Selchow who observes, " The Liberal aggression aims at depriving the holders of power of their self-confidence " (" The Civil and the Heroic Man ", 1934).
† See M. J. Bonn, " The Crumbling of Empire ", pp. 152, 190.
‡ Op. cit., p. 222.

stabbing interests. They felt the curse of the blood-guilty on them.

" Their terror and personal timidity ", wrote Keynes, " is now so great, their confidence in their place in society and in their necessity to the social organism so diminished, that they are the easy victims of intimidation. Now they tremble before every insult. Call them pro-Germans, international financiers, or profiteers, and they will give you any ransom you choose to ask not to speak of them so harshly. They allow themselves to be ruined and altogether undone by their own instruments, governments of their own making, and a press of which they are the proprietors. Perhaps it is historically true that no order of society ever perishes save by its own hand."

Had he rather put it that, while capitalism forges the weapons of its own destruction, the common people have to make use of those weapons to complete the process, he would have been talking good Marxism. In any case, how ominously his words, written as they were during the peace-making at Versailles, find an echo in the negotiations of Godesberg and Munich.

So severe a nervous breakdown in the capitalists could not be concealed in their relations with the people of the Empire. The spiritual conflict between their moral teaching and inhibitions and their imperial desires made European statecraft incredibly disgusting to the dark-skinned races, and in particular perhaps to orientals. In Asia at least the political prestige which the west had once enjoyed vanished for good. The west may teach how to make guns and ships, how to use steam and electricity. Asia will use this teaching to do without the west, and to gain the strength to cut free from its culture, its religion, and its hypocrisy. Indians, Chinese, and Japanese watched the gospel of peace drowning in a sea of blood and hate on the battlefields of Flanders; and they drew their several conclusions. But all agreed that the mission of western capitalism had ended so far as they were concerned.

In the home country, too, the capitalists were coming to be accepted at their own depressed valuation, or less, by the other classes of society. It cannot be said that the ten years between the Peace of Versailles and the coming of the great slump did much to restore them to their old eminence either in their own eyes or in those of the public. The slump itself served further to discredit not only high finance, but also all those responsible for the management of economic affairs.*

Woytinsky stresses the growth of anti-capitalist feeling during the later period of the slump, even in the more conservative sections of society.† And he proceeds " there can be no doubt that the sense of injustice in the distribution of wealth became more firmly rooted in sections of society that had not hitherto objected to the class system. The capitalists were held responsible not merely for business stagnation and the continuation of the depression that seemed to be insoluble, but also—and this accusation was even more bitter—for the fact that the losses resulting from the depression were not borne by those who were held to be responsible for them."

To sum up, then, the natural strains and stresses tending to the collapse of the pre-war type of empire were finding British imperialism out. Those strains and stresses were embodied in the triple challenge from the oppressed people in the colonies, from the democrats and pacifists at home, and from the unsatisfied powers abroad. Old-fashioned conservatism, itself more or less deeply infected with liberalism and seeking in defence of remaining strongholds merely to obstruct change and progress, was evidently in

---

* It should be remembered that the slump was no mere fluctuation of the trade cycle. It was one of the major catastrophes of human history. Between 1930 and 1934 it involved the world economic system in a total loss, as far as production, commerce, and transport were concerned, equal to the total cost of the great war. (See Woytinsky, " Social Consequences of the Economic Depression ", p. 300.)

† Op. cit., p. 297. See also Gaetan Pirou, " La Crise du Capitalisme ".

poor case for meeting a challenge so multiform and so persistent. In 1927 the provocation of the general strike was answered by that judicious blend of prudence and revenge which is the Trades Disputes Act. To the many-headed menace of the post-slump world such a spirit of gentlemanly reaction was quite inadequate. But how was the deficiency to be made good? British conservatism of the easy-going Baldwin kind seemed unable to fill the gap from its own resources. Shaken to the core by its experiences during the previous twenty years, it was acutely aware of the need of some good strong shoulder to lean on.

§ 3. THE HEALING TOUCH

This explains why Chamberlain and his followers like snuggling up under the wing of Hitler. National Socialism is not, like conservatism in England, just plain reaction: it is full counter-revolution. It does not tinker about with Sedition Acts or whittle liberty away with a pocket-knife; it blots out at a stroke the whole system of liberal thought and tradition. " The present state of the world is confused ", wrote Franz Haiser in 1926, " because there is neither a master state above the states, nor a master class above the classes." The Nazis have set both these matters to rights.

In doing so they have made the reactionaries of all countries feel a good deal easier. Franco in Spain, Daladier in France, and Chamberlain in England are all great patriots—and greater oligarchs. Like Coriolanus, they prefer oligarchy to patriotism if the ideal of having both together proves unattainable. No doubt they would rather not have a master state above them in the external field. But if by accepting such inferiority they can ensure the continued mastery of their own class over other classes on the home front, they think the bargain not ill driven. The general effect on them is a tonic effect. Contact with the bracing ruthlessness of Hitlerism gives a sense of release from the paralysing conscience that had been threatening ever since the war to make cowards of them all.

They touch the hem of their saviour's garment and their own bloody issue is stopped.*

In this case, however, the arrangement is not unilateral. Virtue does not go out of the saviour; on the contrary, it is added to him. For Chamberlain cannot rejuvenate British capitalism by means of Hitler's healing touch and monkey-gland injections without at the same time committing Britain to the support of Hitlerism. Mental reservations may, of course, be attached and the extent of the support restricted in that way. But it is doubtful whether any reservations or restrictions can be maintained in practice. The totalitarian character of Hitlerism itself precludes eclecticism on the part of its auxiliaries.

It is therefore vital to all of us, Chamberlain included,

* Many middle-class people in England have a genuine difficulty in understanding how largely the class interests of our rulers have, particularly in recent years, determined British foreign policy. The difficulty is not felt by foreign observers. The continental and American press is full of references to this central fact (as it is taken to be). As a typical example, chosen at random, take the following extract from the October 1938 issue of the Dutch monthly *Bevrijding*. The author, H. Kuijsten, is a pacifist, not a Marxist:

" We know that the exigencies of the geopolitical situation of a country may sometimes be in conflict with the interests of the ruling classes (or rather, castes); we have seen how this contrast induced France and England to adopt an attitude in the Spanish conflict which is at variance with the interests of France and England as a political unit as empires, and thus in the final instance also with the interests of the ruling classes.

" We must assume that we have a contrast here which will be lasting; the ruling classes of all countries are no longer able to give a consistent solution to the problems which arise; they become entangled in untenable contradictions. To help Italy is against England's imperialist interests; not to help Italy is also against the interest of the English ruling classes; for the collapse of Italy means the strengthening of the revolutionary tendencies in Europe.

" Thus besides the reasons explained above which led England to assist Germany and Italy, there is another motive which directs its international policy, and which of course also holds good for France; to prevent the collapse of these countries, occasioning a new wave of revolution. Therefore English policy can only be contra-revolutionary in every sense of the word."

With this factor of class allegiance Chamberlain no doubt mingles a pressing desire to conciliate Hitler in order to turn his nose to the east and to convert the German military machine into a one-way gun to know precisely what Hitlerism involves not only as a political regime, but also as a social philosophy.

---

pointing at the Soviet Union.　Chamberlain's hope perhaps is that his ideological rival (U.S.S.R.) and his imperialist rival may thus go down together, while a good old-fashioned conservatism of the continental type emerges in their place.

CHAPTER XXI

THE ISSUE

§. 1. DEMOCRACY AND SOCIALISM

HITLERISM could no doubt command the solid approval of the ruling class in England and much of the middle class too, if it merely meant (a) a denial of the Christian doctrine that there is no true social progress except the re-organisation of society in the interests of the unprivileged, and (b) the determination to make that denial good by force. But if Hitlerism means the repudiation of *all* Christian doctrine and the denial of *all* that we have hitherto understood as civilisation, would it still find England so responsive?

Hitler has observed that " western democracy is the forerunner of Marxism, which would be entirely unthinkable without it ". And again elsewhere, " Democracy in politics and communism in economics are based on analogous principles ".* He proclaims the utter incompatibility between democratic equality in politics and private property in the means of production in economic life to be the main cause of the present world crisis. Indeed, the general conviction throughout continental Europe is that socialism must come if only the authority of representative democracy is left unimpaired, a conviction firmly grounded in the historical experience of the continent during the post-war period. It follows that if socialism is not to be,

* Othmar Spann, one of the leading philosophers of the new German spirit, gives the following as the natural succession: " Moral decay in Liberalism, cultural paralysis through Democracy, and final degradation by Socialism ". For this reference see Karl Polanyi's Essay on " The Essence of Fascism " in " Christianity and the Social Revolution ", from which much of the material in the following paragraphs has been drawn. Students are also recommended to consult " The War Against the West ", by Aurel Kolnai, to which I am also indebted.

democracy must go.   So far so good; and so far Chamberlain and his supporters see.

But there is more.   Representative democracy is singled
out as a point of attack by Hitlerism because it is the
institutional link between socialism and individualism.
The unanimity of all fascist schools of thought on this point
is impressive.   It is not too much to say that the guiding
principle of them all is their common anti-individualism.
Take the negation of socialism as your starting-point, and
you soon find yourself driven to negate not only democracy
but the reality of the individual into the bargain.

This same charge of being anti-individualist is often
laid at the door of socialism.   That bolshevism is the end of
personality is a stock phrase of middle-class literature.
Here the Nazis profoundly disagree.   They invariably
insist that individualism leads to, and is responsible for,
bolshevism; they are anti-individualist precisely because
they are anti-bolshevist. " Democratic and Marxian
movements ", says Alfred Rosenberg, " take their stand on
the happiness of the individual." Bolshevism, as Spann
puts it, carries over the individualist doctrine of the natural
rights of man from the political sphere to the economic.
Far from being the opposite of individualism, it is its
consistent fulfilment.   It is the economic system under
which alone the substance of individualism can be preserved in an age of production by mechanical power.
What is more, it is but a different formulation and a stricter
interpretation of a reading of life generally accepted in
western Europe for almost 2,000 years.   This reading is
what Hitlerism proposes to destroy.

The view frequently held in England that fascism is a
" right " extreme and communism a " left " extreme
which meet in a common lack of respect for the individual,
is vehemently repudiated by communists and fascists alike,
and is beyond question wholly erroneous.   The antagonism
between the two is absolute.   Both, it is true, attack
bourgeois capitalist society.   But by their attack com-

munists mean that the values professed by liberal civilisation are not, but ought to be, realised in actual practice; the Nazis mean by theirs that such a realisation is as impossible as it is undesirable, and that therefore the values of liberal civilisation ought openly and completely to be dethroned.*

§ 2. MORALITY AND REASON

We may take some brief examples of what the high priests of Hitlerism have to say on some of those functions which we think of as being distinctive of human personality. Ludwig Klages disapproves of the odious fancy of morality. He even calls it the kernel of Judaism and Christianity, both of which must therefore be wiped out. The efforts of moral mania to improve men and conditions are, in his view, doomed to hideous failure. They represent a fussing of man in the face of Nature. They constitute an unwarrantable interference with Life. The moral imperative is the very principle of all offence against Life. The educator aiming at morality is an unconscious but systematic offender against Life.

Again, we are told that " the basic pattern of human existence is not the understanding of things and a mutual understanding between men; it is the growth and struggle of vital energies in their anthropological manifestations ". In plain English this means that what is important in human life is mere life, and not its human character. The fact of life being embodied in men is an accident, without more significance than its embodiment in plants and animals. Human nature is just one species of animated nature among others. Concepts such as civilisation or a rational order of society are essentially false because they can only worsen the natural conditions of life by leading to rebellion against the immutable laws that govern it. This is the fundamental creed professed by Hitler in " Mein Kampf ". The call is therefore to fight the very ideas of objective truth and

* See Kolnai, op. cit., p. 206.

H

universal reason, and to destroy man's inborn claim of access to them.

Further, in regard to the basis of Christian ethics, Franz Haiser gives this assurance. The axiom that no man should serve as a mere tool for another breathes destruction. There is no such thing as a right to happiness or the good life or freedom; only a relative right to existence. " Thou art but a tool of nature, a station of transition and decay destined to serve higher ends. Life lives on life."

Even consciousness, that awareness of self which has been thought to mark off the life of man from that of the beasts, cannot be allowed to stand. "We no longer believe", says Oswald Spengler, " that reason controls life. We have realised that life controls reason. Life has no goal. Mankind has no goal. We witness the sublime aimlessness of a great performance. Ideas act irrationally through the blood. Consciousness is a matter of indifference. Life is the alpha and omega, and Life is devoid of all system, all progress, all reason. It exists simply for its own sake." In this Spengler agrees with Klages, for whom the principle of consciousness is a hostile irruption into man's proper life; in fact a disease. The psychologist, Prinzhorn, puts the same point in a different way when he states that " infra-human nature is the prototype of all life, appropriate order and true community ". The reality of man (the phrase is Polanyi's) lies in his capacity not to be a person.

We can see, then, that this new, or rather refurbished, counter-revolutionary gospel exhales a spirit of deliberate barbarism, of knowing and final despair as to all aspirations of man towards enlightenment and happiness and being at peace with himself. Such thoroughgoing anti-rationalism cannot be fully understood, so Kolnai suggests, unless one perceives that its moral despair reflects a refusal to relinquish power. It has been left to a German anti-Nazi writer to make the final comment on this despair and this refusal.

" Barbarity as a mannerism is the climax of evil. It is bad enough to persevere in barbarous forms of living; to relapse into them is worse; but worst of all is a conscious return to them. This, however, is the object of National Socialism." *

Polanyi has a passage which sums the whole matter up.

" The Christian idea of society is that it is a relationship of persons. Everything else follows logically from this. The central proposition of fascism is that society is *not* a relationship of persons. This is the real significance of its anti-individualism. The implied negation is the formative principle of fascism as a philosophy. It is its essence. It sets to fascist thought its definite task in history, science, morals, politics, economics and religion. Thus fascist philosophy is an effort to produce a vision of the world in which society is *not* a relationship of persons. A society, in fact, in which there are either no conscious human beings or their consciousness has no reference to the existence and functioning of society. Anything less leads back to the Christian truth about society. But that is indivisible. It is the achievement of fascism to have discovered its whole scope. It rightly asserts the correlatedness of the ideas of individualism, democracy and socialism. It knows that either Christianity or fascism must perish in the struggle." †

Such in brief outline is the social content of Hitlerism. Its Utopia lies not in the future, but in the past. Its ideal is regressive, harking back beyond the renaissance, beyond the beginnings of Christianity, beyond antique paganism, beyond all yesterday's seven thousand years, back to the dim ages before man walked upright. Quite simply the Nazi says to himself, " If I must live in a world of destruction, let me be its agent rather than its patient ". This may

* Thomas Murner, quoted in Kolnai, op. cit., p. 210.
† " Christianity and the Social Revolution ", p. 370.

be called making a virtue of an imaginary necessity with a vengeance. It is the fully developed expression of what Freud terms the death instinct, and brings home in a way to move our pity how utterly the Nazi has abandoned all hope of making his world a creative one.

Kolnai reminds us that this attitude is a new departure in the sense that counter-revolution is for the first time here upheld as an experience of positive revolution claiming to remodel society from its foundations on the basis of a complete renunciation of freedom.

§ 3. UNIVERSAL MISSION OF FASCISM

Nor is Hitlerism as a social theory and a reading of life just a collection of philosophical wares displayed in the German shop-window to catch the fancy of passers-by. It is not just a swarm of ideas floating like disease germs in the air, by which one may or may not become infected, according as one is lucky or unlucky. It is a system of faith backed by one of the most powerful military states in the world, whose leaders have declared a holy war against the empire of reason—that realm of corruption which is governed by the Christian superstition that animal life is not enough, and which therefore regards rationality, and not mere life, as the cardinal point of human conduct and values.

Since the German state-machine (and incidentally those of Italy and Japan too) has been seconded for service in this holy war, the faith can be broadcast all over the world, either by beam to single countries in turn, or in full diffusion to all at once, with the compelling appeal and authority that material power can lend. The men who control these state-machines do not seek to persuade the world that their holy faith is true. They are missionaries of another kind. They smash the world in the face with their fists and belabour it with rubber truncheons, until it admits that it can feel Hitlerism flowing in its veins.

Such a faith so supported will not tolerate the continued existence of its adversaries in any place to which its own influence can effectively extend. Its key formula is the relativity of values and the absoluteness of power. Both Hitlerism and western humanism couch their message in universal terms; their ultimate claim is to the allegiance of the whole world. Since neither can abate its claim without denying its own nature, this is necessarily a case of pistols for two, coffee for one. One must conquer the other. Good kind English people who say, with Anthony Eden, that they are not concerned in the ideological struggle, may mean that they do not mind who wins it, or that they believe the side they favour is going to win anyhow. Pacifists who hold that we should treat our ideological enemies with even greater forbearance and kindliness than we show to our ideological friends forget in their overflowing love for the sinner their duty to hate the sin.* Objectively speaking, everyone assists the advance of Hitlerism who does not develop and organise some form of resistance to it. Those who act as allies of Hitlerism, whatever lip service they may pay to democracy, will all be found to be disbelievers in the people's power in the literal meaning of the term.

It is an essential part of the humanist case that the progress of mankind is possible. Fascist irrationalism denies that it is either possible or desirable. We in the so-called democracies have irrationalists of our own who suppose that human progress is necessary or, as it were, automatic. We still suffer grievously from the idea of progress. It comforts us to picture destiny as one of those neat and friendly lift-girls ever conducting humanity to an ever higher floor.

We look over that pitiful tale of senseless horrors which is modern political and social history, and complacently we read its most appalling passages as some temporary stoppage of the unending heavenward motion. No failure of human kind is too gross or too unredeemed to be written off as a brief fluctuation in a general upward trend. Or,

* As Heine remarks, one should forgive one's enemies, but not until they are brought to execution.

worse still, we grow callous and deny that the horrors are horrible, patting one another on the back and saying, " It doesn't do to take these things too tragically ". Or we turn cynic and ask, " Why should I break my head in efforts to amend an incorrigible world ? " Or perhaps we shuffle off the responsibility on to the broad shoulders of God, and pretend that if only we are patient and use his time-scale, everything will come right in the end, either here or hereafter. After all, do not deserts of vast eternity lie before us? What need for urgency or haste? This we call faith.

We may fly to notions even more trivial and confused than these in our determination to forget such relevant positive knowledge as we possess—namely, that the course of evolution has generally been downwards. The usual fate of species in the past has been not progress but extinction, often after slow degeneration through long periods. The animals and plants alive to-day, measureless as their profusion and variety sometimes seem, are nevertheless the descendants of a minority of species which have escaped this fate. There is small reason to think that man will escape it unless he desires to, and knows the cost involved, and is prepared to pay it.

Whether that desire shall become vivid enough and general enough in human consciousness to induce much of the world's population to act on it, and, if so, whether man shall discover in time the means to realise it, are questions whose answer perhaps depends on the events of the next century or so. For the last half-century the world has been in the throes of a great crisis, which so far has only become more complex and more intense. If, as it deepens, it conducts us much further down the slope of barbarism and unreason than we have already descended, it may end in the destruction of civilised culture all over the planet.*

* " Civilisation is a highly complicated invention which has probably been made only once. If it perished, it might never be made again." See J. B. S. Haldane, " The Inequality of Man ", p. 141.

People speak of it as a political and economic crisis, a crisis of international relations, a crisis of the maldistribution of population and resources; it receives a different label according to the several aspects in which it is viewed. Certainly it is all these things and it deserves all these names. But it is much more also. It is a crisis of civilisation. Not the flow of wealth merely, but the whole rational capacity of man is being strangled.

The effort of entrenched privilege to confine the group-life within the framework of economic and social relations which are essentially false can succeed only if it enlists the co-operation of falsehood throughout the whole cultural field. Thus the area within which the energy of the rational can freely operate is in our time becoming more and more closely restricted. The process of restriction is reluctant and hesitating in the so-called democracies; enthusiastic and deliberate in the fascist countries. Science, honoured less and less as the explorer and conqueror of new worlds, is degraded more and more to a mere adjunct of army, factory, or hospital.*

Civilised man is failing more and more conspicuously to adjust the organisation of his society and the structure of his thought so as to harmonise with the scientific methods and ideas which are struggling to remould the material basis of his life. The ancestors of oysters and barnacles had heads but lost them. By a similar process of biological degeneration man may just as easily shed the function we have made bold to dignify with the name of intelligence. The extracts from Nazi philosophy given above suggest, indeed, that he has begun to do so.

For these reasons man is challenged to fight, and fight now, for his own survival; or at least to prevent a loss of specifically human characters and a degeneration into barbarism and thence into animality. It seems likely that a critical point has been reached in humanity's striving towards the light. So far from time being automatically

* Probably military hospital.

on our side, it is almost certainly against us, unless we show
the skill and the resolution not to waste it.

§ 4. THE ENEMY WITHIN

Man's fight is now against no threat from another
species or the brute power of inanimate nature; over such
foes he has already the whip hand. It is against himself.
His enemy is within. The tendencies of thought and
action which Hitlerism has drawn together and developed
into a system in so striking and incisive a way are always
present in human nature; just as the neo-vitalist philosophy of the Nazis is but a disguise and a modification of
theories which have always animated reactionary opposition to Christian civilisation, liberal society, and social
progress.

In every society and in every individual, therefore,
they can be sure of raising some response that gives
them a *point d'appui* from which with luck the whole mind
and the whole society may one day be conquered for
the fascist cause. These tendencies are in a rational
society inhibited by forces in the mind which have been
commonly identified with culture or civilisation. Culture
or civilisation, as Freud insists,* has to call up every
possible reinforcement in order to erect barriers against
them and to hold their manifestations in check by reaction-
formations. When these barriers fail, men are revealed
as savage beasts to whom the thought of sparing their own
kind is alien.

These are the barriers which Hitlerism has pulled down
so far as official Germany is concerned. Nor does Hitlerism
stop there. It is the Messiah which has come to preach
their pulling down the world over. " The fateful question
of the human species seems to me to be whether and to
what extent the cultural process developed in it will succeed
in mastering the derangements of communal life caused by
the human instinct of aggression and self-destruction." †
* " Civilisation and its Discontents ", p. 86.   † Freud, op. cit., p. 144.

Fascist practice and ideology have raised that instinct to the highest concentration which it has yet achieved in the social life of mankind.

The first task of people in England who believe in civilisation is to control and to transmute that instinct in themselves and in their society. That is why it is of crucial importance that they should make a clean break with imperialism. For imperialism is merely one of the developed forms which the instinct assumes. None of us can be said to stand plainly for civilisation against aggression and self-destruction, so long as we are ready to condone the deeds that won and maintain the Empire. Indeed, as we shall see in Part V, fascism and imperialism are in a certain sense bound together in mutual interdependence. British and French imperialist policies were the occasion of Hitlerism's ascendancy in Germany; and so long as the British and French Empires persist in their present forms and organisation, Hitlerism is unlikely to fall into eclipse.

I have emphasised the extremity of peril for human life which fascism embodies, not because I like to be alarmist, and still less because I want to shock people into despair. All the same I recognise that some may feel that to stand up to the fascist attack is too much trouble or too much risk—that the game, in fact is hardly worth the candle. " How can we ", they may ask, " puny atoms in a gigantic social organism hope to modify the structure of the system we live in ? You call us to take up a supreme challenge to the courage, the nobility, and the reason of mankind. We are but poor forked creatures, not Titans trained to be storm-troops of heaven."

If anyone, at this juncture of history, acts on such modest doubts, I wish him joy of the destruction to come. He will learn from it what risk and trouble are. In truth, grave as our danger is, there is no cause for brave men to despair. We know the path to victory. Victory can and will be ours if we take that path, which is the path of the interest of the common people of every land.

H 2

People have a natural inclination to wish to believe that
their having been born is to make some kind of difference to
the world. Normally, too, they like to think of the difference as beneficial. For our generation the beneficial
difference can be real on one condition—that we identify
ourselves fully and actively with the cause of the unprivileged. Fascism is a ferocious power, but also an unstable
one. It is unstable because it lives on privilege. The
common people are interested not in privilege but in
equality, and when they become conscious both of their
danger and of their power they can and will break privilege's back. The social value of each individual among us
to-day is proportionate to his love for and faith in the common
people who do the productive work of the world.

" At such an hour and in such a manner that ye think
not, and in alien guise, the Lord comes." For our generation the coming of the Lord consists in the consciousness
that the common people hold the keys of human advance.
The wisdom of the world and the cleverness of the mighty
are, as always, unprepared for such a coming. It is
recognised and greeted by the few; and they are Samaritans,
Roman centurions, publicans and sinners, outcasts, heathens,
and harlots. In a word, they are the kind of people whom
the complacent, the timid, and the proud are likely to
scorn and mistrust most, the kind of people who form the
membership of the Communist Party.

Those who recognise and greet that coming, minority
though they be, are diffused throughout the whole world
and work as a powerful leaven in every part. In the
aggregate they already represent a very formidable force.
The task they are engaged on, the task in which they need
every ounce of help that every man and woman who
believes in humanity can give them, is the building of a
progressive movement united enough, alert enough, and
intelligent enough to prevent the crushing out of rationality
from man's life by the embattled champions of privilege.
This task is interdependent with the development of the

people's power in the five continents. The Chinese people, the Spanish people, the people of India and the colonies, the people of France, and above all the people of the Soviet Union are the allies in whose success our own progress and liberty will be assured.

By such a united and co-ordinated movement of the common people the extension of fascist organisation and ideology has to be opposed, wherever and whenever it may occur. The links between Hitlerism as a state power and Hitlerism as a social philosophy are such that the two cannot be separated in practice. That is what totalitarianism means. It follows that the rejection of the social philosophy, if it is to be more than a silent motion of the individual mind, must involve resistance to the state power. Conversely, non-resistance to the state power prepares the way for the spread of the social philosophy. To say therefore that it is no concern of ours what state system the people of Germany care to live under is simply untrue. On the practical success or failure of Hitler's state system depends the possibility or otherwise of the Nazi social philosophy conquering the world, as the world was conquered for the valuations of bourgeois capitalism during the nineteenth century.

Snuggling up to Hitler has as one effect the strengthening of Hitlerism as a state power. It is a good policy for Chamberlain if he happens to accept Hitlerism as a social philosophy. But it is a disastrous policy for all those people in England whose concern for civilisation impels them to reject Nazi social philosophy. Hitlerism, the state power, can be resisted by British policy, but it can only be overthrown by the German people who are at present both the victims and the vehicles of Hitlerism, the social philosophy. The primary test of every phase of British policy to-day is thus how far it effectively offers such resistance and assists the German people to restore the control of rationality over the German social mind.

A generation may have to pass before the full implications

of the arrangement between Hitler and Chamberlain at Munich unfold themselves. It is already clear that whatever remained of political liberty between the Rhine and the Black Sea was then destroyed. Some people may feel that this fact, epoch-making as it may be in itself, has little relevance to the colonial issues with which this book is particularly concerned. That attitude is profoundly mistaken. The impulses that drive Hitlerism to the domination of 300 million Europeans spring from the same economic and psychological sources as the impulses that drive the rulers of Britain to maintain dominance over 400 millions of Asiatics and Africans. Durable peace is impossible while either set of impulses remains unsuppressed. There will be no such peace in Europe while we hold India and Africa in bondage.

The converse is equally true. Liberation of the subjects of the Empire is unlikely to be achieved if liberty perishes in Europe; so close and so vital are the links which now couple our fate with the fate of the victims of our greed. Those links imply a common cause, and, therefore, the need for a common course of action. Our failure now to recognise and be faithful to that common course of action will involve Asiatics and Africans in a new servitude. Freedom, like peace, is more indivisible than most men yet dream. If those who call themselves champions of peace and freedom were indivisible too, the Hitler–Chamberlain alliance would not be the deadly danger it now is to the common people in every country in the world.

PART V

POLICY

CHAPTER XXII

A NEW DEAL?

§ 1. APPEASEMENT BY CONCESSION

WE come at long last to consider policy. Difficult as it may seem to many of us who only want to know how this colonial issue is going to affect our own lives and persons, it is against the larger background sketched in the last chapter that we should bring ourselves to focus the question. Colonial policy, like all other branches of social policy, is to be judged by its effect on the disposition of forces in the world crisis, in man's fight for survival as man.

Imperialism has no random link with this crisis and this fight; it lies at the heart of them. The issue is not who shall own certain wide-open spaces in remote corners of the earth. It is whether colonies are to be used to advance Hitlerism and its planned descent to sub-human levels of life; or whether the work that the colonial people are both eager and competent to perform is to be thrown open to them—the work of overturning the last barriers that stand between them and the life of free men. As far as human freedom is realised, so far is Hitlerism defeated. Colonial freedom is one of the safeguards of our own.

The possible policies are reducible to four.

1. The cession of colonies to Germany.
2. The refusal to cede colonies to Germany, and the backing of this refusal by armed force if necessary.
3. International control of colonial areas.
4. Independence for colonial areas.

Let us discuss these possibilities in turn. In the first place, then, a German colonial empire might be re-created by the cession of territory in Africa and perhaps elsewhere. It makes little difference in principle whether the ceded territory was formerly under German sovereignty or not.

This is broadly what the Germans are asking for, and presumably, therefore, what they want. By giving them what they want, one might be said in some sense to be satisfying them. So whatever is to be said for placating German dissatisfaction in general is to be said for giving them colonies. There can be few people, however, who still suppose that this would be likely to moderate the future demands that Germany might feel moved to put forward.

Again, it cannot be said that any power has an equitable claim to any colonial territories. For this reason, their present possessors enjoy no better title to them than do rival claimants. Both titles, being equal to nought, are equal to one another. But while this may afford negative grounds for an all-round expropriation of colonial ownership, it affords no positive grounds for the transfer or re-distribution of such ownership.

Looking at the matter from the other side, there is the obvious general objection that the colonies are not ours or anyone else's to transfer. They properly belong to their indigenous inhabitants.* There is something fundamentally repulsive about all proposals that we should do a cattle deal with them in the interests of European diplomacy. Some of us may try to conceal the repulsiveness by calling it political realism, but the trick does not wash well, and the shady look remains in spite of the whitening.

* Needless to say, this is not the legal position. How neatly the law dovetails in with the interests of dominant groups can be seen from the Southern Rhodesia land case of 1919. There was a dispute between the Crown and the British South Africa Company as to the ownership of unalienated land in the colony. The Judicial Committee of the Privy Council had no difficulty in deciding that whomever the land belonged to, it did not belong to the natives of the country.

Occasionally idealism too is dragged in to justify a trans-action which seems unable to justify itself. We are told that to surrender some of our colonies (after all we have a great many of them) would be " only fair ", and would be a step farther along the road to general international appease-ment. There is here a strange mixture of true and false. It is true that Britain has far too many colonies and ought to be divested not only of some, but of all of them. But what sort of logic is it that infers from this that Germany ought to pick up what we put down?

If there is any substance whatever in the central argument of this book, re-division of colonial territory designed to give dissatisfied powers a share of the spoils, so far from improv-ing the prospects of peace, will merely perpetuate the rival-ries that drive the world towards war. What is required in the interests of peace is not a share-out of the right to exploit, but the all-round abolition of exploitation as an operative principle. If imperialism is what is wrong, how are you likely to improve matters by adding a new German empire to the other empires that already exist?

There is a serious danger that many of the millions in Britain who devoutly long for peace, and would do almost anything to preserve it, may fall into this trap. The case may be put to the country after the following fashion. " Chamberlain saved peace at Munich—God bless him. But unhappily at a fearful price. That price was paid by the Czech people. It was magnificent of them, but really we British must not allow others to sacrifice themselves on our behalf again. We are a proud race and insist on standing on our own feet. If peace is to be saved by a second Munich, we ourselves must make whatever sacrifices have to be made."

The transfer of certain African territories and peoples to the swastika will then be dressed up as " our " sacrifice. Actually, the only difference between this second Munich and the first will be that we shall have thrown Africans instead of Czechs to the wolves. But we are likely enough to do it cheerfully, and think ourselves fine fellows into the bargain, because our realists and idealists alike will swallow the suggestion that the universal interest is being served at some cost to Britain. What will have really happened is that the writ of Hitlerism will have been extended over, and the possibility of democracy excluded from, yet another section of the world. The world situation will have shifted against the people's cause to that extent.

There are further objections of a purely practical order. Any British Government which proposes to return ex-German colonies will, as we have seen, have to face great trouble among British subjects living in Africa. And any British Government which proposes to secure the cession to Germany of African territory not under British control will have great difficulty with the French, or the Belgians, or the Portuguese, or all of them. The former policy would tend to split the empire, while the second would tend to disunite still further what remains of western democracy.

Finally, the anti-Jewish measures which official Germany took in November 1938 ostensibly in revenge for the assassination of vom Rath, hardened opinion in many parts of the world against allowing Germans control over any race which they regard as inferior. Indeed, one could hardly ask for a more spectacular proof of German unfitness to exercise colonial rule. There is no harm in the British and French insisting on this unfitness provided they do not suppose it to vindicate the continuance of their own imperial systems. In any case, it represents another obstacle in the way of any policy which contemplates colonial concessions to Germany.

Judgement, then, goes against such a policy on the grounds that (a) colonies and their inhabitants may not be treated as cattle at a market; (b) the creation of new empires alongside old ones can do nothing to build up peace, and would in the present world situation merely weaken the instruments on which democracy must rely; (c) official Germany has furnished a conclusive demonstration that its unfitness to hold colonies is, if possible, more complete than that of the present imperial powers.

§ 2. NO CONCESSIONS

The second possible policy is " What we have we hold ". This was until recently the policy of the conservatives in England, and still is that of the conservatives in France. It implies a willingness to fight, single-handed if necessary, for the maintenance of the British Empire in its present shape. In practice, it is pretty certain that Britain and France would be fighting alone, since they would enjoy no sympathy from anyone else in such a cause. India certainly, Canada probably, and New Zealand perhaps, would stand out from such a fight. The attitude of South Africa and Eire would be, to say the least, doubtful. The anti-Comintern pact would come into play, and the old imperial powers would find themselves engaged simultaneously with Japan in the Far East, with Italy in the Mediterranean, and with Germany on the home front. Their defeat would be highly probable and richly deserved.

This policy, like the first, would also weaken democracy, as it means risking everything for the maintenance of those elements in our own system which are undemocratic. We should be undone by our own falsehood. It would perpetuate the troubles that have landed us in our present perplexities, and would in its results be just as fatal as giving colonies to Germany.

If peace cannot be served either by making colonial concessions to Germany or by returning a blank negative to her claims, we are driven to the admission that such claims can only be constructively resisted if Britain, as an imperial power, is prepared to renounce her own exclusive control over colonial territories.

Hence arise various schemes for linking colonies up with an international collective system, generally by means of an extension of the mandate principle. In its more fully developed forms the case for internationalisation is presented somehow as follows.

§ 3. INTERNATIONALISE THE COLONIES

The renunciation of exclusive control can be made in two ways. The first, the most obvious, and in some aspects the most important way is by bestowing genuine independence on those countries, now dependent, which are ripe for its exercise. There is no other method by which " the colonial problem " can be finally disposed of, nor ultimately any other way of satisfying justice. India, Burma, Ceylon, and some of the West Indian islands are parts of the British Empire to which this principle could be applied with only the briefest of transitions.

But there are other Empire peoples, the argument continues, who for the present neither desire full self-government nor are ready for it. The renunciation of exclusive imperialist control over peoples at this stage of development must take a different form—a form which vests the old *imperium* in an international authority under some such device as a mandate system. This extended mandate system should cover the great bulk of those colonial areas to which the principle of independence is not applicable in the immediate future; though in their case, too, it should be regarded as an interim arrangement designed first and foremost to train the native peoples concerned for self-govenment in the shortest possible time.

There are, at any rate on paper, four essential features of the present mandate system which would have to be retained in any revised system. They are, first, that the interests of native inhabitants should be the primary concern of the mandatory power; second, that the Open Door for trade and finance should be maintained in mandated territories; third, that there should be no militarisation in mandated territory in the sense either of training native troops for military service or of building naval bases and defences, etc.; and fourth, that the League of Nations should exercise supervision over the administration of the mandatory Power.

These four key points, it is suggested, have to be reinforced and supplemented by four new points, which are these. First of all, the Mandates Commission, or other supervising international authority, should have the power (which it does not at present possess) of sending its representatives into mandated countries to see what is happening there and to carry out their own inspection in their own time as they think fit. Next, representatives of the mandated races themselves should be given a place on the Mandates Commission. Third, the natural resources of mandated countries should be placed in public ownership in those countries—the ownership of the communities who inhabit them. And finally, capital investment and capital supply for the development of those countries should be internationalised by the establishment of a League loans authority which should raise funds for re-lending to mandated territories for their development.

The last two points are revolutionary in the sense that they are designed to make it impossible for colonial territories to be used any longer as redoubts and bolt-holes of private capitalism. If they were properly put into action, their effect on the British capitalist order would be similar in kind to the effect of nationalising some important means of production at home. The proposal is, indeed, that a League loans authority should assume responsibility for financing all colonial developments, not only public works in the usual meaning of the term, but also developments which under the present system are made over to private concessionaires. Such a loans authority would issue stock internationally. All League Members would be free to participate equally as investors. An analogy is provided by the Public Works Loans Board in Britain, which issues Local Loans stock, and re-lends to local authorities that are too small to raise public loans for themselves.

It is claimed that this type of scheme also has advantages

which are not revolutionary. It facilitates genuine international equality, both as regards investment and as regards contracts placed in European countries in consequence of loan developments. It maintains the advantage of relatively cheap borrowing which colonial public authorities enjoy at present, and extends it to the field now covered by private concessionaires, who often have to pay heavily for their capital requirements. This burden on private enterprise is one of the factors tending to the extraordinarily slow growth of the internal market in colonial areas. Public enterprise would not be called upon to bear such a burden, and the prospects of expanding the consuming power of poverty-stricken colonial populations would be to that extent improved.

Further, to give the League control of the supply of capital is, we are told, to place in its hands a weapon for dealing with refractory mandatory powers. We know, or ought to have learnt, that League supervision and rules are of little use if unsupported by any power of exerting coercive pressure. Such control would also do away with many of the openings for abuse and exploitation of native peoples which the present colonial system offers. And last and perhaps most important of all, it would enable an enlightened Mandates Commission to vary the rate of advance of the industrial revolution in colonial territories in accordance with the advancing capacity of native society to adapt itself to the changes involved.

Such a scheme, its exponents suggest, could be operated in various ways and by various agencies. In descending order of idealism, which is not necessarily an ascending order of practicability, one might put

(*a*) International administration by the League, i.e., a revised mandate system from which the national element should have been removed, and which should have been made fully international both from the economic and political points of view.

(b) Joint administration outside the League system by the various imperial powers.

(c) Administration as with the present mandates by national authorities accountable to the Mandates Commission.

Programmes of this general type are honest idealist constructions intended to solve without disorder or upheaval the problem of colonial emancipation. Whether they are utopian as well as idealist we shall discuss later. But we should recognise that the liberation of empires is a far harder task than their conquest, and one which has never yet been peaceably achieved.* If anyone imagines that the trick can be done by waving a wand and crying " Emancipate ", he is assuredly mistaken. We should therefore salute with respect the kind of scheme outlined above as a serious attempt to deal with a serious question.

§ 4. WEAKNESS OF THE MANDATE SYSTEM

At the same time it has to be admitted that such schemes involve a somewhat simple-minded reliance on the efficacy of the mandate principle. Take a typical instrument such as the British mandate for Togo, and you will find that the clauses directly affecting Africans are as follows :—

> Article 2, which deals with material and moral wellbeing and social progress.
> Article 3, which prohibits the recruitment of natives for military service outside the mandated territory. (Note, however, that the French in respect of their African mandates have knocked the bottom out of this ban by the proviso " except in case of general war ".)

---

* The case of the Dominions, though often cited, is not really in point, for those territories of the empire which now rejoice in self-government were never colonies in the sense in which India and tropical Africa were and are colonies. Their subjection and exploitation, such as it was, was of a kind and degree so different as to be scarcely comparable.

Article 4, which deals with slavery, forced labour, traffic in arms and liquor.

Article 5, which is concerned with the land question.

Article 6, which stipulates for the Open Door.

Article 10, which calls for an annual report to the League.

Of these six clauses, Article 2 is a pious aspiration which may mean anything or nothing. Article 3 does not touch the question of the use of native troops for the " preservation of law and order ", punitive expeditions, and the like. In any case, as the French example shows, it may be modified to suit the general military convenience of the mandatory power. Article 4 merely requires the application to mandated territories of measures already generally enforced in colonies.

Article 5 leaves virtually unfettered discretion in the matter of native lands to the mandatory. Article 6 may be important to Africans as enabling them to buy imports in the cheapest market and to sell exports in the dearest, and in certain other respects. For a large part of Africa, however, the Open Door is already provided for by other international agreements. Article 10, with its acceptance of the principle that the mandatory is accountable to an international authority, introduces a new conception into colonial administration, though in an embryonic form.

It can hardly be said that the total effect of the above provisions is epoch-making, or that from the African point of view it involves any vital differentiation between the status of a colony and that of a mandated territory. It is well too to remind ourselves that the whole scheme of mandatory control, though it may have been born in repentance, was, as we have seen, conceived in flagrant sin, of which the marks are still traceable in its working. Many observers would go further, and say bluntly that mandates have proved weak and ineffective in practice.

§ 5. INTERIMPERIALISM

There is another type of international control which may bear some outward resemblance to the first, but which stands in fact opposite to it, and tends not to colonial freedom, but to a more systematic colonial exploitation. Hobson has given it the name of interimperialism.* He points out that " if capitalists in the several western powers were capable of intelligent co-operation instead of wrangling among themselves for separate national areas of exploitation, they would have combined for a joint international enterprise in Asia, a project which might have given the whole of western capitalism another generation of active profitable survival ".

We see the same type of co-ordinated imperialism sketched in the van Zeeland Report, where it contemplates the creation of privileged or chartered companies " whose activities would be strictly limited to the economic sphere and whose capital would be divided internationally in such a way as to offer real guarantees of impartiality ".

There seems to be a genuine probability that the capitalists may somewhat belatedly accept Hobson's advice. Japanese energy has perhaps rather monopolised the development of Asia, but there is still ample scope for intelligent co-operation in Africa. As long ago as October 1937, *The Times* was holding that there was " a strong case for enlisting the co-operation of all the best European experience " in the solution of the problems of the native races. " That did not necessarily mean an extension of the present mandatory system to all the African native territories." An alternative was " the establishment of an international bureau of the powers concerned ".

On November 16th, 1938, just at the height of the savage outburst of the German government against Jews, *The Times* recurred to the theme and suggested the appointment of Germany to the international bureau referred to. This

* Op. cit., p. xx.

striking passage is worth quoting verbatim. After confessing how attractive it found the notion of " a common undertaking by the powers concerned in African colonisation ", the paper continued :—

" Such an undertaking would recognise that, midway between the great self-governing communities in the South of Africa and those others to the East and on the Mediterranean seaboard which are on the way to self-government, there exists a vast continent of backward races whose future must lie, *perhaps for centuries to come*, in the guidance of Europeans. It would rule out once for all the theory that these backward races were ever again to be regarded as a factor in the power politics of Europe. It would utterly ban ' black armies ' raised from their tribes and naval bases established on their coasts. It would eliminate economic barriers between them, and between Europeans trading with them, and regulate their production on a common system. It would ensure, in short, that the rôle of Europe towards uncivilised Africa was that of trusteeship in fact as well as in profession. In such a common undertaking Germany might well find an honourable place side by side with the other colonising nations."

The assumption here that the fate of " uncivilised " Africa is to jog patiently along under European tutelage for hundreds of years shows on the side of fact a strange ignorance of actualities in Africa, and for that matter in Europe too, while on the side of motive it shows the old-fashioned imperialist spirit at its worst. The strategic ideas embodied in this scheme are (*a*) a defeat of African liberationism so decisive as to stand beyond challenge for centuries to come, and (*b*) an agreement between exploiting powers which will stop them " wrangling among themselves " about their colliding ambitions.

The Times, in a word, is saying, " Let's have a nice quiet empire no longer subject to the stresses which arise from

native independence movements and the jockeying of great
states for power positions ". *The Times* does not directly
refer to the third source of anti-imperialist challenge—
namely, the democratic and pacifist movements in the
home country. Nor is any direct reference necessary, since
if the other two sources are quenched, the third also will dry
up. All three feed one another. This is just another way
of saying that liberationism in the colonies and democracy
at home are allied causes which sink or swim together.

It is perhaps not without significance that *The Times*
leader appeared on the very day when Oswald Pirow, the
Minister of Defence in the South African Government, left
London for Berlin. In Berlin Pirow had discussions with
Hitler, Goering, and the Finance Minister, Funk. He had
spent the previous fortnight in London, where it was no
secret that he talked over with British Ministers a plan,
already discussed in Kenya and Portugal, for meeting the
German colonial demands.

One of the contemporaries of *The Times* is a penny paper
called the *Daily Mail*. It sometimes blurts out in plain
English information at which *The Times* prefers merely to
hint in the oblique and esoteric language of diplomacy. So
it happened on this busy morning of November 16th. At
the precise moment when Pall Mall was decoding *The
Times* leader from which we have quoted, the *Daily Mail*
startled the world with details of the so-called Pirow Plan
for giving Germany colonies and big economic advantages
in Africa.

Pirow, so the story went, was to argue in Berlin that the
old German colonies—South-West Africa, Tanganyika, and
so on—would be more trouble than they were worth.
Hitler would do better to accept new territory on the west
coast—e.g., a bit of the Cameroons, a bit of the Belgian
Congo, and a bit of Portuguese Angola. Pirow, according
to the same source, had an economic scheme too, whereby
Germany might obtain raw materials from a common
colonial pool, administered jointly by an international

board representative of all European powers interested in Africa, including Germany.

Pirow went to Berlin, the *Mail* added, " with a clear view of Downing Street's views of his plan for appeasing Germany's colonial ambitions ". This phrase was interpreted by foreign observers as meaning with Chamberlain's fullest approval. The plan failed because Hitler wanted more than it provided for.*

In these calculated indiscretions of *The Times* and the *Mail* we have revealing evidence of the impulse of the British ruling class to snuggle up to Hitler in order to compass the blessed ruthlessness to which they are unable to screw up their own unaided courage. In the same way and in the same spirit, an old-established business firm, when it feels too keenly the draught of unrestricted competition, will arrange a merger and take into partnership some of its sharpest rivals. The new blood, new capital, and new methods thus introduced give to the combined concern a vitality and power beyond what any of the partners could have achieved singly. So Germany, *The Times* proposes, is to be let in on the imperialist racket to the profit of the German ruling class and the rejuvenation of that of Britain. The process is described, with that mastery of diplomatic phrase for which this great journal is justly admired, as ensuring that the rule of Europe towards the poor untutored African should be one of trusteeship " in fact as well as in profession ".

The conception, then, which seems to be taking shape in the minds of our rulers is that of a Holy Alliance of the four powers directed towards a decisive ham-stringing of the people's power throughout Europe, and based on the extinction of Spanish Republican resistance and the organised communal exploitation of the dark-skinned races. Such joint coercion could be more intensive and more durable both at home and in the colonies than any that the older empires are now able to exert by themselves.

* *Izvestia*, December 21st, 1938.

Here we have the totalitarian stage of imperialism in action. It is not mere accident that the *Hamburger Fremdenblatt* remarked almost simultaneously with *The Times* leader, " European domination in Africa cannot be maintained without German co-operation ".*

Interimperialism so conceived has obvious attractions for Chamberlain and his supporters. Presumably it has also for Mr. Pirow, the Tanganyika League, and the settler interest in general. From the standpoint of Europeans domiciled in Africa, it would guarantee white supremacy and scotch, if not kill, the nagging bogey of a native rising. It would do these things without jeopardising, possibly even while actively improving, the prospects of self-government for East Africa under a white settler oligarchy. Nevertheless, any British Government that proposes to attend this kind of diabolical supper-party would do well to take in its pocket for use in emergency a spoon with a specially elongated handle. What is likeliest to happen at such a feast is that Germany having helped herself to the lion's share of the dishes provided, will turn cannibal and swallow her fellow-guests into the bargain.

§ 6. DANGEROUS CONFUSION

If you take the scheme which we have called internationalisation and the scheme which we have called interimperialism, and if you put the two side by side and compare them, it turns out that they are clean contraries at their far edges, but that they shade into one another towards their near edges. Where they touch, they merge and become indistinguishable. That the scheme propounded by *The Times* is radically different in spirit and intention from the scheme for extending the mandate system that we outlined before it, is clear enough. But look at some of the other formulations that are being put forward, and you will find that it is not always easy to tell to which camp they belong. Take, for example, the following extract from a

* Quoted in *The Spectator*, November 25th, 1938.

speech by Tom Johnston in the Debate on the Address in November 1938 :—

" The colonial territories, the non-self-governing territories, which represent 13 per cent. of the population of the world that has no share at present in its own government—Portuguese, Dutch, British, French, and American—should be placed under an international trust, and these colonies should be run for the benefit of the people in them, we should jointly use our efforts to raise the status, the standards of living, the conditions of these people and increase their purchasing power.

" If we can do that we shall have a great free trade area and a great new demand for goods. There would be no special privileges for any State. Germany, as well as Great Britain and the United States, would have an equal seat on the board."

Compare this with another set of proposals made by Sir Daniel Hall in a letter to the *Manchester Guardian* on November 17th, 1937 :—

" The only solution of promise to Africa and the Africans is for the nations to renounce the exercise of their separate sovereignties and to create a trust, under the League or otherwise, for the administration of all Africa between Rhodesia and the Mediterranean territories.

" A board of management would be nominated by the nations chiefly concerned; the civil service would be similarly recruited on a quota basis, with due safeguards as to capacity. Ownership of territories need not be disturbed until it is seen how the experiment would work, but the new Administration would assume all the undertakings entered into by the present Governments, such as the treaty between Great Britain and the Masai nation and the reservation of the Kenya highlands for white settlement.

" Commercial concessions would be equally binding,

and if it were desired to extinguish any of them in the interests of native welfare it must be by process of law. Trade would be equally free to all nations; customs duties and export taxes would be levied only for the Administration and for the service of the necessary loans, since at present the African colonies are responsibilities rather than assets."

It may be that Johnston intends internationalisation and that Hall intends interimperialism. But it is impossible to be certain. There are elements of both in each scheme. The ease with which the two blend and become confused accounts for the solid suspicion with which both are greeted by educated Africans and for the indiscriminate welcome which idealists and pacifists in England are apt to extend to either.

It is essential for policy to cut clear of this confusion. Interimperialism is so dangerous a scheme that internationalisation may have to be rejected also, if only on the grounds of an unfortunate superficial resemblance between the two. The main thing is to ensure that interimperialism is not sold to the British public under a bogus label.*

* Lenin discusses interimperialism, and vigorously criticises certain writers who had suggested that such " peaceful partitioning " of the colonial world might offer an assured basis of permanent peace. He has no difficulty in showing that, regarded from the long-term point of view, interimperialism can afford no more than a breathing space between imperialist wars. He does not deny, of course, that on a short-term reckoning it may be a useful means of killing the germs of colonial freedom (see " Imperialism ", pp. 106 ff.).

CHAPTER XXIII

COLONIAL INDEPENDENCE

§ 1. THE SPIRIT AND THE FLESH

THE actual difference between internationalisation and interimperialism in their practical operation would depend less on organisation and machinery than on the spirit in which they were worked. If you had a democratic board of saints, impervious to all imperialist influences, to carry out your international scheme, things might pan out admirably for all concerned. Even given a batch of left-wing progressive governments in Europe, many features of the internationalisation programme could perhaps be made to work. But in so far as the tradition and outlook of imperialism might still colour (under whatever pseudonyms or disguises) the aims of those who controlled the international machinery, the tendency would be for the whole scheme to degenerate with greater or less rapidity into mere interimperialism.

There is involved here the whole problem of the social dynamics of colonial rule. People who favour the extension of mandatory control start from the unavowed hypothesis that it is possible to set up an international authority with a driving power of its own which can, if necessary, run counter to the interests that determine the policy of the individual states responsible for its formation. Such a hypothesis is seen to be fallacious as soon as it is stated. It is in fact twin brother to the liberal fallacy about the League of Nations that we discussed in Chapter XIX. Moreover, both fallacies are closely related to the fallacy which supposes that the British raj (or for that matter imperial rule of any other country) is beneficial or injurious to the colonial peoples according as it is exercised by enlightened and progressive officials or by obscurantist and reactionary ones.

No one would deny that a bad system becomes worse when it is worked by bad agents, but it does not follow that good agents can turn a bad system into a good one. The primary factor making for social change in the colonial world is the coupling of its people to the economic and financial machinery of industrial Europe. The people of the colonies are being put to work as it were inside the capitalist machine. Work of this kind is the most powerful instrument of economic, cultural, and spiritual modification. Schools, churches, and governments undoubtedly have their importance, derivative in character though it be, when they function as parts of that machine. If, however, they seek to work in opposition to it, it at once becomes evident that there is no driving force behind them except the personal faith of a handful of individuals.

Relatively then to the economic forces thus introduced into colonial life, policies adopted by colonial governments are altogether secondary. Indeed it is not too much to say that colonial governments can be and are a primary source of influence on colonial life only in so far as they cease to be colonial.

§ 2. THE CASE OF KENYA

Let us take by way of illustration a well-known fact such as the efforts of the Colonial Office to impose an income tax in Kenya. These efforts were successful in the formal sense that income tax legislation was passed, but they failed in the practical sense that the Kenya government never managed to collect the tax. Normally the chain of authority runs from the consolidated interests that dominate the British economic structure, through the Colonial Office which is their agent, and on to the

I

colonial government which is in turn (within limits and with qualifications which vary in different colonies) the agent of the Colonial Office. In the case of Kenya income tax, the chain broke at the point of the colonial government.

The colonial government, instead of acting in the usual way directly as agent of the Colonial Office, and indirectly as agent of particular British industrial and financial interests, acted as agent of another party altogether—namely, the European settlers in the colony on whom the tax would have fallen, and who therefore resolved that it should not come into force.

What happened in fact was a repetition in a somewhat different form of the experience of Canada during the 1840's, when Britain, having abandoned in favour of free trade the old mercantilist system of monopoly and production, called on Canada to adopt free trade too. The Canadians on their side were very clear that they wanted to foster their own infant industries, and to protect them not only against foreign manufacturers, but against British manufacturers as well. " Self-government ", declared the Canadian Minister of Finance, " would be utterly annihilated if the views of the imperial government were to be preferred to those of the people of Canada." The imperial government, which did not want another American Revolution on its hands, gave in. The state machine that governed Canada and controlled Canadian policy had been snatched from the grasp of British manufacturers and their agents and captured by settler interests on the spot. To this extent the government of Canada ceased to be colonial and became independent.

Now, Kenya does not formally enjoy self-government, but the settler interest there claims a relative, and still somewhat restricted, right to self-determination in certain matters. What is more, it exercises that right with a bold disregard of constitutional forms. Its conquest of the state or public power in Kenya has hitherto been spasmodic and occasional in the sense of being carried out for *ad hoc* and limited purposes. It is none the less real for being incomplete.

The point is that, as far as the conquest has been made, just so far has the government of Kenya ceased to be colonial and become independent. This is to say, it has become the instrument of interests localised in Kenya instead of being the instrument of interests localised in Britain. Some alliance of course may be established between Kenya interests and British interests, or they may be in full mutual rivalry. These are complications we need not now pursue. In general, any machine or government or control must remain a mere machine, lifeless and inert, until it is connected by some particular driving-belt to some particular source of power. In the usual colonial case the driving-belt is the operations of various European trading and producing concerns in the colony, and the source of power is those group interests which may be described succinctly and adequately, if not with rigorous precision, as the City, the Lords, and the F.B.I. In the case of Kenya the driving-belt is the settlers' threat to start a civil war, or kidnap the Governor, or otherwise inconvenience the colonial government, and the source of power is their group interest as owners of the best land in the colony, and therefore as monopolists of 85% of the colony's exportable produce.*

§ 3. DRIVING-BELT AND MACHINE

Apply these considerations to the question of international control in Africa. No board set up to exercise such control could be independent of the interests represented by the

---

* That these two sources of power are recognised by our ruling class as being the material factors in the colonial question can be illustrated by the following example.

When at the Paris Peace Conference it was proposed to cede Jubaland (then part of British East Africa) to Italy, Milner wrote to Lloyd George saying, " There is certain to be a great outcry about the proposals, both from the British settlers in East Africa and the cotton-growing Association at home " (see " Truth About the Peace Treaties ", by D. Lloyd George, Vol. 2).

governments that established it, for it has no other driving-belt or source of power. These interests will work it in their way and for their purposes or not at all—just as they worked the League of Nations so long as it suited their selfish concerns and then dropped it. To talk in such a case of guarantees, etc. (for example, that Germany should undertake to accept the principle of trusteeship), is just playing with words. Guarantees have never availed much, as the history of the native franchise in the Union of South Africa abundantly proves, and certainly would avail nothing at all with National-Socialist Germany.

Internationalisation and interimperialism are in practice one and the same thing, so long as the driving-force behind the operation of either remains governments of the political complexion of those in power in Europe to-day. The development of Africa can only take place by means of a merger of land and labour on the one hand with capital and technology on the other. The land and the labour will be provided by Africans, and the capital and technology by Europeans. In the view of democrats the object of the merger is to give Africa mastery of the technology and capital, and not to give European capitalists mastery of African labour and African land. But so long as you are dealing with governments of the existing colour, any form of international control of colonies will simply be designed to secure and perpetuate precisely that European mastery of African labour and land and natural resources.

If you want to achieve the opposite result, what must you do? Surely you must see to it that the colonial government machine is hitched to the only other available source of power—namely, the group interests of the African people themselves. In other words, you must consciously and directly encourage the liberationist movements, train them for power, and work the independence principle for all it is worth. Not otherwise can democracy in the world either strengthen itself or demonstrate its fitness to exert strength.

§ 4. THE ENDING OF EMPIRE

The position we have reached, then, is this. In the first place, the formulation and carrying out of a policy calculated to strengthen the forces of democracy in the world is complicated by a relatively novel circumstance of the highest importance—namely, that the Hitlerism which the peace forces and the people's power must destroy if they themselves are to survive, has for its closest accomplices the present national leaders in Britain and France.* The question of peace is therefore also a question of internal political power in these countries (and ultimately, of course, in Germany and Italy as well).

Secondly, we have found ourselves obliged to postulate a common war guilt of all nations which pursue the path of imperialism. All economic policies that aim at the exclusive control of markets and raw materials by powerful special interests make a constructive and stable peace system impossible. The British Empire is a highly elaborate network of such exclusive controls. Hitlerism in one aspect represents the resolve of German envy and covetousness to break down these exclusions and replace them with exclusive controls set up in the interests of Germans. Had it not been for British and French imperial policy scouring the world for economic privileges at the expense of every prospect of free international co-operation, Hitlerism could hardly have arisen in Germany. Conversely, Hitlerism is unlikely to disappear so long as the British and French empires survive in their present economic and political structure.

Once that admission is made, there is no avoiding the inference that the main task of the democrat is to abolish the old-style imperial systems. Such abolition, we argued, cannot mean returning colonies to Germany, for that is merely to increase the number of old-style imperial systems by one. It is, if possible, one degree more fatal than answer-

* This is written in January 1939.

POLICY

ing the German claim with a flat negative on the basis of " what we have we hold ". Interimperialism, or the merger of the chief empire-minded powers for the joint co-ordinated exploitation of colonies, is still more dangerous to the prospects of democracy than the two former courses. Even the various idealist schemes for internationalisation proved to be unacceptable because there was no sure ground for supposing that in practice they would do more than provide sheep's clothing for the interimperialist wolf. What, then, is left? Nothing but the principle of colonial emancipation. Our remaining task, therefore, is to inquire what are the concrete practical steps by which the principle can be applied to the British Empire.

CHAPTER XXIV

INDIA THE CRUX

§ I. OUR NEED OF INDIA

THE first, most obvious, and most important step is independence for India; in other words, popular Indian responsibility for the defence policy and the foreign policy of India in accordance with a constitution framed by popularly elected Indians themselves. To erect self-determination into a sacred principle in Europe and to ignore it in other continents is not a defensible discrimination. Indeed, as some hold, it was precisely the attempt to discriminate in this way that made the League of Nations a falsehood, carrying the seeds of failure from the beginning. India may be a problem for Indians. It is none for the people of Britain. For them it is a godsend at this juncture of our history precisely because it is both the greatest of all colonies and one ripe for independence and capable of exercising it without delay. The freeing of India to-morrow might well mean the liquidation of half the empires of the world the day after.

Indian independence would be quickly followed by independence for Burma, Ceylon, and, after the introduction of adult suffrage, the West Indies. A self-governing African federation would be gradually built up on a similar model. A precedent guaranteeing the destiny of all British dependencies would have been established, and perhaps a mortal blow dealt at the whole policy of imperialism.

Indian independence would have other far-reaching effects on the world situation. Whereas India, the colony,

is dragged protesting at the heels of Hitler–Chamberlainism
in matters of foreign policy, a free India would throw its
powerful support into a new collective defence system
which would be the military answer to what has now become
primarily the military question of the restraint of Hitlerism
—a defence system to be built round a nucleus formed by
Britain, France, and the Soviet Union. The Indian
National Congress has repeatedly declared its willingness
to unite with popular movements anywhere on the only
policy on which the peace forces of the world can possibly
unite, resistance to aggression on whatever country it
may fall.

Indian independence would be the answer, the only
decisive answer, to Hitler's demand for the return of
ex-German colonies. If that demand comes when the
National Government is still in office, we are likely to find
either that it is acceded to in some form or other, or that
we are called upon to fight a world war in order that the
Union Jack may continue to fly in Dar-es-Salaam. Both
alternatives are almost equally disastrous, for the creation
of a new German empire on the old imperialist principle
would reinforce and complicate the factors which have
thwarted all efforts at the organisation of peace in the last
twenty years. A free India would be the final proof
that the age of empire-making was coming to its end, that
the people had grown stronger than vested interests, and
that, perhaps for the first time in the history of the world,
peace among men had become a possibility.

Indian independence is now the crux of the whole problem
of imperialism. It is necessary for the defence of democracy,
and the defence of democracy is part of the defence of
peace. It is necessary, not because it would be pleasant
for the Indians to have, but because the rule of law in the
world, on which our own liberties and those of Indians
and Africans alike depend, cannot be secured without it.

§ 2. A BLUE-PRINT OF INDIAN FREEDOM

And what are the terms on which India might mount from its present subordination to the status of a free country? This is evidently a question to which no answer is possible but one which has been agreed to by the chosen representatives of the Indian people. But as some rough guide to reflection and discussion among democrats in Britain, it may be useful to give the skeleton of a possible scheme: possible both in the sense of being practicable in itself, and also in the sense of being the kind of scheme which a truly democratic government in Britain might invite Indians to consider without dishonour to either side.

THE CONSTITUENT ASSEMBLY

1. An instruction from the British Government to the Viceroy to collaborate with the Indian people for the summoning of a Constituent Assembly.

2. The Viceroy to ask the Provincial Governments or the Lower Houses of Provincial Legislatures to nominate a committee to sit with him to organise elections.

3. Arrangements for elections on the basis of adult suffrage, with acceptance of existing communal constituencies and other similar bases of representation.

4. The actual conduct of elections to be in the hands of Provincial Governments.

5. Provincial Constituent Councils to be set up, each of which should elect its quota to the National Constituent Assembly on the basis of proportional representation.

6. If any of the Princes should accept the foregoing principles, his state would be admitted to the Constituent Assembly on the same basis as the provinces of British India. States or Princes not accepting them would be excluded from the Constituent Assembly.

6a. Parallel with the instruction under (1) there would

I 2

be an announcement of intention to renounce the treaties with Princes, such renunciation to be operative on promulgation of the treaty of cession between India and Britain (see 9 below).

7. In the period of transition the Provincial Governments would carry on as fully responsible governments.

8. The Constituent Assembly to consist approximately of 600 members.

THE TREATY

9. The constitution as framed by the Constituent Assembly to be the subject of a treaty between India and Britain. This would involve, besides the treaty itself, (a) an act of abdication on the part of the British Crown in respect of India, and (b) ratification of the treaty by the House of Commons.

10. The treaty would make provision for:

(a) The transitional period.
(b) The holding of new elections.
(c) The financial adjustments.
(d) Transition in defence.
(e) Mutual non-aggression clauses.
(f) A Commercial Agreement.
(g) The position of British Indians resident and domiciled outside India in British possessions.
(h) An affirmation of racial equality.

11. The treaty would be registered at the League of Nations.

12. Ceylon and Burma would not be affected by the treaty. All other Indian islands and territories under the Government of India would pass out of British control with the coming into force of the treaty.

13. Under 10 (d) provision would be made for a mutual defence alliance, to which Burma and Ceylon would also be parties, in relation to Burma and Trincomalee.

FINANCE

14. The new Government of India would accept responsibility for that part of the public debt represented by assets within British India.

15. The valuation of such assets would be made in the first instance by a joint Committee of Indians and British. Where agreement could not be reached by such a Committee, valuation would be undertaken by an impartial tribunal, consisting of three jurists of high international repute appointed by the Permanent Court of International Justice.

16. In respect of the Indian Public Debt not represented under (14) the Indian Government would undertake to purchase in Britain over a period of years manufactured goods to an equivalent amount.

17. Provisions to cover pensions charges, actual and prospective, arising out of the service in India of British Officials.

§ 3. MILITARY DEFENCE

Schemes of this kind are often criticised even by liberal-minded people in Britain on military grounds, the suggestion being that a free India would be incapable of defending itself. A dilemma is posed in the following form: If the Japanese or the Germans march into India as the British march out, how will the Indians profit by the change?

This question of the military defence of India deserves some attention, since it is so great a stumbling-block to many. And the more Britain's general state policy centres on rearmament and the maintenance of national and imperial interests, the more vexatious does the stumbling-block prove.

The root of the trouble is simple enough. It is just this; that in present circumstances the armed force of which Britain disposes in India is there for two reasons:

1. to defend Indian territory against invasion from without;

2. to defend the British Empire in India, if need be, against the Indian people.

Evidently (1) is an aim which it is in the interest of British democrats to promote, and (2) is one which it is vital for British democrats to repudiate. The distinction is fully grasped by the leaders of the liberationist movement in India. Subhas Chandra Bose, President of the Indian National Congress, has declared that " the establishment of a socialist order in Britain is impossible of achievement without the liquidation of colonialism, and we who are fighting for the political freedom of India and other enslaved countries of the British Empire are incidentally fighting for the economic emancipation of the British people as well ".*

Any policy for India, therefore, which is to be adequate to the conditions of our time, has to start from the clear realisation:

(a) that the Indian liberationists are active allies in the defence of democracy in Britain, and that consequently it would be suicidal for democrats to oppose liberationism in India;

(b) that the military security of the Indian people is a problem utterly distinct and separate from the defence of British imperial interests in India, in spite of the apparent confusion between the two which the imperialists (with, from their own standpoint, such magnificent completeness) have contrived to produce.

As to (a), our progressives find it relatively easy to see the need for supporting the Chinese liberationist struggle against Japanese imperialism. They understand less readily the need for supporting the Indian liberationist movement against British imperialism. Psychologically this may be curious and interesting; politically it is

* See *Empire*, June 1938.

disastrous. For imperialism everywhere—British, Japanese, German, or Italian—is just as fatal to the basic aspirations of unprivileged classes in the colony-owning countries as it is to those of the subject peoples at the colonial end. The plain fact is that the defence of British democracy has been sustained in the last few years at least as gallantly and effectively by the Indian National Congress, the negro strikers of Trinidad and Jamaica, and the cocoa-farmers of the Gold Coast, as by the Trade Union Congress and the Labour Party at home. The forces of British capitalism recognise this with complete frankness, and take their repressive counter-measures in the Gold Coast, the West Indies, and India.

§ 4. FREEDOM AND SECURITY

Now consider (b). Can policy provide for the defence of Indian territory against foreign aggression without at the same time involving the continued subjugation of the Indian people to British military rule?

Here we must begin by discarding the illusion against which Jawaharlal Nehru has entered a caution—the illusion that if India ceased to be subject to British domination, it would fall a prey to Japan or Germany or Italy, and that therefore the British are justified in still holding India by the sword. Nehru shows how that illusion is merely evidence of a latent imperialism colouring the outlook of those who call themselves democrats and socialists. Moreover, he dismisses unhesitatingly the view that a Japanese, German or Italian invasion of India falls within the field of political reality.* He supports his reading of the situation by the following arguments:

"Japan is further away from India, for all practical purposes, than England is. The land route is entirely closed and impossible of passage, even for aircraft. The sea route is very long and terribly dangerous and cannot be negotiated till Japan is master of the sea and

* *Empire,* loc. cit.

air and Britain and the United States have been wholly
disabled. Japan cannot think of coming to India till
she has absorbed the whole of China, a task almost
certainly beyond her competence and resources. Even
after that, the next countries on the list are Australia,
the Philippine Islands and Netherlands India.

" It is equally fantastic to think in terms of a German
or Italian invasion of India. Both these countries will
have their work cut out for them in Europe and their
objectives lie in Europe or North Africa. But if by any
chance the fascist Powers gain an overwhelming victory
in a world war and the world lies prostrate before them,
then of course anything might happen. Even so India
will not go as a gift to anybody. She will resist the
invader to the utmost and, in spite of lack of military
and such like resources, she has developed enough
strength and technique of her own method of struggle
to make an invasion a terribly burdensome operation.
We have to struggle to-day with an entrenched system
which has dug itself deep into our very soil. It will be
far easier to deal with a newcomer who comes with
hostile intentions."

The contrast may be expressed thus. So long as India
is maintained as a subordinate item in the British Empire,
its fate in a general war will be decided on the battlefields
of Europe. While such a war is in progress, India will be
a sideshow from the standpoint of her British " protectors ",
who will have their hands extremely full elsewhere, and
for whom the Mediterranean route will almost certainly
be closed. The British forces in India will have as their
main duty the crushing of the Indian bid for independence
which Nehru assures us will be made. In the process
India will be bled even whiter than she was in 1914–18.
In the event of a British defeat in Europe, India would
by reason of this bleeding be in poor shape to resist the
entry of Britain's conquerors; though, as Nehru shows,

even then a new invader need not expect to have everything his own way. If Britain came out on the winning side, the question would be whether a war-worn Britain were too weak to fasten its grip afresh on India, or whether a drained India were too weak to throw off finally the dead-weight of the British yoke.

Suppose, on the other hand, the case of an independent India, and estimate as a military enterprise its invasion by a power whose home base was in western Europe or the western Pacific and which had no foothold inside India. In this case, it would be necessary for the issue to be fought out, not on any European field or on the high seas, but actually on Indian soil.

The entire attacking force would have to be transported by sea. Even had the power in question to meet no naval challenge and no challenge from the air along its whole line of communications (an unlikely supposition), it would first have to build up a secure land base within striking distance of India; next to break through India's coast defences and effect landings on a number of wide fronts in India itself; and finally from these advanced bases to proceed to the conquest and military occupation of a vast country solidly hostile and better trained than any other in the discipline of passive resistance. Even if the aggressor were a great world power, this would be at the best a very formidable military adventure, fraught with all and more than all the perils and difficulties that confront the Japanese in their war with China.

§ 5. THE POOLING OF INDIAN DEFENCE

If Nehru's view of the matter is correct, the present " defence " arrangements in India will, then, serve little purpose but to maintain the British raj against the wishes of the people of India themselves. Even if he is wrong, it is doubtful whether those arrangements could actually protect India from foreign aggression in the kind of concrete situation which in that case we should have to visualise.

During the last six years, British foreign policy has been a major factor in putting the collective system out of action, in disintegrating international solidarity in Europe, in isolating the Soviet Union, in reducing France to impotence, in driving the U.S.A. and many small states back to neutrality, in combining the three fascist powers, strengthening them by the surrender of vital strategic positions, and inspiring them with the conviction that the world is their oyster.

One cumulative effect of this trend is that it has become physically and materially impossible for the small island of Britain to defend the whole vast British Empire single-handed against the triple danger that now threatens it. Once again, it must not be forgotten that the anti-Comintern pact is one of the key factors in the current international situation, and is quite as capable of being employed against the British and French Empires as against the Soviet Union.

What is more, the defence of British imperial egoism against rival imperialisms is, as we have seen, not a cause that commands anything like unity within the Empire or among the British people. In India particularly it would cause large-scale disaffection. Congress, which has the masses behind it, has declared its intention of resisting any attempt to " defend " India for imperialist purposes, and of using the situation created by an imperialist war to make a bid for independence.

For these reasons, there can be only one form of guarantee for the defence of the people and territory of India, as distinct from the maintenance of British rule in India. It consists in the pooling of Indian defence in the defence of an " open " group of States within the League, with France, the Soviet Union, and Britain as the nucleus, based on arbitration, non-aggression, mutual assistance, economic co-operation, and an agreement to solve the colonial problem by way of the abolition of colonial status.

But—and this is the crucial point—such a scheme involves a free India. By free is meant not merely enjoying autonomy in respect of internal affairs, but free to conduct its own foreign policy, to make its own arrangements for defence, and to accept membership of the League of Nations in its own right. Such a scheme cannot be shared in by an India faced with the problem of intensifying mass discontent with imperialist exploitation and repression, and at the same time preventing mass disillusionment with Congress ministries because of their inability to terminate that repression and exploitation; nor by an India promoted to a junior partnership in the firm of British imperialism and thereby obliged to identify itself with the repression and exploitation of the non-self-governing parts of the Empire.

CHAPTER XXV

TROPICAL AFRICA

§ 1. SELF-GOVERNMENT—HOW SOON?

As we have already suggested, there are other parts of the dependent empire besides India which are capable of exercising self-government either at once or after the introduction of adult suffrage. Burma, Ceylon, and the West Indies were given as examples. If these places were to follow India in completing their liberation, the total population freed would be in the neighbourhood of 400 millions out of a total of less than 450 millions of subject people inside the British Empire. The whole shape and size of the colonial question would have been changed. There could be no more convincing proof of a decisive break with the traditions and policies of imperialism. The importance of such changes for the course of world events could hardly be exaggerated.

But they leave on our hands the question of tropical Africa —the very region to which Germany's present claims mainly relate. Some people will feel that it is no answer to these claims to say that India is to achieve independence. How, it will be asked, can constitutional changes in India either negate or fulfil German colonial ambitions in Africa?

What has been said above is, I hope, enough to show the profound relevance of Indian freedom to the prospects of freedom for Africa. But there is no gainsaying that it does not in itself provide any complete or direct solution of the immediate African problem, although I believe that problem cannot be solved without it.

The next question, then, is this. Why cannot the

methods we have suggested for India be extended to Africa immediately, particularly if they are not only suitable for India but also capable of extension to such places as Burma, Ceylon, and the West Indies? And if their extension to Africa is impossible, what is the alternative? Are we really going to be driven to take up the same position as *The Times* and the imperialists—namely, that tropical Africa is to be under European tutelage for as long as we can foresee or longer?

The favourite imperialist form of expression is that Africa is not yet ripe for self-government, the implication being that the revolving years and seasons will in God's good time bring ripeness if we all patiently serve by watching and waiting. Having thus adjourned the whole matter *sine die* to some heaven-ordained millennium, the imperialists go on to tighten up their sedition ordinances and recondition their penal codes, in order that they may be well placed for treating as criminal disaffection every evidence of the increasing capacity and willingness of Africans to manage their own affairs. In the same spirit they develop the technique of what they call indirect rule, not as a road to the democratic control of Africa by Africans, but as a substitute for it.

It need hardly be said that what we have in mind is something poles apart from this. If, therefore, we are going to accept the thesis of African unripeness for other reasons of our own, we must not only be very clear what our other reasons are; we must also offer concrete positive pledges that African independence is to be the guiding principle, and that Africans themselves are to do the main work of carrying the principle into effect. In other words, while Indian freedom is a *sine qua non* of African freedom, the circumstances require that we should offer Africa more than a precondition. What is called for is a guarantee. We must not let go of independence as a principle, even if it is not immediately realisable.

§ 2. THE INTERNAL OBSTACLES

The real reasons why it is not possible to speak of independence for Africa *now* in the same way that we have spoken of independence for India are these.

First come the social reasons. Africans have not the art of writing or reading; they are only now acquiring it slowly from Europeans. I mean reading and writing not necessarily English, but even their own languages. There are scores of such vernacular languages in every colony, a fact which hinders the growth of the unity that is itself a necessary preliminary to self-government. Not, of course, national unity in the sense of all thinking alike, but simply in the sense in which people living in Lancashire or Yorkshire, without forgetting the colour of their roses, still think of themselves as Englishmen.

The lack of literacy means, too, a very narrow basis even for the mere office-work of administration, let alone for the planning and co-ordinating of the varied and complex phases of government policy. As the figures given in Chapter XIV show, not 10% of the Africans in any British colony are literate in any language, and in most colonies the literates are less than 5%.

The system of indirect rule intensifies local tribalism to a vicious degree and keeps the people of one local government unit from almost all contact with their neighbours in the next. It also props up the decaying authority of the chiefs who have a vested interest now in the system and who would strongly oppose a central government which overrode their tribal privileges. We should not under-estimate the danger of steps which, while masquerading as advances towards African independence, would in fact mean placing power over millions of illiterate natives in the hands of a set of rival African chiefs or landlords already sufficiently despotic even under British restraint. Measures of this kind would defer rather than hasten the achievement of that national unity which will be the one firm foundation of African freedom. Africa too has its class struggles; enemies of the people may have black skins as well as white. It behoves us to see that the banner of freedom is not abused so as to increase their strength. In short, no organised social force has yet developed enough head of steam to keep the machine of government revolving in the interests of the common people of Africa. In no African colony is there even a substantial middle class (though one is growing up in West Africa). For this and other reasons, what the Indian National Congress can do, and is doing, for the Indian people can be done for the African people by no type of organisation that yet exists. Events in the colonies are of course tending all the time to work up this head of steam and to prepare channels for its release. The first task is to co-ordinate and quicken the two processes, a task which requires the close co-operation of the democratic movement at home with the liberationist movements in the colonies.

Next come economic reasons. The industrial, commercial and financial links which couple up the colonies with big business in Britain are highly complex. In the main they are also highly undesirable. African freedom will come as and when these links in their present form are broken. But they cannot be broken until an Africa which is consciously preparing its own freedom has something ready to put in their place. This taking over and reconstituting the economic machinery that forms the foundation of African productive life cannot be achieved overnight, but only after a difficult transition during which African-managed institutions will have to employ European technicians and experts at the same time as Africans are being trained to succeed them.

Third are reasons connected with geography and ethnology. The present political boundaries which mark off British, French, Belgian, and Portuguese Africa from one another were settled in the midst of a hectic international scramble for the continent. They were settled

purely by the exigencies of the contemporary diplomatic
situation in Europe, and have little or no relevance to
African life. It is hardly an exaggeration to say that every
international boundary in Africa violates a tribal or ethnical
group to a greater or less extent.* For example, the old
Anglo-German boundary between Togoland and the Gold
Coast cuts through tribes for the whole of its length, leaving
villages on one side, and farming lands on the other.†
Similarly, the Masai tribe is cut into two fragments by the
Kenya–Tanganyika border. Such anomalies are typical
of the African scene everywhere.

In circumstances like these, it is doubtful whether to
speak of independence for, e.g., the Gold Coast really means
very much. At any rate, it begs the question whether the
Gold Coast as it stands is a social unit capable of forming an
independent state; or, more accurately, whether it is the
most suitable ethnic unit on which to build up independence
for that part of Africa. It is a safe assumption that full
political and economic freedom in tropical Africa will only
become actual in the union of autonomous groups in a
federal state. The question that needs to be answered
therefore is what is the most appropriate composition of
the groups which are to exercise autonomy.

In the present state of our knowledge no one can say
what the answer is. It is, on the face of it, highly unlikely
that the limits of these groups coincide with existing colonial
frontiers. We need a general revision of these frontiers
by an expert commission in the light of ethnological considerations, and of the political need for rapid advance to
cultural autonomy as a step towards the higher reaches
of self-government and self-determination. If the governments concerned will not appoint a commission for the
purpose, then African leaders themselves should take steps
to see that the inquiry is undertaken unofficially.

* See W. M. Macmillan, " Africa Emergent ", pp. 392 ff.
† See A. W. Norris, late Provincial Commissioner of the Gold Coast,
in the *Daily Telegraph*, November 8th, 1938.

Fourth are military reasons. The immediate abandonment of political control by Britain would mean for British Africa a return to the anarchy of the scramble period. Round every seat of native authority the blue-bottles and the scallywags would come buzzing again, as Rhodes' men once buzzed round Lobengula's kraal. The licensed and oblique methods by which white men cheat Africans of their copper in Rhodesia, their tobacco in Nyasaland, and their cocoa in the Gold Coast would at once give way to the direct and quite lawless methods of the gangster. Independence for Kenya, for instance, would beyond question mean nothing but the government of Kenya Africans by the white oligarchy for the white oligarchy. The slight restraint which Downing Street rule puts on the destructive exuberance of the settlers would be removed. That is all. Similarly, in West Africa undesirables of every type and every nationality would flock in, many of them agents of the great mischief-making foreign powers. The end of the process would presumably be reconquest by one European power or another.

Africa's position in this aspect differs widely from India's. As we saw, the foreign invader of an independent India would have a very formidable military nut to crack. Similar difficulties, at least in part, would confront the invader of Burma or Ceylon. The West Indies, again, are in effect covered by the broad wings of the Monroe doctrine. But in Africa Mussolini, Franco, and the Portuguese are already established. For all of these gentlemen, and therefore for Hitler also, many parts of the continent are available at once as bases for an expeditionary force. Military security for tropical Africa, even of the relative and provisional kind which is all that anyone can expect in the modern world, is not an easy problem.

Clearly the one prospect of combining it with freedom for Africans lies in a collective system in which the defence of many countries is pooled. So African independence, in any complete sense, cannot in practice precede the establishment of the collective system of which we spoke in an earlier section, that system which is to comprise Britain and France and the Soviet Union as its nucleus. India, on the other hand, if supported vigorously and without reserve by progressives in Britain, might force independence even from a Conservative Government, and even in the absence of any fully developed collective defence system.

§ 3. THE PRIMARY NEED

If we put the above four sets of considerations alongside one another and look at them together, they compel us to recognise that the permanent foundations of African self-government have still to be laid. The primary need now is that Africans should be given a chance of organising themselves as citizens, as producers, and as consumers, in accordance with the requirements of the modern world. Group organisation for any of these purposes is very difficult without political and educational advances far beyond any point yet reached in Tropical Africa. This is proved equally by the relative failure so far of trade union and co-operative movements in India and Africa, and by their success in the Soviet Union. The contrast is not invalidated by the fact that free trade unionism is encouraged in the U.S.S.R. and largely illegalised in British colonies. All the fostering in the world could not have built up the Russian movement if the foundation of popular understanding and popular capacity had not been there. Real trade unions or co-operatives which should combine efficient management with the democratic authority of the rank and file membership can hardly be created in a society composed of voteless illiterates, however much alive and however worthy of respect their traditional culture may be.

The precise forms which such organisations should take in Africa are the business of Africans. On the political side, for instance, it may be questioned whether the parliamentary and municipal institutions peculiar to western democracy are the most suitable forms for Africa. It is quite possible that the original Soviet system of village and occupational councils forming a fully democratic base on which a pyramid can be built up by indirect election may be preferable.* Or again, it might be more practicable to press for the development of the existing Legislative Councils accompanied by proper African representation on them. These are matters for Africans to decide, but it is high time we began consulting them. The pretence that they have no views on them is absurd, and has been recognised to be absurd even by imperialists themselves ever since the Joint Committee on Closer Union in East Africa (1931) listened to its African witnesses.

The immediate question for Africa is not independence, but the quickest possible progress towards independence. This will have to be fought for less in the international field than within each colony-owning nation by democrats in alliance with Africans themselves against the imperialists. Ultimate victory will be guaranteed if the independence precedent can be promptly established in India and certain other colonies.

For the moment political control in Africa will have to go on as it is. But only for the moment. Deplorable and indefensible as are the effects of the British colonial system, its grip has the advantage of being relatively weak. It is susceptible to the joint pressure of African nationalists and British democrats, whereas neither would be able to exert any serious influence on an interimperialist combination such as *The Times* hopes to see. An element of international co-operation there will assuredly have to be before the end. But not one which provides for political control. It had better be avoided altogether until we can ensure that it should take the form of abolishing frontiers and preparing the federation of Africa on a self-governing basis.

* See "Soviet Communism", by Sidney and Beatrice Webb, Chapter 2.

§ 4. TIME = EFFORT

All this is simply saying that Africa is a victim of imperialism which has suffered perhaps more grievously than any other, and which is still sorely disabled by its wounds. It obviously does not mean that in a revolutionary situation some indigenous form of government might not successfully come to the front in Africa. This indeed might well happen, and what is more such a government might well manage the day-to-day affairs of Africans with less waste and inefficiency and common hardship than now mar the beauties of British trusteeship. But we are not speaking here of revolutionary situations.

In trying to weigh up fairly the difficulties which at present stand in the path of African independence, I shall no doubt be suspected in some quarters of wishing to put off that independence until the Greek Kalends. Such a postponement is not necessarily implied in an acknowledgment of the difficulties, and is certainly the last thing intended by me. The time needed to bring the neglected, wronged, and harassed peoples of Africa to at least the level of unity and literacy now attained in India, Ceylon, or the West Indies is not some fixed and unalterable quantity. It depends entirely on the effort put into the task. The authorities of the British Empire put the minimum compatible with certain theories held by a bemused public opinion at home. In this way they have done in 150 years for Indians, Ceylonese, and the people of the West Indies a great deal less than the Soviet Union has done in one tenth of the time for socially comparable populations within its frontiers. However, the authorities of the British Empire can hardly be expected to hasten the day of their own undoing.

That constructive task a genuinely democratic government in Britain would gladly undertake. To its undertaking a genuinely democratic movement, which understood how the survival of civilisation is wrapped up with the waxing of the people's power, would gladly pledge itself in advance. Such a government and such a movement would attach a time-limit to the charter of African freedom. They would plan the completion of African liberation by specified stages within a specified space of time—say two ten-year periods.

The work of the first ten-year period would be to carry out the points of the charter relating to mass education, civil liberties, and popular franchise; to limit and reduce the power of alien economic interests; to ensure that all new development of natural resources, industries, and public utilities, should be undertaken by African public enterprise instead of European private enterprise; to put an end to the unrestricted drain of tribute to absentee investors, and in general to keep African-produced wealth in Africa, except in so far as Africans themselves might choose to organise its exchange abroad on a co-operative basis.

The second ten years would be devoted to building up African economic interests in organisational forms based on popular control; to completing the manning of the public services by Africans; to transferring one by one the various departments of administration and spheres of policy to the responsibility of African representative institutions; and to preparing the way for and finally negotiating a treaty with African states on lines similar to the treaty suggested for India in Chapter XXIV.

CHAPTER XXVI

WHAT CAN WE DO?

§ 1. THE IMMEDIATE TASKS

OUR last word must be to point to some of the immediate tasks that lie to hand for those who accept the broad argument of this book.

To all such I would say first and foremost, " Get people thinking about the whole question of colonies and their meaning. Arrange meetings in your locality; get hold of speakers; distribute literature. There are half a dozen good booklets on the subject which can be had for sixpence or less. There is a little monthly paper called *Empire*. It costs threepence. Get it, read it, and pass it on to your friends. Break down the Land-of-Hope-and-Glory complex wherever you come across it in your circle of acquaintance. You would be more than surprised, you would be amazed, at how much Kipling junk is still lying about in people's minds. Fetch it out into the light of the facts, and burn it. Cultivate the sense of individual responsibility both for getting a grasp of colonial issues, and for acting in support of the coloured peoples." All these things are pre-eminently jobs for Left-Book-Club groups, for Co-operative Guilds, and for study circles of every kind. They are the educational side of our struggle. Learn, learn, and learn; then patiently explain.

Next, readers who are active in the co-operative and the trade-union movements can usefully make it their business to press for direct pioneering work in the colonies by the Trade Union Congress and the Co-operative Union. Such work might take the form suggested at the end of Chapter XVI—that is to say, direct help to colonial workers and consumers in organising and building up trade unions and co-operative societies. This would often lead on to the fight for civil liberties, for in many colonies such organisation of the workers is subject to serious legal disabilities. The home movements can be of the greatest assistance in getting such disabilities removed and in ensuring that their colonial opposite-numbers enjoy the same legal rights as they do themselves.

The co-operative movement, through the Co-operative Wholesale Society, is itself a part of the colonial world. The Co-operative Wholesale Society owns tea plantations, for example, in Ceylon and elsewhere, and is directly engaged in the cocoa business in the Gold Coast. In such capacities it is in a position to play, and to some extent does play, a really democratic rôle. When in 1937 the Unilever combine and others sought to form a ring with a view to securing control of the West African cocoa market (a manoeuvre designed in the worst imperialist manner to exploit the negro cocoa farmer and vehemently resented by him), the Co-operative Wholesale Society very properly refused to have anything to do with " the ringers ".

Similarly, the Trade Union Congress has in recent years shown an awakening interest in, and concern for, colonial labour problems. It has sent representatives to report on labour matters in India; it has helped at Geneva in the drawing up of conventions on forced labour and the recruitment of native labour; and it has set up a special advisory committee, with a special officer, to keep under continuous review the whole range of labour problems and to advise the colonial workers how to build an independent trade-union movement.

These are admirable beginnings, and they afford admirable opportunities. They need to be extended and amplified. One obvious possibility would be a plan by which the Co-operative Union and the Trade Union

Congress should collaborate to make the Co-operative
Wholesale Society estates in the colonies strongholds of
trade unionism and models up to which capitalist employers would be challenged to live. Both movements
might run summer schools of instruction for colonial
organisers either in this country or in the colonies.
Fraternal delegates from the colonies might be invited to
the annual conferences of the movements here. Provision might even be made for the direct representation
of colonial labour movements on the National Council
of Labour.

In these and a hundred other ways a tradition and a
technique of working alliance could be built up between
workers in the colonies and workers at home. Many such
suggestions will prove impracticable, and it may often
happen that the carrying out of one will make another
unnecessary. The important thing is that suggestions of
the kind should be deliberated upon by both movements
(jointly, where appropriate), with a view to action being
taken. Rank-and-file members of either movement can
well get together in their localities, and see that such
matters are raised and carried to a decision by the proper
authority.

Third comes the question of general political action.
What is the maximum colonial programme on which the
progressive parties and groups might be induced to combine? I suggest the following outiine.

(*a*) independence for India on the lines proposed in
Chapter XXIV;

(*b*) ditto Burma and Ceylon;

(*c*) for the West Indies adult suffrage leading rapidly
to self-government;

(*e*) for tropical Africa, a liberal charter of democratic
rights, including (1) compulsory free education, (2)
freedom of speech, movement, and association, (3) a
minimum level of labour and social provision, (4)

popular African representation in the Colonial legislatures.

There is nothing here that a democrat can object to,
except by throwing overboard his democratic principles.
That does not mean that many so-called democrats will
not object to it. The job for those of us who are members of
political parties or peace movements is to press for the
incorporation of some such scheme in the official platforms
of the Labour and Liberal parties, and in the policy
declarations of such bodies as the League of Nations Union,
the National Peace Council, and the Peace Pledge Union.
This means getting the issue raised in a multitude of local
organisations. Political work, like charity, begins at
home. Let us try to influence the national organisations,
not directly, but by an agitation starting in the groups at
the base of the pyramid and working upwards.

In a word, we should endeavour, along the three main
lines indicated, to ensure that the whole progressive and
democratic movement in its various organisational forms
should throw itself into active collaboration with the
kindred movements in the colonies, and seek agreement
with its colonial allies on the concerted steps by which the
above programme of colonial liberation could be carried
into effect.

It will be well to lay emphasis throughout on this point
of the need for framing policy and taking action in concert
with the colonial movements. It is unreasonable to expect
their policies and ours to coincide automatically. If we do
not advance step by step in agreement with them, one of
two things will happen, and each is dangerous. Either
they and we will come to follow conflicting courses which
impede one another's progress instead of assisting it; or
we shall give the impression of trying to lay down a line
for them as well as for ourselves. It is always fatally easy
for Englishmen to think they know what is best for Indians
and Africans. In point of fact, they are as a rule singularly

deficient in such knowledge. But their calm and almost instinctive assumption of it naturally makes Africans and Indians wild and fruitful co-operation with them needlessly difficult.

§ 2. LESSONS FROM SPAIN AND FRANCE

One can scarcely over-state the urgency of the need to tackle these jobs now. There are melancholy examples around us of the perils of supposing that they can be safely deferred. A democratic Spanish Government went into office early in 1936 with no clear colonial programme and has had colonial troops used against it ever since. Not its fault of course. But just the kind of thing that might happen to anyone who failed or was not in a position to prepare the ground in good time. The fact that the advent of the republic in Spain in 1931 did not lead to any appreciable change in Spanish colonial policy and that Spanish Morocco continued to be governed by reactionary generals explains both why the Spanish colonies became centres from which Franco's revolt of 1936 was planned and why these generals were able to lead their Moorish troops against the Spanish people. It is not hard to imagine circumstances in which Indian troops might similarly be used to crush a too-vigorous democracy in Britain. The surest way of forestalling any such danger is to take in good time steps which will make it impossible for the progressive movement in this country to be identified in Indian minds with the imperialist machine that oppresses India. If such steps are taken now, any progressive Government which might be formed in Britain in the next year or two would find that much had been done to safeguard its position against sabotage and attack from the colonial end.

Again, the history of the French Popular Front in its relations with the French Empire is full of lessons about how unpreparedness on the colonial issue may bedevil the efforts of a progressive Government at home. The

Popular Front included elements which were anxious to give effective support to the political and economic demands of the colonial people. But the Popular Front forces as a whole had no agreed colonial programme worked out in advance, and therefore no understanding with the colonial movements as to how the democratic cause was to be advanced in the colonies.

No doubt it is true that a composite alliance such as a Popular Front from its nature precludes any complete or revolutionary policy either at home or overseas. Yet it is also true that the defence of democracy is the one reason for the formation of the alliance; so that, given time for adequate preparation, the possibility of drawing up a forward democratic policy for the colonies exists. In any case, the actual colonial record of the French Popular Front in office proved to be a disappointing mixture of good and bad.

Much good was done. The social reforms introduced in France in 1936 were applied to North Africa. They included the forty-hour week, recognition of collective bargaining, and holidays with pay. For the rural population there was a guaranteed price for wheat, a minimum wage for agricultural workers, and decrees against usury. The earlier repression of liberationist and working-class activity was somewhat relaxed. Trade unions and the Communist Party came to enjoy legality.

On the other hand, the obstruction of employers and reactionary officials was allowed to render some part of the reforms inoperative. The political demands of the liberationist movement were not granted, although the French Government had formally promised that they would be. The Algerian franchise reform scheme was dropped. The Arabs continued to suffer under the penal laws of the " Native Code " and the " Forest Code ". There was corresponding backsliding in Syria, after a good beginning.

The result was inevitably a certain disillusionment among the politically active sections of the colonial people, some

K

of whom, ironically enough, edged towards the fascist countries as more likely deliverers. This tendency in turn was forcibly checked by the French Imperialist police administered by the Popular Front. Certain groups, such as the Neo-Destour party in Tunis, the People's party of Messali-el-Hadj in Algeria, and the Committee of Action in Morocco (all of which had made direct approaches to Italy), were banned; and the ban had the approval of the progressive movement in France, which could not tolerate a colonial link-up with fascism. Thus colour was given to the cry that the Popular Front was repressing the freedom movement in the colonies.

Such a cry was only a half-truth, or less. The trade unions in Tunis increased their strength five-fold while the Popular Front was in office. In Algeria the formation of the Moslem National Congress was directly assisted by the Popular Front parties. In all the circumstances it is probably true to say that under the Popular Front the colonial people received concrete benefits and a stimulus towards free democratic organisation such as could not have reached them by any other channel during the period in question. We must remember that the threat of fascist aggression overshadowed all North African politics, while the Popular Front had to face not only economic crisis at home, but also the solid and furious hostility of French and North African reaction. Conditions were not exactly favourable to a general sweep towards colonial independence.

All the same, it is difficult not to feel that a great opportunity was missed, and that consequently the progressive forces in North Africa were tragically left at sixes and sevens and reduced through internal bickering to impotence. I mention these matters not in order to tarnish the good repute of the Popular Front, but merely to emphasise a truth I have drawn attention to before—namely, that the liberation of empires is a much harder task than their acquisition. So hard a task, indeed, that even progressives readily fall into the error committed by certain left-wing groups in Holland, who lately took up the position that Japanese fascism is more an enemy to the people of Java and Sumatra than the Dutch imperialism that already rules and exploits them.

Obviously there is a sense, though a very restricted one, in which this is true. Nevertheless the judgement is quite illegitimate if it is taken as justifying the perpetration of the rule of the present imperial owners. It is also one which English people are very liable to accept in thinking of British colonies. Fear of a hypothetical fascist invasion cannot be met by saying that colonies had better continue under the control of their present masters, and by leaving the independence issue on one side until the fascist danger shall have blown over. The proper conclusion is, on the contrary, that the rate of progress towards independence should be speeded up to the highest practicable pitch. The crucial significance of India in the present crisis is due partly to the fact that India is the one important colonial country in the world where the independence problem can be tackled without either delay or such confusion and cross-issues as, thanks to fascist intervention, are at work in North Africa and the Dutch East Indies.

Let us, while a margin of time remains, profit by the mistakes and the difficulties that have troubled our friends in Spain, France and Holland. It can be done if we get our own progressive movement and those of the colonies marching in line and in step with one another.

SELECT BIBLIOGRAPHY

BARNES, LEONARD: " The Duty of Empire."
  " Skeleton of the Empire."
  " The Future of Colonies."
BEAUCHAMP, JOAN: " British Imperialism in India."
BOSE, SUBHAS: " The Indian Struggle."
BRAILSFORD, H. N.: " Property or Peace."
  " Why Capitalism Means War."
  " Rebel India."
BRITISH YOUTH PEACE ASSEMBLY: " The Bengal Peasant."
DILLEY, M. R.: " British Policy in Kenya Colony."
DUTT, R. P.: " India To-day " (forthcoming).
EMERSON, R.: " Malaysia."
GREEN, J. E. S.: " Rhodes Goes North."
HOBSON, J. A.: " Imperialism."
HORRABIN, J. F.: " How Empires Grow."
  " Atlas of Empire."
  " Outline of Economic Geography."
LABOUR RESEARCH DEPARTMENT: " British Imperialism in
  Malaya."
  " British Imperialism in East Africa."
  " British Imperialism in West Africa."
  " British Imperialism in Egypt."
LAMBERT, R. S.: " Modern Imperialism."
LEYS, NORMAN: " Kenya."
  " A Last Chance in Kenya."
LENIN, V. I.: " Imperialism."
LOVELL, R. I.: " The Struggle for South Africa."
MACMILLAN, W. M.: " Africa Emergent."
  " Warning from the West Indies."
MIDDLETON, LAMAR: " The Rape of Africa."
MOON, P. T.: " Imperialism and World Politics."
OLIVIER, LORD: " White Capital and Coloured Labour."

PADMORE, GEORGE: " Africa and World Peace."
PALMER, RICHARD: " Science and World Resources."
PLOMER, WILLIAM: " Cecil Rhodes."
RAPHAEL, L. A. C.: " The Cape-to-Cairo Dream."
REYNOLDS, REGINALD: " The White Sahibs in India."
RUDIN, H. R.: " Germans in the Cameroons."
SOUTHWORTH, C.: " The French Colonial Venture."
STALIN, J.: " Leninism."
TOWNSEND, M. E.: " The Rise and Fall of the German Colonial Empire."
VULLIAMY, C. E.: " Outlanders."
WARD, BARBARA: " The International Share-Out."
WOOLF, LEONARD: " Imperialism and Civilisation."
    " Economic Imperialism."
    " Empire and Commerce in Africa."

Empire : A Monthly Record.
The Labour Monthly.

INDEX

INDEX

Lightning Source UK Ltd.
Milton Keynes UK
UKOW03f2235170914

238772UK00001B/11/P